Berlitz HANDB ☑ KU-005-229

FRANCE

Contents

Top **25** attractions

1 **Historic Paris** The Seine and the monuments and streets of old Paris have a unique blend of grandeur and charm (see p.65)

2 **Eat local in Lyon** Get to grips with generous specialities at a traditional *bouchon* in one of France's culinary capitals (see p.170)

3 **The lavender fields of Provence** Exquisite landscapes around the rugged stone villages of the south are full of ever-changing colours (see p.226)

4 **The Côte d'Azur from Eze** From this gem of a hilltop village you can see why the Riviera is famous (see p.239)

5 **Champagne** Savour the 'the wine of kings' in the champagne houses of Reims and Epernay (see p.107)

6 **The royal valley of the Loire** The great châteaux rise up out of a verdant landscape (see p.148)

7 **The Camargue** Discover vast wetlands that are home to white horses and millions of birds (see p.229)

8 **The cloisters of Toulouse** The city's two medieval jewels have a wonderful tranquillity (see p.205)

9 People-watch in Paris The city's cafés provide enjoyable viewpoints on its life and style *(see p.64)*

10 Burgundy's plenty Discover some of the world's finest foods and wines in idyllic countryside *(see p.163)*

12 The Gorges du Tarn Hike to the top for spectacular views, or canoe down the river below *(see p.224)*

11 The Normandy battlefields The invasion beaches of 1944 remain enormously evocative *(see p.45)*

13 Stroll through La Rochelle One of the liveliest of France's many beautiful Atlantic harbours *(see p.155)*

15 **Brittany's granite coast** The coastal path will take you past unforgettable seascapes *(see p.134)*

14 **Old-world Alsace** Explore the fairy-tale villages and vineyards of the Alsatian 'wine route' around Colmar *(see p.113)*

16 **Have a seafood feast** Washed down with chilled white – an essential Breton experience *(see p.141)*

17 **Majestic Versailles** Louis XIV's dream home and its elegant gardens are a sumptuous symbol of royal power and ambition *(see p.87)*

18 Ski the Alps Beneath towering Mont Blanc, the French Alps contain some of the world's most stylish and most exciting ski resorts *(see p.172)*

19 Corsica's golden beaches Sun-worshippers can find miles of empty beaches along Corsica's north coast *(see p.242)*

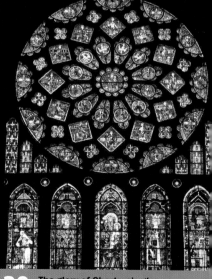

20 The glory of Chartres's glass Telling stories in intricate detail, the stained glass of Chartres is truly breathtaking *(see p.145)*

21 **Impressionist Giverny** Claude Monet's famous garden and lily pond is entrancing *(see p.37)*

22 **Market-going in Aix-en-Provence** Relish the colours at Provence's most exuberant market *(see p.229)*

23 **Great art** Explore Paris's treasure-houses of art in the Louvre and the Musée d'Orsay *(see p.72 and 80)*

24 **The Dordogne** The ancient villages around the placid river are a by-word for rural beauty *(see p.194)*

25 **Magnificent Mont St-Michel** Climb up to this monastery built upon an ocean rock *(see p.131)*

France fact file

France is the largest country in Western Europe, bounded by three seas – the English Channel, the Atlantic and the Mediterranean – and three mountain ranges: the Alps, the Pyrenees and the Jura. Three quarters of the population live in towns and cities, with around 13 million in and around Paris, while the rest are spread thinly over huge areas of countryside, working mainly in agriculture.

BASICS
Population: 62 million
Area: 551,500 sq km
(212,935 sq miles)
Official language(s): French
Majority religion: Roman Catholic
Capital city: Paris
President: Nicolas Sarkozy
National anthem: *La Marseillaise*
National symbols: Seal of State, Marianne, cockerel
National sports/art forms: Football/cycling/haute couture
National airline: Air France

CURRENCY
Euro (€)
€1 = 100 centimes (50 centimes = €0.50)
The following figures are approximate:
£1 = €1.11
€1 = 88p
$1 = €0.69

TIME ZONE
GMT + 2 hours (late March to late October) GMT + 1 hour (late October to late March)
In January:
New York: 6am
London: 11am
Paris: noon
Sydney: 10pm
Auckland: midnight

In July:
New York: 6am
London: 11am
Paris: noon
Sydney: 8pm
Auckland: 10pm

KEY TELEPHONE NUMBERS
Country code: +33
International calls: 00 + country code + number
Police: 17
Ambulance (SAMU): 15
Fire: 18
European emergency line: 112

AGE RESTRICTIONS
Driving: 18
Drinking: 16
Age of Consent: 15

Smoking: Banned in public places (museums, cinemas, etc, public transport)

ELECTRICITY
230 volts, 50 hertz
2-pin round-hole plug

OPENING HOURS
Banks in Paris: Mon–Fri 10am–5pm
Banks in regions: Tue–Sat 10am–1pm, 3–5pm
Shops: Tue–Sat 9 or 10am–7 or 8pm in large towns. Regions close for 1–3 hours from noon
Museums are generally closed all day on Mon or Tue and for 1–2 hours from noon

POSTAL SERVICE
Mon–Fri 9am–noon, 2–7pm, Sat 9am–noon.
Post boxes: yellow boxes marked *Postes* attached to a wall
Standard post: €0.56
Airmail: €0.85

Trip planner

WHEN TO GO

Climate

The French climate is varied and seasonal and, in most of the north, it is typically temperate with moderate summer temperatures, damp autumns, early springs and chilly winters. Around the Atlantic coasts, especially northern Brittany and Normandy's Cotentin Peninsula, the ocean weather is extremely changeable, while in southern Brittany and the Loire Valley, the climate is milder and noticeably warmer; there can also be occasional heavy storms.

The east, including the Alps and the Massif Central, tends to have warm summers and cold winters with snow, as do the Pyrenees, and at any time of year there are big temperature differences between low and high altitudes. The

Public holidays	
1 January	New Year's Day
1 May	Labour Day
8 May	VE Day
14 July	Bastille Day
15 August	Assumption Day
1 November	All Saints' Day
11 November	Armistice Day
25 December	Christmas Day
Easter Monday	March or April
Ascension Day	May or June
Whit Monday	May or June

On these days, most shops, banks, post offices, government departments and attractions are closed. If a public holiday falls on a Thursday or Tuesday, it is common practice for offices to faire le pont (bridge the gap) and take the Friday or Monday as holiday too.

Vineyards in Alsace

Mediterranean coast is characterised by very hot, dry summers and mild, showery winters; strong winds can be annoying when they whip up. With the exception of this coast, rainfall is sporadic all year round, with the most precipitation between January and April and the least in July and August; Mont Aigoual in the Cévennes National Park is the wettest place in France.

The weather in Paris is generally good, especially during spring; summer is often hot, autumn warm and winter tolerable, although the city has been dusted with snow in the last few years.

Crowds in front of the Louvre's star attraction – the *Mona Lisa*

High/low season

France is a great country to visit, whatever the time of year. However, it's best to avoid the south in August when the French traditionally take their holidays and the roads can get very busy.

Many shops and restaurants close in Paris in August, but this quiet period can be a good time to explore the French capital as hotel rates are generally lower then.

High season in popular areas runs from mid-June to mid-September; July and August elsewhere. The ski resorts operate from mid-December to May, but avoid British and French school holidays when prices rise, lift queues are long and the mountain roads are jammed.

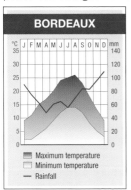

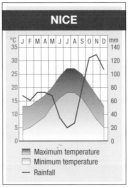

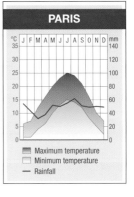

ESSENTIAL EVENTS

Glamour at the Cannes Film Festival

January–February

La Grande Odyssée, January, Savoie and Haute Savoie
Mushers head to the Alps to take part in one of the world's most challenging dog-sled races.

La Folle Journée, February, Nantes
France's largest classical music festival celebrates different composers each year. Music recitals, each no longer than 45 minutes, take place in non-traditional surroundings.

Nice Carnival, February
This, one of the world's major carnivals, has existed since at least 1294. More than a million visitors descend upon the city each year for two weeks of rambunctious fun.

March–April

Spi Ouest-France Regatta, April, La Trinité-sur-Mer, near Carnac
Europe's largest gathering of yachts sees around 400 vessels sail into this picturesque port in southern Brittany for a week of races.

International Kite Festival, April, Berck-sur-Mer (Pas-de-Calais)
Kite enthusiasts from around the world visit this family-friendly resort in northern France each year for Europe's largest kite-flying festival.

May–June

Cannes Film Festival, May
This upmarket yet charming seaside resort hosts the world's glitziest film festival in one of the ugliest buildings on the Côte d'Azur. Glimpsing an A-lister is almost guaranteed.

French Open Tennis Tournament, May–June, Paris
Top tennis stars battle it out on the clay courts at Roland Garros to land this prestigious Grand Slam title.

Feria de Nîmes, June
Five days of bullfighting and *courses camarguaises* (non-mortal bull baiting) in Nîmes's magnificent Roman arena. Most tourists visit for the atmosphere and street parties.

Rendez-Vous aux Jardins (Garden Open Days), June, national
Some of France's finest public and private gardens offer guided tours to

visitors during three days. There's a different theme each year.

July–August

Bastille Day, 14 July, Paris
An impressive military parade in Paris marks the start of the Revolution, but the whole of France celebrates.

Tour de France, July
This annual three-week international cycle race covers around 3,600km (2,200 miles) in about 20 stages, including arduous Alpine climbs.

Interceltic Festival, August, Lorient
Seven days of music, art, literature and dance celebrate Europe's Celtic cultures in the town that also happens to be France's second-largest fishing port.

Lorraine Hot Air Balloon Festival, July, Chambley-Bussières
The world's largest hot air balloon festival attracts around 3,000 pilots and more than 400,000 visitors over 10 days.

Avignon Festival, July
France's most important theatre festival takes place in one of the country's most beautiful cities.

September–October

Journées du Patrimoine, September
Public and private buildings of artistic or architectural importance open their doors to the public on the third weekend of September.

November–December

Christmas Market, mid-November–31 December, Strasbourg
France's oldest Christmas market is in an atmospheric location in the city's old town. The Children's Village will delight little ones.

Fête des Lumières, December, Lyon
The Festival of Lights celebrates the Virgin Mary with a candlelit procession, illuminated facades and artistic light displays. Legend has it that she saved Lyon from the plague in 1643.

Thousands of balloons take to the air at the Lorraine Hot Air Balloon Festival

ITINERARIES

To get the most out of a week, it's probably best to pick one region to explore: from the rugged coasts and Celtic traditions of Brittany to the stylish beaches of the Côte d'Azur, and from Mont Blanc, the highest mountain in Western Europe, and the snow-topped Alps to the châteaux and vineyards of the Loire. You could consider a themed stay, such as following the route that Napoleon took after he returned to France from exile in Elba in 1815; this happens to be in one of the prettiest parts of Provence.

One week: Brittany's megalithic coast

Days 1–2: Explore the pretty medieval walled town of Vannes; check out the local archaeological finds in Château Gaillard and stroll around the harbour. Take a boat trip around the little islands in the Gulf of Morbihan.

Day 3: Head to Larmor-Baden to take the boat to the Ile de Gavrinis, known for its ancient dolmen whose walls are decorated with megalithic art, then continue to the oyster-fishing port of Locmariaquer to see the fallen menhir – it's thought to be the largest standing stone ever erected by Neolithic man.

Day 4: Stop off at Auray to admire the pretty port of St-Goustan – its waterside restaurants are a great spot for lunch – then check out the famous megalithic avenues in Carnac; the village's visitor centre and museum offer fascinating insights.

Days 5–6: Explore the windswept Quiberon Peninsula. Try some windsurfing or sand-yachting (char à voile) or walk its Côte Sauvage; there are some dolmens and the remains of an Iron Age fort along the way.

Day 7: Enjoy a seafood lunch overlooking the record-breaking round-the-world catamarans in La-Trinité-sur-Mer, and visit the gallery of nautical photographer Philip Plisson.

10 days: coasts, châteaux and vineyards of Bordeaux

Days 1–2: Start at the Bassin d'Arcachon, an ideal destination for

Vineyard at St-Emilion, Bordeaux

beach lovers and outdoorsy sorts, and check out the Dune du Pilat – Europe's largest sand dune.

Days 3–4: Head up to the Gironde estuary, the largest in Western Europe, and explore its islands by boat – Ile Margaux is covered with vines whose grapes produce Médoc wines, while the Ile du Fort Pâté has a 17th-century fort built by Vauban.

Days 5–6: In Bordeaux, a Unesco World Heritage Site, check out the elegant 18th-century architecture and visit the Musée des Beaux-Arts, which houses one of France's most impressive art collections. Find out about the area's history, including the wine trade, in the Musée d'Aquitaine.

Days 7–10: Explore the surrounding vineyards, especially the estates of Lafite-Rothschild and Margaux, and the charming village of St-Emilion.

Lac de Ste Croix in Provence

Trip planner

Two weeks: in the footsteps of Napoleon in Provence

This follows the route Napoleon took on his return from Elba in 1815. Part of the RN 85, it is marked along the way by statues of golden eagles.

Days 1–3: Explore the lovely old town of Antibes, not missing the Picasso Museum and the Musée Napoléonien. Head inland to Grasse and visit the lavender fields and perfume museum.

Day 4: In Saint-Vallier-de-Thiey to the north, check out the megalithic sites and cave – the Grotte de Baume Obscure. The town's large park is a good place for a picnic.

Days 5–7: Enjoy some swimming, kayaking or climbing in the Verdon Gorge; admire the view of Castellane from the terrace of Notre Dame du Roc chapel, then head to Digne-les-Bains, a centre for lavender growing.

Days 8–9: Eat some highly prized local lamb in Sisteron; the more adventurous can try hang-gliding here. Visit the Alpine garden at the Domaine de Charance in Gap.

Days 10–11: Make a detour off the Route Napoléon into the Parc National des Ecrins. The park is famous for its glaciers and offers plenty of walking opportunities, as well as typical villages to explore.

Day 12: Enjoy a journey on the scenic tourist train in La Mure.

Days 13–14: In Grenoble, take the cable car up to the Bastille fort for stunning views, then end the trip with a gastronomic feast at the Auberge Napoléon; the emperor stayed here briefly in 1815.

BEFORE YOU LEAVE

Visas and entry requirements

European citizens only need a national identity card to enter France, but those without them, such as UK and Irish citizens, must have full a passport. Visitors from Australia, Canada, New Zealand and the USA must have a full passport but do not require a visa for stays of less than 90 days. Visitors from South Africa require a visa as well as a passport. This must be obtained from the country's consulate before travelling.

Nationality	Visa Required
UK	✗
US	✗
Canada	✗
Australia	✗
New Zealand	✗
Ireland	✗
South Africa	✓

Embassies and consulates

Australia: Level 26, 31 Market Street, Sydney NSW 2000, Australia; tel: 02 92 68 24 00; www.ambafrance-au.org.
Canada: 42 Sussex Drive, Ottawa, Ontario K1M 2C9, Canada; tel: 1 613 789 1795; www.ambafrance-ca.org.
Ireland: 36 Ailesbury Road, Ballsbridge, Dublin 4, Ireland; tel: 01 277 5000; www.ambafrance-ie.org.
New Zealand: 34–42 Manners Street, Wellington 6142, NZ; tel: 04 384 25 55; www.ambafrance-nz.org.
South Africa: Johannesburg: Standard Bank Building 3rd Floor, 191 Jan Smuts Avenue, PO Box 1027 Parklands, 1021 Johannesburg; tel: 011 77 85 600; www.consulfrance-jhb.org. Cape Town: 78 Queen Victoria Street, Gardens – PO Box 1702, 8001 Cape Town; tel: 021 48 85 080; www.consulfrance-lecap.org.
UK: 21 Cromwell Road, London SW7 2EN, UK; tel: 020 7073 1250; www.ambafrance-uk.org.

US: 4101 Reservoir Road, NW Washington DC 20007, USA; tel: 202 944 6000; www.ambafrance-us.org.

Vaccinations

No vaccinations required.

Booking in advance

It's a good idea to book accommodation well in advance, especially for visits during August high season and major events.

Tourist information

ATOUT France; www.franceguide.com
Australia: Level 13, 25 Bligh Street, Sydney, NSW 2000, Australia; tel: 02 9231 6277.
Canada: 1800 Avenue McGill College, Suite 1010, H3A 3J6 Montreal, Canada; tel: 514 876 9881.
New Zealand: As Australia.
Ireland: 30 Upper Merrion Street, Dublin 2, Ireland; tel: 01 662 9330.
South Africa: 3rd Floor, Village Walk Office Tower cnr Maude and Rivonia, Sandton; tel: 011 523 8292.
UK: Lincoln House, 300 High Holborn, London WC1V 7JH, UK; tel: 09068 244 123.
US: 825 Third Avenue, New York, NY 10022, USA; tel: 1 514 288 1904.

On the beach at Cannes

www.dordognetoday.com English-language paper for Dordogne expats
www.francemag.com Monthly British magazine about France
www.francetoday.com US magazine about French culture and travel
www.frenchentree.com Guide to property, holidays and more
www.fusac.fr Weekly listings and classifieds for Paris expats
www.meteo.fr French weather
www.monuments-nationaux.fr/en Guide to France's historical monuments
www.normandyadertiser.fr English-language newspaper for Normandy
www.rivieratimes.com English-language newspaper for Riviera expats
www.gallicbooks.co.uk Gallic Books publish fiction by new French writers in English translation

Maps
Basic city and regional maps can generally be obtained free of charge from tourist offices. More detailed maps are sold at newsstands and in bookshops. The best road maps are by Michelin, while those by IGN (France's equivalent of Ordnance Survey) are recommended for cyclists and walkers.

Useful websites
http://france.angloinfo.com
Listings and classifieds for most French regions
www.connexionfrance.com
France's national English-language newspaper
www.diplomatie.gouv.fr/en
Informative website from the Ministry of Foreign Affairs

Books to get you in the mood
A Year in Provence, Peter Mayle. A hugely successful account of moving to rural southern France.
French Provincial Cooking, Elizabeth David. Pioneering guide to traditional French cooking by the *grande dame* of cookery writers.
Labyrinth, Kate Mosse. An atmospheric and haunting novel set in modern and medieval Carcassonne.
Parisians, Graham Robb. A fascinating journey through Paris via historical anecdotes.
The Secret Life of France, Lucy Wadham. Another autobiography of an expat in France, this one more interesting than most, providing an insightful look at French mores and customs.

Trip planner

UNIQUE EXPERIENCES

Foods and wines of France

Wines, cheeses, meats, even lentils – French ingenuity has created thousands of variations on these apparently simple terms over the centuries. Intertwined with the landscape, each has its own special place of origin, and there are few better ways of discovering the French countryside than through each region's scents and flavours.

Quality in French food and wine comes from attention to certain basics: a willingness to take trouble, as seen in the painstaking craft of local chefs and cheesemakers, and a concern to use the best and the freshest ingredients. Inseparable from this is the idea of *terroir*. From *terre*, earth, this means the particular earth of each place or region, with the implication that each *terroir* has its characteristics and is best suited to producing particular foods. It follows that any distinctive wine or food will be a unique product of the *terroir* that created it, and will always be finest closest to its source.

Many specialities are regulated by the methodical system of *appellations d'origine contrôlée* or AOC, which stipulates that only products made within a specific area and by producers observing tightly policed quality standards can use a particular name. This is now equivalent to the EU-wide *appellation d'origine protégée* (AOP, or 'Protected Designation of Origin' in English), but in France you will usually see the traditional AOC.

Comprehensive for wines and cheeses, this system is much less so for other products – though this doesn't mean these cannot be proudly proclaimed specialities. Some say the

At Cave Saumur in the Loire Valley

AOC system is outmoded, but in general it's still a good guide to quality.

Described here are only some of France's most rewarding *terroirs* to explore. Foods and wines are essential to each area's identity, and French people experience any part of their own country through its specialities. Hence local tourist offices provide plentiful information to help find them. Health restrictions now make cheese farms hard to visit, so the best places to find their products may be local markets, but many other places welcome visitors. At grander vineyards, especially in Burgundy and Bordeaux, reservations are advisable.

The north and east

Maroilles, from the Nord, is a wonderfully pungent cheese, and French Flanders produces France's most interesting beers; **Brasserie d'Esquelbecq** (tel: 03 28 62 88 44; www.brasserie thiriez.com) in the village of the same name is an excellent small brewery.

Champagne

Attention tends to go, though, to France's northernmost wine region, the first given legal protection, in 1891, and one of the most beautiful. The grand names of champagne are in Reims itself, with **Taittinger** (tel: 03 26 85 84 33; www.taittinger. com) and **Veuve Clicquot** (tel: 03 26 89 53 90; www.veuve-clicquot.com) among others, or to the south in Ay and Epernay, with **Moët & Chandon** (tel: 03 26 51 20 20; www.moet.com). The classic *Routes du Champagne* run between the two main towns through the lovely Montagne de Reims, with offshoots north and south. Most big champagne houses offer tours of their magnificent cellars (reservations recommended), but it's fun also to visit smaller producers, such as **Champagne Corbon** (tel: 09 66 42 34 93; www.champagne-corbon.fr), in Alize in the Côte de Blancs south of Epernay. At Hautvillers, north of Epernay, is the grave of Dom Pérignon, the 17th-century friar credited with inventing champagne.

France produces hundreds of different cheeses

Foods and wines of France

Alsace

The Alsace *Route du Vin* runs north for 180km (110 miles) from the Vosges mountains near Mulhouse, through postcard-pretty timber-frame villages. Wines often use German white grapes like Gewürztraminer or Riesling, and can be sampled in traditional taverns called *winstubs* with hearty Alsatian cuisine. Some Alsatian wines are *grand crus*. **Domaine Weinbach** (tel: 03 89 47 13 21; www. domaineweinbach.com) at Kaysersberg near Colmar is an impressive larger estate, and **Dopff au Moulin** (tel: 03 89 49 09 51; www.dopff-au-moulin.fr) in Riquewihr is known for Crémant d'Alsace, the region's sparkling wine.

Normandy and Brittany

Normandy is one French region that until recently never attempted to make wine. Instead, apples and dairy products are its symbols of abundance.

Ciders and calvados

Most cider farms also produce calvados, a very refined apple brandy, and *pommeau*, a cider-and-calvados liqueur. The Pays d'Auge around Cambremer is the only area to have AOCs for both ciders and calvados, and has a well-arranged *Route du Cidre* around farms open for visits and sales. Cider farms are generally much smaller than vineyards, and the route is a delightful way to explore a ravishing area of Norman countryside. One distinguished larger producer is **Calvados Pierre Huet** (tel: 02 31 63 01 09; www.calvados-huet.com), in a magnificent half-timbered manor outside Cambremer.

Other less renowned areas also produce excellent dry ciders, notably the Perche and the Cotentin Peninsula. Breton ciders have been less esteemed, but Cornouaille, around Quimper, now has a cider AOC. The best times for cider touring are spring and early summer.

Normandy cheeses

Of the four great Norman cheeses only one is from north of the Seine, **Neufchâtel**, from the Pays de Bray northeast of Rouen. It is still produced only on small farms, and the best place to find it is the Saturday market in Neufchâtel-en-Bray. The others – **Livarot**, **Pont-l'Evêque**, and **Camembert de Normandie** (the name of the AOC, to distinguish it from industrial camemberts) are all from the Pays d'Auge, mostly from

an area south of the main cider route. As everywhere, health regulations mean that few farms admit visitors, but arrays of cheeses can be seen at markets, such as the spectacular Monday market in St-Pierre-sur-Dives or special *marchés à l'ancienne* every summer Sunday in Cambremer and Pont-l'Evêque. Camembert village, where milkmaid Marie Harel is said to have invented the famous cheese in 1791, has the **Maison du Camembert** (tel: 02 33 12 10 37; www.maisondu camembert.com), with an exhibition and shop.

The Loire Valley

South of the Loire, goats'-cheese country begins, with delicious variations such as **Crottin de Chavignol** and **Valençay**.

Normandy cider

Loire Valley goats' cheese

Wines of the Loire

The Loire runs through one of France's most varied wine regions, with many small *appellations*. Wines are often aged in chalk caves that have been used for centuries, adding to the fascination of vineyard visits. In the eastern Loire, Sancerre is known above all for superb Sauvignon Blanc whites, but also produces reds and fine rosés; the **Maison des Sancerre** (tel: 02 48 54 11 35; www.maison-des-sancerre.com) in the town is a good point to begin visits. Vouvray, outside Tours, is famed for *pétillant* (slightly sparkling) whites: **Domaine Huet** (L'Echansonne, tel: 02 47 52 78 87; www.huet-echansonne.com) is an attractive vineyard.

The small AOCs west of Tours such as Bourgueil and Chinon mainly produce beautifully subtle reds. In Restigné outside Bourgueil, the Caslot family have been making wine in fabulous cave cellars since 1640 at **Domaine de la Chevalerie** (tel: 02 47 97 46 32; www.domaine delachevalerie.fr). Around Nantes is Muscadet, home of France's favourite white wine. **Domaine de Bel-Air** (tel: 02 51 70 80 80; www.domaine-de-bel-air.fr) in St-Aignan-de-Grand-Bleu provides imaginative tours.

Cognac

On the lovely River Charente, this historic town is inseparable from its famous product. The great cognac houses – **Hennessy**, **Martell** – are impossible to miss, and all offer tours. **Cognac Otard** (tel: 05 45 36 88 86; www.otard.com) has stunning cellars

Wine and food tours

Below is just a selection of specialist tour companies. Tourist offices in all the main wine regions also offer tours.
Arblaster & Clarke, tel: (UK) 01730 26311; www.arblasterandclarke.com. Prestigious wine-travel specialists, with tours to every region.
French Wine Explorers, tel: (US) 1 877 261 1500; http://wine-tours-france.com.

Luxurious gourmet tours.
Grape Escapes, tel: (UK) 0845 643 0860; www.grapeescapes.net. Tours to all the main regions.
Insider Wine Tours, tel: (US) 1 800 449 7147; www.insiderwinetours.com. US operator with tours of the major regions.
Voyages Millefleurs; www.customwine tours.com. Informal small-group tours.

world-famous for Chardonnay whites,
is north of the main region near Auxerre; **Maison Lamblin** (tel: 03 86 98
22 00; www.lamblin.com) in Maligny
is one notable producer. The most celebrated Burgundy wine area, the **Côte
d'Or** or 'golden slope', runs south
from Dijon to Santenay, with two
halves, the Côte de Nuits to the north
and Côte de Beaune in the south,
meeting at the gorgeous wine town of
Beaune, where the **Musée du Vin de
Bourgogne** (tel: 03 80 22 08 19; www.
musees-bourgogne.org) occupies a
14th-century mansion.

The classic *Route des Grands Crus*
runs down the N74 road, passing villages legendary for supreme reds such
as Gevrey-Chambertin or Nuits-St-
Georges (try **Dufouleur Père & Fils**;
tel: 03 80 61 21 21; www.dufouleur.

Burgundy vineyards

incorporating part of a 13th-century
castle. **Courvoisier** (tel: 05 45 33 55
55; www.courvoisier.com) is in nearby
Jarnac, with a sleek modern museum.

Burgundy and the northern Rhône

A culinary heartland, Burgundy's beef,
hams, creamy cheeses such as **Cha-
ource** and **Epoisses** and, of course,
Dijon mustard are all celebrated.

Wines of Burgundy and Beaujolais

Burgundy has the oldest, most intricate system of *appellations*, making
tours particularly helpful. Chablis,

com), and, to the south, Pouligny-Montrachet, esteemed for its whites (**Olivier Leflaive**; tel: 03 80 21 37 65; www.olivier-leflaive.com, offers tasting sessions, with lunch).

A possible detour is the *Route du Cassis* west from Nuits-St-Georges, through villages that produce the blackcurrant liqueur crème de cassis. A small amount served with white wine makes kir. When mixed with champagne you have the ideal summer apéritif, kir royal.

Further south the *Route des Vins Mâconnais-Beaujolais* runs down through beautiful villages towards Lyon. The light reds of Beaujolais, famous for early Beaujolais Nouveau available each November, are produced over a wide area, but the **Maison des Beaujolais** (tel: 04 74 66 16 46; www.lamaisondebeaujolais.com) in St-Jean-d'Ardières has an ample selection.

The northern Côtes du Rhône

South of Lyon, the northern part of the Rhône wine region extends from Vienne to Valence, with hillside vineyards down the west bank. Condrieu, near Vienne, produces exceptional whites; Tain-l'Hermitage wonderful, delicate reds (Hermitage and Crozes-Hermitage). **Cave de Tain** (tel: 04 75 08 20 87; www.cavedetain.com) offers friendly tastings.

The southwest
Wines of Bordeaux

The Bordeaux winelands extend either side of the Gironde river and Bordeaux city, with, as in Burgundy, a bewildering variety of sub-regions

Taking notes at Le Weekend des Grand Crus in Bordeaux

and *appellations*. Ample facilities are provided for wine tourism. In Bordeaux the **tourist office** offers tours (Cours XXX Juillet; tel: 05 56 00 66 00; www.bordeaux-tourisme.com; booking ahead is recommended), and opposite it the **Maison du Vin** (tel: 05 56 00 22 66; www.bordeaux.com) is an excellent information source and has a chic wine bar.

Grandest of Bordeaux wine areas is Médoc along the Gironde's left bank, which is home to very aristocratic reds: Château Margaux, Château Mouton Rothschild and more. Wine estates, all called *châteaux*, spread along the D2 road to Pauillac, where the **Maison du Tourisme et du Vin** (tel: 05 56 59 03 08; www.pauillac-medoc.com) has a useful information centre and shop.

Estates are commonly as impressive as their wines, as in the Louis XV-style

Foods and wines of France

Château Beaumont (tel: 05 56 58 92 29; www.chateau-beaumont.com) near Cussac. South of Bordeaux is the Graves area, known mainly for reds, but which leads down to Sauternes with its sweet whites. At **Château Filhot** (tel: 05 56 76 61 09; www.filhot.com) there are lively tours. East of Bordeaux is charming St-Emilion, another home of historic reds. The **Maison du Vin de Saint-Emilion** (tel: 05 57 55 50 55; www.maisonduvinsaintemilion.com) is a good place to start.

The Dordogne and its truffles

The gorgeous countryside of the Périgord or Dordogne is less known for wines than for other specialities: duck, *foie gras*, walnuts, forest mushrooms and especially truffles (black here; white ones are found in Italy). The little village of Sorges, north of Périgueux, has a truffle market every Sunday in the December–January truffle season, and the **Ecomusée de la Truffe** (tel: 05 53 05 90 11; www.ecomusee-truffe-sorges.com; open all year) offers tastings and guided walks.

Armagnac

The area east of Mont-de-Marsan is the origin of France's oldest *eau-de-vie* or brandy, much older than cognac. In the medieval village of Labastide d'Armagnac there is an **Ecomusée de l'Armagnac** at **Château Garreau** (tel: 05 58 44 84 35; www.chateau-garreau.fr), one of the main producers. Armagnac producers also make lighter *Floc de Gascogne*, delicious as a chilled aperitif.

Wine tasting in St-Emilion

Unique experiences

Mediterranean France

Languedoc-Roussillon actually produces more wine than any other part of France – a good deal of it cheap *vins de table*. However, big efforts are being made to improve quality, and there are interesting smaller *appellations* (at accessible prices). Fitou, in Roussillon, produces full-bodied reds. Several vineyards are along the road north from Perpignan, and inland at Tuchan the **Mont Tauch** cooperative (tel: 04 68 45 44 73; www.mont-tauch.com) has a friendly visitor centre.

Most famous of southern Rhône wines are the powerful reds of Châteauneuf-du-Pape, between Orange and Avignon, where the **Château Cabrières** (tel: 04 90 83 75 55; www.chateau-cabrieres.fr) is an enjoyable estate to visit. To the east are two small AOCs with mostly red wines of great character, Gigondas and Vacqueyras. Nearby too is Beaumes-de-Venise, source of the fragrant dessert wine Muscat de Beaumes-de-Venise. **Balma Vénitia** (tel: 04 90 12 41 00; www.beaumes-de-venise.com) is the local cooperative.

Périgord specialities

Côtes-de-Provence behind the Côte d'Azur is known for fine, light rosés, ideal for summer drinking. Les Arcs, near Fréjus, has imposing estates like **Château Sainte-Roseline** (tel: 04 94 99 50 30; www.sainte-roseline.com).

Foods and wines of France

AOCs to look out for

The appellation system to indicate superior quality goes well beyond just wine and cheese. Also included:

Chasselas de Moissac, table grapes from around Moissac near Toulouse

Coco de Paimpol, white haricot beans from Paimpol, Brittany

Lentilles vertes du Puy, Puy lentils, from Puy-en-Velay in the Auvergne

Oignon doux des Cévennes, sweet onions from the Cévennes north of Montpellier

Noix du Périgord, the Dordogne's small, tasty walnuts

Piment d'Espelette, sweet red peppers from Espelette, near Bayonne

Poulet de Bresse, from around Bourg-en-Bresse east of Mâcon, considered the world's finest chickens

Foin de Crau, hay from around St-Martin-de-Crau in the Rhône delta – the only AOC animal feed, a gourmet treat for your horse(!)

Exploring the landscape

Western Europe's largest country, the only one that is both fully northern and Mediterranean at the same time, France has an unequalled variety of landscapes and microclimates, from sun-baked rocky crags in Provence to wind-blasted Atlantic cliffs. They provide a backdrop to a great range of outdoor activities.

Many French people feel no need to holiday outside their own country, because they find so much variety within it. France has plenty of busy cities, yet large areas remain thinly populated, their only centres charming small towns. Some of its most beautiful landscapes have been carefully crafted by human intervention – vineyards of Champagne or Burgundy, the dense green *bocage* farmlands of Normandy – but elsewhere there are great stretches of marsh, forest or mountain that feel wild and empty, with no sounds but wind and wildlife.

The French are enthusiastic fans of outdoor pursuits – especially hiking, cycling, climbing and skiing – but such is the range of options that few places get crowded, except perhaps in August. Local tourist offices provide extensive information on activities in their area. France has six national parks, in the southern mountains, and 44 *parcs naturels régionaux* (regional nature parks). A comprehensive network of well-marked long-distance (*Grande Randonnée* or GR) footpaths extends throughout the country – some strenuous, some easy – and there are exceptional facilities for cycling, with long-distance 'Green Ways' (*Voie Vertes*) off-road or away from main roads. Tourist offices have

View over Les Calanques near Marseille

maps of current routes. For watersports in different areas, *see p.56*.

Coastlines

France's two coastlines – plus Corsica – extend for 3,427km (2,130 miles). Beaches are naturally a centre of attention, but there is also spectacular coastal scenery. The most dramatic Atlantic scenery begins in western Normandy, in the Cotentin Peninsula. The **GR223** path runs all along the coast from Honfleur, behind the D-Day beaches and around the Cotentin, above rugged cliffs at Cap de la Hague and through dunes and empty beaches on the west side. At Mont St-Michel it meets the **GR34**, the Breton coastal footpath. Often following old *chemins des douaniers* or customs paths, it continues around Brittany, finest of all France's coastlines, past wooded beaches and bizarre rock formations on the Côte du Granit Rose.

Much further south, another popular area for walking is around **Arcachon** near Bordeaux. Just south is the Dune du Pilat, Europe's biggest sand dune, 107m (350ft) high.

On the Mediterranean, there are delightful small coves in Roussillon near the Spanish border, while most of the Languedoc coast is open and windswept, excellent for sunbathing or windsurfing but less attractive for exploring. By contrast, the fabulous beauty of the cliffs, rocky inlets (*calanques*) and beaches of the Provence *corniche* and Côte d'Azur are rightly celebrated. The **GR51** or *Balcons de la Mediterranée* is a classic footpath from Menton to Marseille, traversing crests behind the coast and accompanied by breathtaking views. Near Marseille it's also possible to hike to *calanques*, on winding rocky paths.

Wetlands

France's expanses of marsh and wetland form very special areas, with immense horizons and an irresistible stillness. On the Channel, the **Baie de la Somme** is a giant arc where the tide retreats 12km (7 miles), leaving

Europe's largest sand dune, Dune du Pilat

placid channels and marsh grasses. In St-Valery-sur-Somme, **Rando-Nature en Somme** (tel: 03 22 26 92 30; www.randonature-baiedesomme.com) leads guided walks across the sands, and **Baie des Phoques** (tel: 03 22 60 08 44; www.baiedesphoques.org) leads kayak trips to seal colonies.

Most magical of all coastal wetlands is the **Baie du Mont St-Michel**, a vast theatre around its extraordinary island-abbey, where at low tide the sea disappears from view. The most memorable way to visit the Mont is to walk

Wetland safety

Never, at any time, attempt any low-tide walks into tidal wetlands such as the bays of the Somme (northeast France) and Mont St-Michel (Normandy) without an experienced guide. The tides are fast and immensely powerful, making unguided walking extremely dangerous.

across at low tide from Genêts on the east side, the medieval pilgrims' route. **Chemins de la Baie** (tel: 02 33 89 80 88; www.cheminsdelabaie.com) is a reliable guides' organisation with walks in English. The **Ecomusée de la Baie du Mont St-Michel** at Vains and **Maison de la Baie** centres in Genêts and Courtils provide information.

France's largest wetlands are the **Camargue** in the Rhône delta – 930 sq km (360 sq miles) of open pasture, dunes, lagoons, marsh and salt flats. Its distinctive cattle and horses are kept by *gardians*, France's cowboys, and the bird species include flamingos. For information, go to the tourist office in **Arles** (tel: 04 90 18 41 20; www.arlestourisme.com) and the Camargue *parc régional*'s **Maison du Parc** (tel: 04 90 97 86 32; www.parc-camargue.fr) on the D570 road to Stes-Maries-de-la-Mer. The traditional way to explore the Camargue is on horseback, and **Cabanes du Cacharel** (tel: 04 90 97 84 10; www.cabanesdu cacharel.com) is one of several centres offering riding excursions. Alternatively, **Le Vélo Saintois** (tel: 04 90 97 74 56; www.levelosaintois.camargue.

fr) in Stes-Maries-de-la-Mer rents mountain bikes. The Camargue is also famous for aggressive bugs, most active in summer.

The largest inland wetlands are south of the Loire near Niort, in the **Marais Poitevin**, marsh islands divided by narrow, tree-shrouded canals. Dubbed *la Venise verte*, 'Green Venise', it's a habitat for a great variety of wildlife. Trips are taken in silent, punt-like boats (from **Embarcadère Cardinaud**, Coulon, near Niort; tel: 05 49 35 85 01; www.embarcadere-cardinaud.fr).

Forests

A vivid indication of how thinly populated some parts of France are is the extent of its woodlands and forest, covering 138,000 sq km (53,280 sq

Riding in the Camargue

miles) and home to deer, wild boar and many other creatures. The **Forêt d'Haguenau** in northern Alsace is one of the biggest undivided forests, with kilometres of oak woods. Paris is still ringed by forests, with the magnificent **Chantilly** with its horse-training runs to the north, and **Fontainebleau** and, above all, the **Forêt de Rambouillet** to the east. Within the latter is the **Espace Rambouillet** (tel: 01 34 83 05 00; www.onf.fr/espace ramb), a nature reserve with birds of prey and other wildlife, ponies for hire and the **Odyssée Verte**, a raised pathway at treetop height. Further south are large forests on the borders of Burgundy and the Auvergne, such as the **Forêt de Tronçais**. Except for the giant conifer plantations of the Landes south of Bordeaux, most are native forests, with beautiful glades of oak, beech and chestnut, giving way to Mediterranean holm oaks further south. Every region has its own forests, such as the **Forêt d'Eawy** in northern Normandy, traversed by a 14km (9-mile) bridle path.

All tourist offices have information on local forests, with suggestions for walks. Many forests are used for hunting, and in hunting seasons – mostly in winter – it's advisable to check where it's safe to walk.

Mountains

France's high mountains naturally have different aspects in summer and winter. The least-known range internationally, the **Jura** by the Swiss border, stretching north into the **Vosges** in Alsace, is relatively low, with a highest point of 1,720m

Footpath signs on the coast near Calais

(5,643ft) at Le Crêt de la Neige above Lake Geneva, but has plenty of superb scenery, especially lakes and waterfalls. The north–south *Grandes Traversées du Jura* (**GTJ**) trails are the longest of many beautiful paths for walking, cycling or riding. In winter, the Jura is France's foremost region for

---

Footpath signs

Categories of footpath are indicated by different colours. If routes are shared by more than one path both signs will be shown.

- **GR**, *Sentiers de Grande Randonnée*, national long-distance paths, indicated by horizontal red and white stripes.
- **GRP**, *Grandes Randonnées de Pays*, regional paths, with red and yellow signs.
- **PR**, *Petites Randonnées*, local paths, marked in yellow.

Exploring the landscape

cross-country skiing. The **Maison du Parc du Haut-Jura** (tel: 03 84 34 12 30; www.parc-haut-jura.fr) in Lajoux is the first stop for orientation.

The sprawling **Massif Central** contains France's largest mountain area, with a feel of real wilderness in its rocky plateaux and extinct volcanoes. The GR441 path along the *Chaîne des Puys*, the line of old volcanoes, is the region's classic hike (for information, **Parc Natural Régional des Volcans d'Auvergne**; tel: 04 73 65 64 00; www.chainedespuys.com), while climbers head for the Massif de Sancy, around the Puy de Sancy (1,886m/6,187ft). To the east and south are spectacular gorges, the Ardèche and Gorges du Tarn. In the south, the **Cévennes** national park has wonderfully rugged scenery at lower altitudes (tel: 04 66 49 53 03; www.cevennes-parcnational. fr). In winter, the central Massif is another cross-country skiing centre, but has downhill ski resorts such as **Mont-Doré** (tel: 04 73 65 20 21; www.sancy.com).

The **Pyrenees** have every kind of mountain scenery, from massive grey peaks to lush Mediterranean valleys. The famous **GR10** footpath runs all the way from the Atlantic to the Mediterranean, with manageable sections along the way. The highest part of the Pyrenees is south of Tarbes, with the Pic de Vignemale (3,298m/10,820ft), the tallest peak on the French side, and the extraordinary natural bowl of the Cirque de Gavarnie. The **Parc National des Pyrénées** (tel: 05 62 54 16 40; www.parc-pyrenees.com) has information

Hiking at Vignemale in the Pyrenees

centres in all the main valleys. The Pyrenees are also a major winter-sports centre, with several stations offering downhill, cross-country and other options.

France's most famous mountains, of course, are the **Alps** around Western Europe's highest point, Mont Blanc (4,810m/15,782ft). As well as hikes, summer possibilities include treks along *vie ferrate* (mountain trails marked with metal cables and steps), white-water rafting and spectacular mountain-bike routes. For winter sports there are naturally countless options, with celebrated resorts such as Chamonix, Val d'Isère and Val Thorens. **Savoie-Mont Blanc Tourisme** (tel: 08 20 00 73 74; www.savoie-montblanc.com) has a state-of-the-art information service.

The southern Alps have less glamour but still fabulous wild scenery. Briançon is another winter and summer centre and the gateway to the **Parc National des Ecrins**, famed for its glaciers, and crossed by the **GR54** path (tel: 04 92 40 20 10; www.ecrins-parcnational.fr). Mountain

The Gorges du Verdon

Exploring the landscape

scenery continues, lower but drier and more rugged, past the spectacular Gorges du Verdon right to the Côte d'Azur *corniche*.

Corsica is virtually one entire mountain, and its **GR20** north–south path is one of France's most gruelling hikes (**Parc Naturel Régional de Corse**, tel: 04 95 51 79 10; www.parc-corse.org).

Further information

Auvergne Tourisme www.auvergne-tourisme.info.

Confédération Pyrénéenne du Tourisme www.lespyrenees.net. Joint site for the whole of the French Pyrenees.

France Montagnes www.france-montagnes.com. Information on all France's mountain *massifs*, whether visiting in winter or summer.

IGN (Institut Géographique Nationale) www.ign.fr. Produces indispensable walking maps of France.

ONF (Office National des Forêts) www.onf.fr. Masses of information, but the majority is mostly in French.

Rhône-Alpes Tourisme www.rhonealpes-tourisme.fr

Ride in France www.rideinfrance.com. Horse-riding tourism specialists providing riding tours in the most scenic parts of France, from beaches and vineyards to gastronomic and castle tours.

On the artists' trail

Scattered around France are places indelibly associated with particular artists from the years when modern art was born. These artists travelled in search of new air, light, landscapes and colours, and following in their tracks gives fascinating insights into the sources of their inspiration.

Paris and France gained their status as the hub of Western art – and above all artistic innovation – after the Revolution, when new freedoms and Romanticism combined to bring about profound changes in the image of the artist. Instead of following aristocratic taste, the idea grew that artists should be individual, questing, radical.

Painters such as Delacroix introduced newly intense subjects and dramatic techniques. Others chose to leave Paris for the countryside, in search of contact with nature, natural light and rural life instead of Parisian *bourgeois* existence. The first 'artists' colony' was born, and as the century passed artists moved further afield, in pursuit of wilder landscapes, or intense southern colours. Another requirement of an artistic colony, before modern art was appreciated, was that it should be cheap to stay there for months at a time.

These artists have become global figures, placing these often once insignificant villages among their regions' biggest tourist destinations. Nevertheless, pick your day (especially at Giverny), and their original attractions still seize the eye.

Millet at Barbizon

In the 1840s a group of artists led by Théodore Rousseau, Jean-François

Artist following the painters' circuit through Fontainebleau forest near Barbizon

Millet and Camille Corot moved to the tiny village of Barbizon, by the Forest of Fontainebleau south of Paris, becoming France's first artists' colony. Anticipating the Impressionists in style and subject matter, the Barbizon artists were immensely influential, especially Millet, whose austere images of peasants such as *The Gleaners* or *The Angelus* were particularly loved by Van Gogh.

Millet and his colleagues are less celebrated today than later artists, so Barbizon is usually fairly tranquil. It still has one long main street, with the **Maison-Atelier Jean-François Millet** (tel: 01 60 66 21 25; www. atelier-millet.fr), his former home and studio, and the **Auberge Ganne-Musée de l'Ecole de Barbizon** (tel: 01 60 66 22 27; www.seine-et-marne.fr/musees-departementaux), the former inn where artists painted rooms and furniture in lieu of rent. A beautiful walk takes you round locations of famous paintings. Barbizon is an easy day trip from Paris, often combined with Fontainebleau.

Monet at Giverny

The most famous artist's house in France is now one of its greatest attractions, at Giverny, where Claude Monet lived from 1883 until his death in 1926. As the **Fondation Claude Monet** (tel: 02 32 51 54 18; www.fondation-monet.fr) the house and garden receive hordes of visitors during their April–October opening season (in winter, the village is utterly quiet). However, the brightly painted house is so charming, and the famous garden with the lily pond that Monet painted countless times so exquisite, that their beauty is undiminished. To miss some of the crowds, avoid weekends, and get there early.

Monet had no intention of founding an artists' colony, but one gathered around him, consisting particularly of young Americans. The **Musée des Impressionismes** (tel: 02 32 51 94 65; www.

Monet's famous lily pond in Giverny

museedesimpressionismesgiverny.com; Apr–Oct only) contains some of their work and hosts temporary exhibitions. Visitors were catered for at the celebrated **Hôtel Baudy**, which remains on Giverny's scarcely altered main street (rue Claude Monet). Now only a restaurant (also Apr–Oct only), it retains a likeable air of Belle Epoque bohemia.

Gauguin at Pont-Aven and Le Pouldu

In the 1880s another cluster of artists sought wilder landscapes and a simpler life in Pont-Aven in western Brittany, with its Breton-speaking peasants in traditional dress. Most famous of the 'Pont-Aven School' was Paul Gauguin, who visited several times from 1886, refining the powerful forms later seen in his Polynesian pictures. In 1889, finding Pont-Aven already too crowded, he and Dutch

Montagne Ste-Victoire, one of Cézanne's favourite subjects

painter Meijer de Haan spent a winter in tiny Le Pouldu, on the coast.

Today Pont-Aven's fame is reflected in its dozens of Breton biscuit shops, and signs identify the locations of particular pictures, such as the mills along the lovely River Aven. The **Musée de Pont-Aven** (tel: 02 98 06 14 43; www.museepontaven.fr) has an excellent collection of pieces by artists who worked here. Next to it, the **Hôtel Ajoncs d'Or**, where Gauguin convalesced after his leg was broken in a fight in 1894, is still a charming small town hotel, not an exhibit. In Le Pouldu, the **Maison-Musée du Pouldu** (tel: 02 98 39 98 51; www.museedupouldu.clohars-carnoet.fr) in the little former hotel has fascinating reconstructions of rooms that, like their forebears at Barbizon, Gauguin and friends painted in lieu of rent.

Cézanne in Aix-en-Provence

Paul Cézanne was born in the south, in Aix-en-Provence in 1839, and after a time in Paris returned in 1870 to paint amid the intense Mediterranean light and landscape. There he undertook most of the exploration of colour and form that made him a founding father of modern art. His equivalent of Monet's garden as a repeated subject was Montagne Ste-Victoire, the giant crag east of Aix that is instantly recognizable from the D17 road.

The guide to Cézanne sites by the **tourist office** (Place Général de Gaulle; tel: 04 42 16 11 61; www.aix enprovencetourism.com) provides a very enjoyable way of getting to know one of the south's most attractive cities, Aix. The largest sites are the **Atelier Cézanne** (tel: 04 42 21 06 53; www.ate-lier-cezanne.com), his last studio, and the slightly dilapidated house **Jas de**

Bouffon (via the tourist office), once owned by his family. Outside Aix, a *Circuit Cézanne* leads to a viewpoint below **Montagne Ste-Victoire**, past the **Bibémus Quarries**, where he painted almost cubist images of limestone rocks, and where the hut he used can be visited (via the tourist office). Access to the three main sites is by guided tour; book at the tourist office.

Van Gogh in Arles and Auvers-sur-Oise

The tragic figure of Vincent Van Gogh is equally inseparable from the places he painted. He became an artist in his thirties, and only a few years later, in 1888, arrived in Arles in Provence, drawn by the sun. He was there a little over a year, but painted scores of pictures in the town, such as the *Café Terrace on the Place du Forum* (now the Café Van Gogh), and a walk around

Café Terrace on the Place du Forum

Arles is enormously evocative. The **Fondation Vincent Van Gogh** (due to move to a new location in Arles; www.fondationvangogharles-blog. com) has exhibits of other modern art (but not Van Goghs). Before they quarrelled Van Gogh was joined in Arles by Gauguin, some of whose works are in the **Musée Réattu** (tel: 04 90 49 37 58; www.museereattu.arles.fr), along with drawings by Picasso.

In 1889 Van Gogh voluntarily entered an asylum nearby at St Rémy-de-Provence, where he continued to paint. His room in the hospital, in the former monastery of **St Paul-de-Mausole** (Avenue Van Gogh; tel: 04 90 92 77 00) can be visited.

In May 1890, Van Gogh returned north to Auvers-sur-Oise, just north of Paris, to be treated by Dr Paul Gachet. In two months before his suicide on

On the artists' trail

Trying your hand

Should you wish to compare techniques with the masters, a variety of art workshops are available. In Giverny, US-based **ArtStudy Giverny** (www.giverny-art.com) organises residential workshops with access to Monet's garden (normal visitors are not allowed to have painting materials). **France Art Breaks** (tel: 06 99 91 86 17; www.franceartbreaks.com) offers a wide range of themed and other courses with mostly British artists from a magnificent villa in Biot, near Antibes, with visits to local artistic destinations naturally an option.

Most art workshops are small operations, but a useful aid in finding some of those available is www.study abroadlinks.com.

27 July, he painted some 70 pictures. The Auberge Ravoux where he stayed is now the **Maison de Van Gogh** (tel: 01 30 36 60 60; www.maisondevan gogh.fr; booking advisable). Visiting Auvers is a particularly poignant experience: the settings of paintings such as *Wheatfield with Crows* are remarkably recognisable, and the intensity of these last pictures stays in the mind. He is buried in the churchyard, with his brother Theo. Auvers is accessible by local train from Gare du Nord or Gare St-Lazare in Paris, usually via a change in Pontoise.

Matisse, Chagall and Picasso on the Côte d'Azur

The draw of the south increased in the 20th century. Henri Matisse, from France's industrial north but in love with Mediterranean light and colour, lived in and around Nice from 1917 until his death in 1954. After World War II others made the same journey, notably Marc Chagall, who from 1947–85 lived mainly in the ravishing fortified hill village of St Paul-de-Vence. Pablo Picasso lived from 1948 in Vallauris outside Antibes, experimenting in ceramics with local craftsmen, and from 1961–73 in a former farmhouse in nearby Mougins (now the tourist office).

By this time modern art was anything but unappreciated: Picasso was one of the Riviera's biggest celebrities, and St Paul-de-Vence, to the west of Nice, became the most famous artists' centre in France. It is now rather touristy, full of art galleries and souvenir shops. More interesting is the **Fondation Maeght** (tel: 04 93 32 81 63; www.fondation-maeght.com) outside the village, one of the finest collections of modern art in the world. With

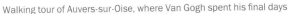

Walking tour of Auvers-sur-Oise, where Van Gogh spent his final days

Musée Matisse in Nice

a collection of works by Chagall, Miró, Braque and other modern masters, it is a wonderful example of the integration of art with architecture and nature. The tourist office, as usual, has marked a route around locations associated with Chagall. In nearby Vence is the **Chapelle du Rosaire** (Maison Lacordaire; tel: 04 93 58 03 26), with remarkable murals by Matisse.

In Nice, the **Musée Matisse** (tel: 04 93 81 08 08; www.musee-matisse-nice.org) is in the hilltop Cimiez district where the artist lived; below it is the stunning **Musée National Marc Chagall** (tel: 04 93 53 87 31; www.musee-chagall.fr). Picasso's presence is still noticeable in Vallauris, where the **Musée National Picasso 'Guerre et Paix'** (tel: 04 93 64 71 83; www.vallauris-golfe-juan.fr) has beautiful murals in a Romanesque chapel.

In Antibes, the **Musée Picasso** (tel: 04 92 90 54 28; www.antibes-juanles pins.com) in the Château Grimaldi centres on 150 works Picasso donated in return for allowing him to use the château as a studio.

The museum majors

Only a few former artists' colonies still contain major works; many of the pieces reside in neighbouring cities. Listed below are the best museums for 19th–20th-century art.

- Centre Pompidou, Paris
- Musée d'Art Moderne et Contemporain, Nice
- Musée d'Art Moderne et Contemporain, Strasbourg
- Musée d'Art Moderne de la Ville de Paris
- Musée des Beaux-Arts, Quimper
- Musée Eugène Boudin, Honfleur
- Musée Malraux, Le Havre
- Musée Marmottan, Paris
- Musée Matisse, Le Cateau-Cambrésis
- Musée d'Orsay, Paris

Marks of war

France has played a peculiarly prominent role in European conflicts for centuries, and the traces of these struggles are found all across the country, in castles, walled towns and battlefields that are dramatic, atmospheric and hauntingly evocative.

The countless fortifications and battle-fields of France are due to internal bickering, invasions, the country's own ambitions and its fateful role as an international battleground. For most of the Middle Ages what later became France was fragmented: local lords fought each other from their own strongholds, while great barons built vast citadels that dwarfed those of the often disregarded kings of France.

Towns were built within tight rings of stone walls. Later, when medieval French kings extended their power, they built more fortresses of their own. English invasion in the Hundred Years War and later wars with Spain and other countries led to further massive fortress-building. Northeast France, Artois, Lorraine and Flanders were a crucible of European power struggles for centuries.

The two modern conflagrations were naturally on an entirely new scale. When World War I broke out in 1914 many expected quick, heroic victories; instead, the new power of artillery and machine-guns pounded attacks into the mud, resulting in the immobility of the Western Front, a long gash of opposing trenches from Switzerland to the sea. World War II was quite different, although the northeast was again the initial battleground: in 1940 the Germans

The flowers of remembrance, poppies grow in profusion on World War I battlefield sites

broke through to the sea along the Somme, before expelling the British through Dunkirk. The Allies' return in the D-Day invasion of Normandy on 6 June 1944 was followed by a bloody three-month battle across the region. Paris fell on 25 August 1944. Fighting may not have been as concentrated for so long in one area as in 1914–18, but its effects, accentuated by bombing, were still more destructive. Some devastated cities, such as St-Malo, have been astonishingly restored; others, such as Brest and Le Havre, were rebuilt in entirely modern styles.

Castles, ramparts and fortresses

Baronial castles from the Middle Ages dot the skyline all over France. The southwest is particularly rich in castles, such as the spectacular stronghold at Foix; in the Gers, near Toulouse, there is one on virtually every hilltop.

Walled towns are equally part of the landscape, from the remarkably preserved ensemble of Carcassonne to walled villages like Vence in Provence and the *villes hautes* in otherwise modern towns such as Boulogne-sur-Mer. Some of the most dramatic castles were built in the titanic struggles between French kings and the great regional lords. In 1196 Richard the Lionheart of England and Normandy built the massive Château Gaillard on a crag high above the Seine at Les Andelys, in an attempt to keep the French out of Normandy. It failed, but from its giant ruins you can still see how it once dominated the river. Another fortified frontier was in Brittany, independent from France until 1532. Dinan and Vitré are among the most fascinating walled towns, and Fougères has one of the largest medieval castles.

After the Hundred Years War the military role of castles within France declined, but a new round of fortress-building began in the 17th century, as France's borders were pushed

St-Paul-de-Vence sits within ramparts

north and east. Defences were added in the new territories and around the coast, above all by Louis XIV's great fortress-builder Marshal Vauban. One of the country's most prominent architects, he built or rebuilt over 300 fortifications, and you can still find his angular creations around the edges of France.

World War I battlefields

The Western Front extended for some 740km (460 miles), north from Alsace, then westwards into France before turning north again to cross the Belgian border. Attention focuses on certain flashpoints, where men were launched forward in massive offensives that cost thousands of lives. One of the most awe-inspiring is Verdun, where the French and Germans each lost over 300,000 men during 1916, in an area 20km (12 miles) wide. Further west, near

Reims, is the Chemin des Dames, a ridge above the River Aisne that saw fierce fighting at many stages in the war. This is one of the most strangely beautiful battle sites, and in a walk through the woods along the ridge you can still get a vivid sense of what happened here.

For British and Commonwealth visitors some of the most emotive battlefields are those of the Somme, east of Amiens, where Britain's volunteer army launched its great offensive on 1 July 1916 and lost 20,000 in the first hour. There are several sites around the area: the giant British memorial at Thiepval, the Newfoundland Memorial at Beaumont-Hamel, the Australian Memorial at Pozières, and others. To the north the Arras sector contains more sites including Vimy Ridge, taken by Canadians in April 1917 and now the Canadian National Memorial, one of the most impressive of the sites, where visitors can tour preserved trenches, terrifyingly close together. Just north of the Belgian border is Ypres, where British troops fought in horrendous conditions for almost the entire duration of the war.

The battle lines are also marked by cemeteries, overwhelming by their sheer size: 40,000 names in the British cemetery in Arras, over 130,000 dead, French and German together, in the ossuary at Verdun. A feature of

World War I memorial grave, Vimy

Reading up

Some of the most accessible titles to fill in the background:

Band of Brothers, by Stephen E. Ambrose. Now-classic account of one US company's experience of D-Day and beyond.

Death's Men: Soldiers of the Great War, by Denis Winter. Powerfully individual testimony.

Fatal Avenue, by Richard Holmes. Traveller's guide to the battlefields of northern France from the 14th century to 1945.

Overlord, by Max Hastings. Classic account of the 1944 Normandy campaign.

Six Armies in Normandy, by John Keegan. An international perspective.

Voices from the Great War, by Peter Vansittart. Covers a remarkable range of material.

Douaumont Ossuary memorial, Verdun

British and Commonwealth graves is that families have been helped to place personal messages, making them especially moving.

Background and visits

If you want to get an overview of the war, a good place to begin is at the **Historial de la Grande Guerre** (www.historial.org) in the castle in Péronne, on the Somme. The **Mémorial de Verdun** (www.memorial-de-verdun.fr) is also hugely impressive. Other museums are more specific: the Somme is covered in the visitor centre at the **Thiepval Memorial** (www.thiepval.org.uk) and the **Musée Somme 1916** (www.musee-somme-1916.eu) in Albert. An essential visit for Australians interested in their role in World War I is the **Musée Franco-Australien** (www.museeaustralien.com) at Villers-Bretonneux near Amiens.

Some sites stand out for their strangeness: the museum of the Chemin des Dames is in the **Caverne du Dragon** (www.caverne-du-dragon.fr), a former quarry used as a refuge by German troops, while in Arras you can tour the **Carrière Wellington** (www.carriere-wellington.com), a maze of chalk tunnels occupied for months by British and New Zealand troops in 1917. No country does so much with its war sites as Canada, and the centres at **Vimy Ridge** and **Beaumont-Hamel** (Somme) provide exceptional free tours.

All local tourist offices provide full information on sites in their area, and in the Somme there is a well-indicated *Circuit du Souvenir* or Circuit of Remembrance.

World War II: Normandy

The D-Day invasion coast runs in an arc some 95km (60 miles) long above Caen, from Pegasus Bridge on the Caen canal, centre of the British airborne landings, westwards through the British and Canadian Sword, Juno and Gold beaches to the American Omaha beach (the location of the film *Saving Private Ryan*) and, separated by the marshes of the Cotentin *marais*, Utah Beach and Ste-Mère-Eglise, where US airborne troops landed. The D514 road runs along the coast from Sword to beyond Omaha, from where there is a detour inland to reach Utah.

In total there are 29 sites in the well-organised **Espace Historique de la Bataille de Normandie** (www.

Marks of war

normandiememoire.com), which allows you to explore particular areas or follow every stage of the campaign, from the landings to the cataclysmic finale in the 'Falaise Gap' in mid-August, when the German armies were trapped in a giant pocket with the only exit between Falaise and Argentan.

Museums and visits

Tourist offices again provide comprehensive information on sites in the Espace Historique, and a **Normandie Pass** gives discounts on admission for an initial charge of €1. Two major museums provide an overview: the **Mémorial de Caen** (www.memorial-caen.com) outside central Caen presents the events in their political context, and seeks to be a 'peace museum' as much as a conventional war museum, while at the **Musée-Mémorial de la Bataille de Normandie** (www.normandie memoire.com) in Bayeux you can follow the campaign itself in abundant detail. Most individual sites also have their own museums. Particularly impressive are the **Mémorial Pegasus** at Pegasus Bridge (www.normandy1944.com), the Canadian **Juno Beach Centre** (www.juno beach.org) at Courseulles-sur-Mer, and the **Utah Beach** museum (www.utah-beach.com). Some of the small privately run museums can be eccentrically tacky.

Long, precise lines of over 9,300 white markers make up the famous US military cemetery above Omaha Beach. British, Canadian and Polish cemeteries are more dispersed and, as in the World War I cemeteries, have personal messages on many graves. German cemeteries, such as at La Cambe, south of Omaha, are huge, dark and very tomb-like.

A sobering reminder of more violent times can be seen on some of Normandy's beaches

Outside Normandy

There are museums recording the Occupation and French Resistance in many parts of France, but the **Musée de la Résistance Nationale** (www.musee-resistance.com) is at Champigny-sur-Marne outside Paris, with branches in other towns. The most shocking monument is at **Oradour-sur-Glane** (www.oradour.org) near Limoges in the southwest of the country, where SS troops massacred over 600 people in 1944. The *village martyre* (martyred village) has never been rebuilt, and so stands as a memorial.

Around the Pas-de-Calais coast, massive bunkers of Hitler's 'Atlantic Wall' have been preserved, while just inland near St-Omer you can be awestruck by two ghoulishly intriguing sites, the **Blockhaus d'Eperlecques** (www.leblockhaus.com) and **La Coupole** (www.lacoupole-france.com). Both are

American military cemetery at Omaha Beach

massive concrete bunkers built to store and launch V2 rockets against London. Neither were ever in operation, abandoned after months of Allied bombing.

Touring the battlefields

Below is a selection of the many tours on offer. There are 'standard' routes – the Normandy beaches – but bespoke and special-interest tours are also available. The Canadian centres at Vimy, Beaumont-Hamel and Juno Beach provide free tours, and the Mémorial de Caen offers D-Day tours (charge).

- **Battlefield Tours**, Birmingham, UK; tel: 0121 430 5348; www.battlefieldtours.co.uk. Tours of all the battlefields of Europe and further afield.
- **DDay Historian/Battlebus**, Bayeux; tel: 02 31 22 28 82; www.ddayhistorian.com. D-Day and Normandy specialists.
- **In the Footsteps Battlefield Tours**, Ross on Wye, UK; tel: 01989 565599; www.

inthefootsteps.com. Tours on request to all the battlefields of northwest Europe, including medieval ones such as those of the Hundred Years War.
- **Normandy Tours**, Bayeux; tel: 02 31 92 10 70; www.normandy-landing-tours.com. Daily D-Day beaches tour, plus other Normandy tours.
- **Somme-Normandy Tours**, Péronne; tel: 03 21 73 46 16; www.somme-normandy-tours.com. Highly regarded tours of the Somme, Flanders and Normandy.
- **Terres de Memoire**, Péronne; tel: 03 22 84 23 05; www.terresdememoire.com. French bilingual guides focusing on the Somme and the Western Front.

French architecture

Yellow-stone Provençal farmhouses, Gothic spires, grand châteaux and small-town *mairies* with shutters and Art Nouveau porches: allowing for many different styles but also instantly recognisable, the architectural symbols of France are as much a part of its identity as its language, cheeses, movies and fine wines.

Modern Europe may appear increasingly homogenised, but France still presents a set of hallmarks in stone, wood and brick that, whichever direction you arrive from, immediately let you know you have entered the Gallic cultural sphere: a particular combination of styles and equally distinctive arrangement of space, a sense of geometry that reflects a very French rationalistic mindset. In cities they can include soaring medieval cathedrals or Baroque mansions, in small towns more likely market squares flanked by a 19th-century town hall.

Some of these styles and features grew up 'out of the ground' in the regions of France; others were extended to every part of the country precisely because of their role as symbols of official Frenchness, notably in areas on the fringes such as Corsica or Alsace, as a tangible sign of their integration into the nation. Visitors to France can see these identity tags mixed together around the country, or pursue a special interest along a particular route.

Rustic traditions

Traditional rural architecture is the most local and most diverse. The massive-walled stone *mas* farmhouses of Provence, Languedoc and

Traditional architecture and well in Josselin, Normandy

Rousillon follow a style recognisable since Roman times. Towards the Alps and the Jura, giant chalets predominate. Further north and in the Basque Country stone gives way to brick and wood, particularly in half-timbered houses or *maisons à colombages*. In this, too, there is no uniformity: classic Norman half-timbering, using thin wooden staves and often thatched roofs, is very different from the loftier houses of Alsace. In western Normandy and Brittany, granite is the main material, producing buildings as rugged as the landscape.

Traditional techniques also served to build imposing townhouses. Half-timbered towns are especially characteristic of Alsace, Picardy, southern Brittany and Normandy, where even Rouen has a half-timbered core. More public buildings – notably churches – generally followed more 'cultivated' styles, with exceptions such as the 'parish enclosures' of western Brittany, where local builders combined Gothic, Renaissance and their own traditions in some of the strangest religious buildings in Europe.

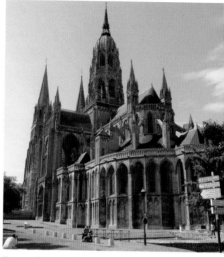
Bayeux Cathedral, a superb example of Romanesque style

Romanesque and Gothic

The first 'cultured' architectural style to become widespread in France since the fall of Rome was Romanesque. Characterised by massive walls, small windows, fine carving and tall, rounded arches, it gives an impression of majestic simplicity.

As the name suggests, it was highly influenced by Roman building, and first appeared in northern Italy, spreading around France from about AD1000. France at this time was fragmented, and the centres of Romanesque were distant from the later hub of French power. The southwest and Burgundy are particularly rich, with treasures such as the church at **Moissac** near Toulouse, the 11th-century basilica of **Vézelay** and **Abbey of Fontenay**, both in Burgundy. Romanesque was also the preferred style of the Norman dukes, who took it to England (where it is often called Norman architecture). The gems of Norman Romanesque are the **Abbaye aux Hommes** in Caen and **Mont St-Michel**, but it was used to magnificent effect in many other buildings in Normandy, such as **Bayeux Cathedral** and the glorious abbey at **Lessay**.

The first real 'French' style, Gothic, fittingly appeared at the time when France's kings were extending their power. Abbot Suger, who commissioned the first true Gothic building at **St-Denis** in 1137, was also the right arm of kings Louis VI and VII. In contrast to the solidity of Romanesque, Gothic builders used innovations such as flying buttresses to create slimmer walls that seem to soar to impossible heights. Larger windows flooded cathedrals with light. St-Denis was followed by **Notre-Dame** in Paris itself. The jewels of French Gothic

French architecture

The 16th-century palace of Chambord in the Loire

can be seen in a trip from Paris through Picardy and Champagne: the cathedrals of **Beauvais** – never finished – **Senlis**, **Noyon**, **Soissons** and, above all, **Reims**, **Laon** and **Amiens**. Elsewhere, Gothic was grafted onto older buildings, as in **Rouen** or **Mont St-Michel**. Larger windows allowed the development of another great art of medieval France, stained glass, at its summit in the cathedral at **Chartres**.

Grandeur

One characteristic of official French architecture is its desire for grandeur, which came to the fore when pleasure châteaux appeared in the Loire at the end of the 15th century. The greatest builder of the age was François I (1515–47), who rebuilt the **Louvre**, **Fontainebleau** and several Loire châteaux, and built his own massive Loire palace of **Chambord**. He also near-imposed the French Renaissance style, combining Italian neoclassicism with an imposing sense of symmetry and very French grey roofs and pointed towers.

Grand building continued after 1600 in France's *grand siècle* or 'great century', and reached a peak, naturally, under Louis XIV with his vast showcase at **Versailles**. The role of French Baroque architecture was to show off its patrons to the greatest glory, and architects such as Salomon de Brosse, Louis Le Vau – who partly defined the style in 1658–61 at **Vaux-le-Vicomte** – François Mansart and Jules Hardouin-Mansart did their best to comply.

A special feature of this grand French architecture is that the geometrical arrangement of surrounding space is as important as the building itself. No grand château is complete

A selection of France's master-builders, in chronological order:

Robert de Luzarches – chief architect of Amiens Cathedral, and one of few medieval builders whose name is known.

François Mansart – an inescapable influence in French architecture, for his châteaux and for his roofs.

Louis Le Vau – at Vaux-le-Vicomte, the Louvre and in the first parts of Versailles he established the model of *ancien régime* opulence.

Jules Hardouin-Mansart – the chief architect of Versailles.

Marshal Vauban – surrounded France with ramparts and fortresses for Louis XIV.

Ange-Jacques Gabriel – completed the classical elegance of Paris in the place de la Concorde.

Eugène Viollet-le-Duc – France's greatest Gothic revivalist, who restored (and prettified) Notre-Dame and built the Château de Pierrefonds for Napoleon III.

Charles Garnier – builder of the sumptuous Paris Opéra and Monte Carlo Casino.

Christian de Portzamparc – creator of Paris's Cité de la Musique and other intricate structures.

Jean Nouvel – one of the current stars of world architecture, who in Paris has built the Institut du Monde Arabe and the Musée du Quai Branly.

without its complementary French gardens, epitomised by André Le Nôtre's elaborate creations at Versailles. Chambord is more majestic as you approach on the tree-lined *allées* than when you actually go inside. This obsession with grand perspectives was extended to urban planning, especially in Paris, from where it naturally spread to provincial France.

Stand in the **place de la Concorde** – from the 1750s – and the sense of design remains breathtaking. In the 1850s, Baron Haussmann's transformation of Paris enshrined the broad, straight **boulevard** as the hallmark of urban refinement, imitated in other cities. In the 1980s President Mitterrand, a man with a strong sense of French tradition, took great care to complete Paris's **Grand Axe** or 'Great Axis', so that from the Louvre pyramid you can see all along the Champs-Elysées to the **Arche de La Défense**, 8km (5 miles) away. Few countries take so much interest in creating straight lines.

51

French architecture

Part of the *Grand Axe* in Paris, from the Arc de Triomphe looking towards La Défense

Grand siècle and Belle Epoque

The abiding influence of the *grand siècle* is not only in châteaux and grand avenues. In 1605 Henri IV commissioned the **place des Vosges** in Paris, France's first modern square, and the **Marais** district around it began to fill with *hôtels particuliers*, town mansions. A few years later, streets of townhouses appeared on the **Ile St-Louis**. Walk around these Paris streets today, though, and they seem more familiar than historic, for the style developed there – shutters, plain facades, mansard roofs (invented by François Mansart), imposing doorways – has remained a template for French building, repeated in countless towns and even in use today. A similar 'official' style developed for public buildings, such as **Rennes**'s grand 1618 **Parlement de Bretagne,** or the **place de la Comédie** in **Montpellier**.

The next building boom to leave an indelible mark came in the Second Empire and Belle Epoque (1871–1914). Napoleon III's empire was most associated with the indulgently ornate Beaux-Arts style, as in the voluptuous Paris **Opéra**. Later, apartment blocks with mansard roofs filled the new boulevards, but from the 1880s architecture – as well as favouring technical innovation, as in the **Eiffel Tower** – departed from French sobriety with eclecticism and even frivolity, as Beaux-Arts blended into curvaceous Art Nouveau.

Small towns across France acquired *mairies* and train stations with Beaux-Arts details; the new seaside gave still more scope for frivolousness, as in the whimsical beach villas of resorts such

Place de la Comédie in Montpellier

as **Dinard** in Brittany, Normandy's **Etretat** or, among the most extravagant, the Côte d'Azur at **Antibes**.

Modern times

Contemporary France is known for its spectacular large-scale buildings, often cultural venues featuring ground-breaking design, symbols of modernity. In a departure from the past, many are by foreign architects, notably the initiator of the wave, the **Centre Pompidou** in Paris by Richard Rogers and Renzo Piano, from the 1970s. Still more were Mitterrand-era *grands projets*, such as the **Opéra Bastille** and the **Cité de la Musique** at La Villette, both in Paris.

In the interests of decentralisation, dramatic cultural showcases have also appeared in the regions, such as the **Centre Pompidou-Metz** and forthcoming **Louvre-Lens** in Lille, both by Japanese architects. The most spectacular modern structure in France, though, is a bridge, Norman Foster's breathtaking **Millau Viaduct** in Languedoc.

By contrast, the functionalist theories of arch-modernist Le Corbusier and cost considerations have both contributed to the creation of France's often notably drab modern low-cost housing. The other side of the coin of the careful preservation of historic centres of towns and cities has been the confinement of cheaper housing (and its often immigrant residents) to the tower-block *banlieue* (suburbs) around most towns, notorious as social flashpoints.

Destinations

Emblematic architectural locations:
Provence – the villages of the Vaucluse for their timeless stone houses.
Central Normandy – for the infinite variety of half-timbering in the Pays d'Auge.
Mont St-Michel – an extraordinary blend of Norman Romanesque and High Gothic, on a rock in the ocean.
Amiens – the most stunning of all the Gothic cathedrals.
Chambord and the other royal Loire châteaux – Renaissance opulence.
Versailles, **Fontainebleau** and **Vaux-le-Vicomte** – the definition of the French grand manner.
Paris: Ile de la Cité – a model of French urban living.
Paris: Grand Axe and **Grand Boulevards** – the French ideal of urban order.
Etretat – apart from Monet's beloved cliffs, its eccentric villas still have the scent of the Belle Epoque.
Paris: Centre Pompidou – the first and still most impressive of *grands projets*.

On the water

Water is inseparable from many of France's most beautiful vistas. With long, broad rivers, rocky gorges, quiet canals and seascapes that run from the granite cliffs of Brittany to Mediterranean beaches, the country offers an enormous range of options for enjoying the water, from slow canal cruising to some of Europe's best surfing.

Along the Atlantic and the Mediterranean coasts of France there are, as well as beaches, hundreds of harbours, especially charming small ports, with excellent facilities for sailing and watersports in a wide variety of conditions. Some locations have specialities, such as surfing on the Basque coast, or sand-yachting in the Pas-de-Calais. France's small ports also have their special style, fresh fish and seafood in harbour-side restaurants being an essential feature.

France's inland waterways consist not only of its great river systems – the Seine, the Loire, the Rhône, the Garonne – but also a remarkable network of canals begun in the 1600s to link them up. The Canal de Briare and Canal du Centre run between the Seine and the Loire; another, the Canal de Bourgogne, links the Seine and Rhône basins, and is one of France's most beautiful canals; and the Canal du Midi runs from the Mediterranean near Sète to Toulouse, where it joins the Canal de la Garonne to continue to the Atlantic near Bordeaux. Intended as 'flowing highways' connecting the Channel, the Biscay coast and the Mediterranean, these canals nowadays provide one of the most delightful ways of enjoying France's changing landscapes.

Sailing school at Etretat, Normandy

The rivers, above all in the south, also provide plenty of opportunity for exploration and entertainment. The Dordogne is lovely for gentle canoeing and kayaking, while the river gorges of the Massif Central, the Alps and Provence are gorgeous locations for white-water kayaking and rafting.

For information on facilities in any part of France, check regional and *département* tourism websites.

Sailing

Sailing facilities in France are world-class, and very well organised. There are attractive ports on the Channel coast, such as Honfleur, but sailors' attention tends to be drawn to the Cotentin Peninsula and Brittany, with their dramatic cliffs, engaging harbours, shifting weather and rocky islands. On Brittany's sheltered south side is the Golfe du Morbihan, a shallow inland sea 20km (12 miles) wide and full of small islands that is ideal for lazy sailing. If you take your own boat, nearly every Breton port has a marina or *port de plaisance*.

Many coastal towns also have a *station nautique* offering a range of activities and tuition. A comprehensive guide to all sea-based activities in Brittany is on the Nautisme en Bretagne site (in French only; www.nautisme bretagne.fr). In addition, Brittany originated the idea (since extended to the Charente-Maritime, Côte d'Azur and Corsica) of **Points Passion Plage**, smaller-scale centres to encourage more casual access to watersports, such as at **Cancale** near St-Malo (tel: 02 99 89 90), or the **Point Passion Plage de Crozon-Morgat** (tel: 02 98 26 24 90) in the sheltered Bay of Douarnenez. There is a joint website for *Points Plage* around France: www. pointplage.fr.

South of Brittany, the area around La Rochelle and its islands is beautiful for exploring by boat, and there are also several *Points Plage* here (see website above). Near Bordeaux, Arcachon, on its giant bay, is another popular centre, where **Activoile** (tel: 05 56 83 82 81; www.activoileocean.com)

Sailing off the Corsican coast

offers boats to rent and training.

In the Mediterranean, strong winds make the Languedoc-Roussillon coast an exciting place to sail, on the sea and the *étangs* or saltwater lagoons; try the **Centre Nautique Cap d'Agde** (tel: 04 67 01 46 46; www.centre nautique-capdagde.com). Further east, yacht rentals, with or without crew, are a speciality of the beautiful ports of Provence and the Côte d'Azur through companies such as **Evasion-Location** in St-Mandrier-sur-Mer near Toulon (tel: 04 94 63 69 70; www. evasionlocation.fr). An easy sail away is Corsica, where the many small harbours are a must for sailors. The **Base Nautique Mare e Vela**, Plage de Portigiolo (tel: 04 95 22 56 67), south of Ajaccio, is an attractive *Point Plage*.

Many companies offer yacht charters. UK-based **Nautilus Yachting** (UK tel: 01732 867455) provides boats in Brittany and the Côte d'Azur.

On the water

Windsurfing, kiteboarding, sea kayaking, sand-yachting

Windsurfing is also available at many – indeed most – of France's sailing centres, and kiteboarding and wakeboarding are fast gaining in popularity. The hottest spots for these are, on the Atlantic, Quiberon in Brittany, where **Carnac Evasion** provides courses (Carnac-Plage; tel: 02 97 52 33 66; www.carnac-evasion. com), and the beaches and lakes west of Bordeaux around Arcachon, where **H2o Kite** (Biscarosse; tel: 06 26 91 21 29; www.h2okite.com) offers high-adrenalin activities.

In the Mediterranean the Languedoc coast is one of the world's foremost windsurf destinations. In St-Pierre-sur-Mer near Narbonne, **SNK** (tel: 04 68 49 22 31; www.snkite.com) provides a full range of services. The tramontane, a local wind, can make for very challenging conditions.

Many centres also offer guided sea-kayak trips or rentals. In the Golfe du Morbihan you can kayak to deserted islands, and the Bay of Arcachon is another favourite.

The huge, flat tidal reaches of the north Channel coast – around Wissant, Berck-sur-Mer and the Baie de la Somme – have made this the world capital of sand-yachting *(char à voile)*. A two-hour introduction is available from **Agora** in Berck (tel: 03 21 89 87 00; www.agora-berck.com).

Surfing

International surfers rate the surf breaks on the Basque coast north of Biarritz as among the best in the world. The main beaches are Lacanau and Hossegor, and you can also surf in Biarritz itself. **Natural Surf Lodge** in Hossegor (tel: 06 74 16 02 28; www.naturalsurflodge. com) offers surf camps and packages. Other surf destinations are in Brittany, at Quiberon and Perros-Guirec. For information, check www.surfing france.com.

Surf school in Finistère

Water-skiing

Water-skis are available in many Mediterranean resorts, and the Atlantic beaches south of Arcachon are popular with more adventurous water-skiers. **Sports Service Lacanau** (tel: 05 56 03 09 01; www.lacanau-loisirs-nautique.com) provides full equipment and training. There are also water-ski centres on many inland lakes, such as at Gravon, only 80km (50 miles) southeast of Paris (**Aqu'aventure**; tel: 01 64 31 27 59; www.skiaquaventure.com).

Scuba-diving and snorkelling

The home of Jacques Cousteau, France is also a fine diving destination. The Provençal coast and the Côte d'Azur are the prime area, with the best diving from St-Tropez to the Ile de Porquerolles, famed for its historic wrecks. **Aqualonde Plongée** (tel: 04 94 01 20 04; www.aqualonde-plongee.com), at La Londe, near

Wakeboarding in Brittany

Hyères, is a highly respected local operator. Inshore, the secluded coves of this coast are great for snorkelling. There is also fine diving around Corsica, particularly near Porto.

The Dordogne/Lot region is one of the best in the world for cave diving.

Boating bureaucracy

- Owners of non-French-registered boats are not required to have a French sailing permit in French inshore waters, but it is advisable to have an **International Certificate of Competence (ICC)**.
- Those in charge of a French-registered boat (including chartered ones) do not require a permit if they are only sail-powered or have an engine of under 6 horsepower, but with a bigger motor one of several classes of *Permis Plaisance* will be necessary. Check with your charter company exactly what paperwork you need.

- Inland, owners of foreign boats entering French canals and rivers must have an ICC endorsed for inland waterways (called a CEVNI). However, this is strangely not required of anyone hiring a canal or river boat. Again, your rental company should provide all papers required, including those needed when passing through locks.
- In the UK an ICC can be obtained from centres approved by the Royal Yachting Association (www.rya.org.uk), which also provides useful advice about sailing in France.

The Canal du Midi which runs through Languedoc in the southwest

Canal and river cruising

France's 8,000km (5,000 miles) of inland waterways offer an array of possibilities. Cruising along the canals at a snail's pace is a wonderful way to slow down and appreciate the countryside. Canal-lovers can choose between modern cruisers or *péniches* and *pénichettes*, converted traditional barges with comfortable accommodation. Some opulent *péniches* are like floating hotels, with attentive crews.

The most popular cruising waterways are the Canal de Bourgogne and Canal du Nivernais through the Burgundy winelands, with the option of continuing to the Seine or the Rhône; the Canal du Centre from Burgundy to the Loire; the River Charente through Cognac; and the Canal du Midi through Languedoc. Other options include canals in Alsace-Lorraine. **Aboard in France** (www.french-waterways.com) is an excellent source of information in English on all aspects of inland boating in France.

A wide variety of companies provide cruises and/or rentals. One of the largest, **Le Boat** (UK tel: 0844 463 3594; www.leboat.co.uk) offers itineraries in every part of the country; **Locaboat**, based at Joigny near Auxerre (tel: 03 86 91 72 72; www.locaboat.com) is a more low-key operation using charming *pénichettes*, but still with a wide range of routes. By contrast, the *Fandango* and *Tango* are two wonderfully luxurious former barges that take guests on gourmet tours through Burgundy and on the Canal du Midi respectively (**Canals of France**; tel: 06 88 81 16 05; www.canalsoffrance.com).

There's also an ample choice of enjoyable day trips on the water. From La Roque Gageac on the Dordogne, **Les Caminades** (tel: 05 53 29 40 95; www.best-of-perigord.tm.fr) take one-hour rides on a traditional *gabarre* or flat-bottomed barge.

Top spots

A pick of France's watersports hubs:

- Côte du Granit Rose from Paimpol to Roscoff, Brittany
- Quiberon and Carnac, Brittany
- Golfe du Morbihan, Brittany
- Les Sables d'Olonne to Ile d'Oléron, Poitou-Charentes
- Arcachon Bay, Aquitaine
- Biarritz to Hossegor, Basque Country
- Leucate to Cap d'Agde, Languedoc-Roussillon
- Hyères to St-Tropez, Côte d'Azur
- Golfe de Porto and Golfe de Sagone, Corsica

Inland kayaking and white-water rivers

The most celebrated river for kayaking and canoeing through exquisite scenery is the Dordogne, with gorgeous locations to stop over. **Canoë-Safaraid-Dordogne**, based at Vayrac (tel: 05 65 37 44 87; www.canoe-kayak-dordogne.com) offers routes from half a day to a week. The Tarn Gorges

north of Montpellier are another unforgettable location, the river winding beneath giant cliffs. These and trips on other rivers can be booked through **Rivières de France** (www.canoe-france.com; also in English).

To get the heart rate up, southern France also has famous white-water rivers for adventure kayaking and rafting. The Ardèche Gorges west of Orange are the most famous, the river passing spectacularly beneath the giant natural bridge of the Pont d'Arc (**Alpha Bateaux**, Vallon-Pont d'Arc; tel: 04 75 88 08 29; www.canoeardeche.com, are local experts). Equally awe-inspiring are the Gorges du Verdon inland from the Côte d'Azur. Adventure sports operations are based in nearby Castellane, where at **Base Sport-Nature** (tel: 04 93 05 41 18; www.basesportnature.com) rafting can be combined with other exciting options. Other rafting rivers include the relatively gentle Gave d'Oloron in the Basque Country, and the challenging upper Isère in the Alps.

59

On the water

Kayaking through Brantôme in the Dordogne

PLACES

UNITED KINGDOM

English Channel

Dunkerque
Calais
Boulogne-
sur-Mer
Étaples
Nord-Pas-
de-Calais Lille
Amiens

Dieppe

Cherbourg   Fécamp
le Havre
Bayeux
Caen
Rouen   Beauvais

Channel Islands
(Îles Normandes)

Golfe de
St-Malo

**NORMANDY
AND BRITTANY**

Pages 120 – 143

Picardie

Soissons

Château-
Thierry

Évreux

Alençon

**PARIS AND THE
ILE DE FRANCE**

Pages 64 – 97

Île
d'Ouessant

Brest   Morlaix

Quimper

Pointe
du Raz

Pointe de
Penmarch   **Lorient**

Belle
Île

Bretagne

St-Brieuc

Loudéac

Pontivy

Vannes

Dinard

Dinan

Rennes

Mayenne

Le Mans

Versailles

Chartres

Orléans

Auxerre

Île de
Noirmoutier

St-Nazaire

Nantes

Cholet

Angers

Pays de
la Loire

Vendôme

Blois

Romorantin-
Lanthenay

Parthenay

Thouars

THE LOIRE VALLEY

Pages 144 – 161

Centre

Bourges

la Roche-
sur-Yon

les Sables-
d'Olonne

la
Rochelle

Île
d'Oléron

Fontenay-
le-Comte

Niort

Châtellerault

Poitiers

Poitou-
Charentes

Châteauroux

St-Amand-
Montrond

BAY   OF

BISCAY

Rochefort

Royan

Pointe
de Grave

Saintes

Cognac

Angoulême

Limoges

Limousin

Clermont-
Ferrand

Auvergne

Issoire

St-Médard-
en-Jalles

Bordeaux

Arcachon

Libourne

Dordogne

Bergerac

Périgueux

Brive-la-
Gaillarde

Tulle

Ussel

Golfe de
Gascogne

Landes

Aquitaine

Marmande

Mont-de-
Marsan

THE SOUTHWEST

Pages 188 – 217

Rodez

Biarritz

Bayonne

Orthez

Oloron-
Ste-Marie

Pau

Dax

Lourdes

Midi-
Pyrénées

Tarbes

St-
Gaudens

Auch

Montauban

Albi

Castres

Toulouse

Carcassonne

Limoux

Béziers

Narbonne

Perpignan

SPAIN   Pyrénées

Getting your bearings

France's unique position as the only European country that is both Atlantic and Mediterranean, northern and southern, gives it an extraordinary diversity of climate and landscape. The towns and villages that have grown out of the landscape are just as distinctive.

For easy reference when using this guide, each major area has a dedicated chapter and is colour-coded for quick navigation. France's great hub of Paris and its surrounding towns naturally form an area apart. The north and east covers several distinctive regions: Picardy, the Nord–Pas-de-Calais, Champagne with its vineyards, Lorraine and Germanic Alsace. Normandy and Brittany both have a special Atlantic flavour. The Loire Valley and Burgundy to the Alps together cover huge areas inseparable from fine wines and good living, from Loire châteaux to Alpine resorts. The southwest includes another great wine region, Bordeaux, with the Dordogne countryside, the Basque coast and the Pyrenees. The final chapter covers the whole of France's Mediterranean coast, with Provence and the offshore island of Corsica.

Detailed regional maps are included within each chapter. With each one there is also a listings section featuring the best hotels, restaurants, cafés and activities the city or region has to offer, covering all budgets.

MEDITERRANEAN SEA

Paris and the Ile de France

A city for romantics, art enthusiasts and lovers of street life, Paris is fascinating at every turn. The site of some of the most stunningly beautiful urban landscapes in the world, Paris is also an earthy, eternally vibrant city of contrasts and rough edges. Nearby is a rich mix of castles, forests and villages to explore – and Disneyland Resort Paris.

Population: 12,800,000

Local dialling code: 01

Main tourist offices: Paris: 25 rue des Pyramides; tel: 08 92 68 30 00; **www.parisinfo.com**. Ile de France: 2 bis avenue de Paris, Versailles; tel: 01 30 97 89 89; **www.new-paris-idf.com**

Main police stations: 4 place du Louvre; tel: 01 53 71 33 00

Main post office: 52 rue du Louvre

Main hospitals: American Hospital of Paris (private), 63 boulevard Victor-Hugo, 92292 Neuilly; tel: 01 46 41 25 25; **www.american-hospital. org**. Hôpital Européen Georges-Pompidou, 20 rue Leblanc; tel: 01 56 09 20 00

Local newspapers/listings: *L'Officiel des Spectacles, Pariscope* (every Wed)

The fascination of the French capital – 'the city of cities' as Victor Hugo put it – is eternal. It has been growing and changing for over 2,000 years, and each of its many layers is rich in history and intrigue. Unlike many European cities, it was left almost unscathed by the two world wars, and its celebrated streets, monuments and museums still work their centuries-old magic today.

Paris is a city ideal for strolling – there is always something completely different around the next corner; begin at place de la Concorde, and before you realise it you can have walked through the Napoleonic arcades of rue de Rivoli and the charming squares and lanes of the Marais to the Bastille, or past the riverside *quais* and street markets on the *Rive Gauche* (Left Bank) of the Seine to the famous bohemian gathering-points in the cafés of St-Germain. Associations with all the thousands of famous past residents – artists, writers, thinkers, musicians, decadents – are intertwined with the life of the city.

Surrounding the capital, the Ile de France offers the glories of the palaces of Versailles and Fontainebleau, the thrills of Disney and the serenity of the forest of Chantilly – all easily reached by train from the city centre.

The heart of Paris

The Ile de la Cité is the birthplace and physical centre of Paris, and has been its spiritual and legislative pulse for more than 2,000 years. Bridges cross over to either side, and on the Right Bank it is an easy walk to the Louvre, the queen of all art museums. In contrast, Les Halles offers modern shopping adjacent to the chic and colourful lanes of the Marais.

The islands

The Ile de la Cité is dominated by the soaring **Cathédrale Notre-Dame de Paris** Ⓐ (www.cathedraledeparis. com; Mon–Fri 8am–6.45pm, Sat–Sun 8am–7.15pm; free, charge for towers),

Art Nouveau métro sign

which fills the eastern end of the island. A masterpiece of Gothic art, it was built during the 12th and 13th centuries, and extensively restored in the 19th. The tall central spire (82m/ 270ft) is flanked by two square towers, and visitors may climb up to see the 16-ton brass bell that the hunchback Quasimodo rang in Victor Hugo's *The Hunchback of Notre-Dame*, and the view is a heavenly reward (*for more on Notre-Dame, see p.70*).

Occupying the northeast wing of the Palais de Justice at the opposite end of the island, the **Conciergerie** (daily, Mar–Oct 9.30am–6.30pm, Nov–Feb 10am–5pm; charge) looks like an intimidating castle. Built in the 14th century, it isn't hard to imagine this fortress as a merciless medieval prison. Later, during the Revolution, it housed nearly 2,600 prisoners awaiting the guillotine, including Marie Antoinette.

Through an ornate 18th-century gate, **Sainte-Chapelle** Ⓑ (daily, Mar–Oct 9.30am–6pm, May–Sept Wed until 9pm, Nov–Feb 9am–5pm; charge) is a glittering jewel of Gothic art built in 1246 to hold the Crown

The Gothic cathedral of Notre-Dame

5ᵉ Arr
PONT
DE
L'ARCHEVÊCHÉ

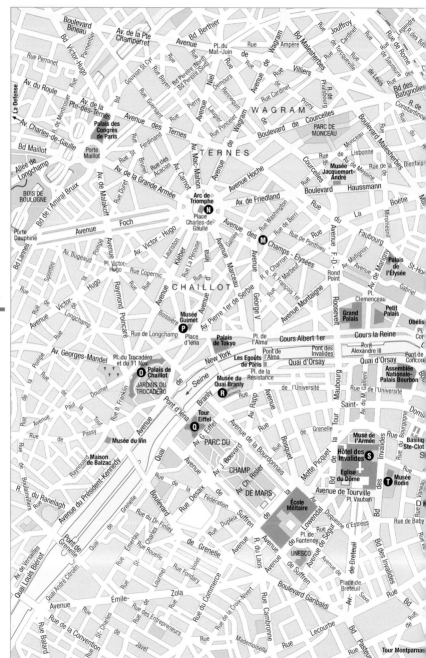

Paris

Airports: Roissy-Charles de Gaulle (CDG), 23km (15 miles) from Paris; Orly (ORY), 14km (9 miles). For both airports, tel: 3950; **www.aeroportsdeparis.fr**. Transport into Paris from CDG: suburban train line (RER), line B every 15 minutes, takes 50 minutes; single €9.40. RoissyBus every 15–20 minutes, takes an hour; €9.40. Noctilien night bus every hour, 12.30–5.30am; €7.50; **www.noctilien.fr**. VEA shuttle to Disneyland Resort Paris every 20 minutes; €18. Taxis take around an hour for about €50. From Orly: shuttle bus and RER line C every 15 minutes, takes 35 minutes; €6.30. The Orlyval shuttle and RER line B every 5 minutes, takes 30 minutes; €13. Orlybus every 15–20 minutes, takes 30 minutes; €6.60. VEA shuttle to Disneyland Resort Paris every 30 minutes; €17. Taxis take about 45 minutes, cost around €45

Métro and RER: Operated by RATP, tel: 3246; **www.ratp.info**. The métro has 14 lines that operate daily 5.30am–12.30am (Sat until 2.20am) identified by number, a colour and the names of the last station in each direction. The RER runs five suburban rail lines, identified as A–E, 5am–midnight, out to the Ile de France. T+ Tickets (€1.70) are valid for métro, buses and RER trains within the city. A *carnet* of 10 costs €12. A Mobilis one-day ticket allows travel anywhere according to zones from €6.10 to €17.30

Buses: Also run by RATP *(see above)* 6am–midnight, when Noctilien night buses (**www.noctilien.fr**) take over. Paris now also has some tramway lines outside the centre, and is building several more

Taxis: Available from almost 500 taxi ranks in the city. For all Paris taxis, tel: 01 45 30 30 30; **www.taxi.fr**

Car hire: Avis: 8 boulevard Davout; tel: 01 0 24 10 20; **www.avis.co.uk**. Rent-A-Car: 23 rue du Départ; tel: 01 43 21 56 50; **www.rentacar.fr**

of Thorns acquired by Louis IX. Try and visit when the sun is shining to appreciate fully the splendour of the stained glass.

Several bridges cross over the Seine from the Ile de la Cité. The **Pont Neuf** (New Bridge) is, despite its name, the oldest existing bridge in Paris (1607) and links the western end of the island to both banks. The pedestrian Pont St-Louis crosses to the smaller **Ile St-Louis 🄲** behind Notre-Dame, a privileged haven of peace and wealth, small art galleries, intimate restaurants and tearooms – and Berthillon, home of what is reputed to be the best ice cream in Paris.

Les Halles and the Marais

Across from the Ile de la Cité, the place du Châtelet lies above one of Paris's biggest metro and RER stations. Head north up boulevard de Sébastopol where to the left, the **Forum des Halles** is a vast underground shopping centre built under a demolished marketplace that had fed Paris from 1183 until 1969.

East of the boulevard looms the **Centre Pompidou 🄳** (www.centrepompidou.fr; Wed–Mon 11am–9pm; charge), an innovative inside-out construction designed by Richard Rogers and Renzo Piano, showcasing modern and contemporary art including

Outside the Pompidou Centre

Carnavalet (www.carnavalet. paris.fr; Tue–Sun 10am–6pm; free, charge for temporary exhibitions), in rue Sévigné, which documents the city's history from its Gallo-Roman days and has a gallery dedicated to Madame de Sévigné, a 17th-century *grande dame*. Nearby, on rue Thorigny, the newly renovated **Musée National Picasso** (www.musee-picasso.fr; reopening in 2012) occupies the 17th-century Hôtel Salé and is filled with Picasso's works, donated by his family in lieu of inheritance tax.

The magnificent, arcaded **place des Vosges** to the south was built by Henri as a showcase for his court. Today, the arcades house restaurants and expensive art galleries as well as the **Maison de Victor Hugo** (Tue–Sun 10am–6pm; free), the writer's Paris home for 15 years. Close by is the **place de la Bastille** , the site of the 14th-century prison destroyed by the people on 14 July 1789, igniting the Revolution. Dominating the square,

Paris and the Ile de France

works by Picasso, Matisse and Warhol. The square outside is often thronged with people and entertainers.

Continuing eastwards, the **Marais** is a *quartier* full of history and local colour. 'Marais' means marsh, and in the reign of Henri IV (1589–1610) the area was drained and homes were built for the aristocracy along narrow streets and alleyways. From the Revolution, the Marais fell into disrepair until 1962 when renovation work began. Today, it is one of the most fashionable – and costly – places to live in Paris, its character defined by mansions and museums, chic boutiques, gay bars and cafés and the kosher groceries in rue des Rosiers.

Many private mansions are now museums, such as the **Musée**

Arcades in the Place des Vosges

Even before it was finished, Notre-Dame had become the venue for state ceremonies; in 1239 Louis IX deposited the Crown of Thorns and other relics acquired on Crusades here. In 1589, Henri of Navarre was crowned in the cathedral, having decided to convert to Catholicism. Come the Revolution, Notre-Dame was ravaged by looters, and at Napoleon's coronation in 1804, the cathedral was in such a shabby state that bright tapestries were hung up to cover the crumbling decor; when Pope Pius VII hesitated at the altar, Napoleon took the crown and – to cheers of 'Vive l'Empereur!' – placed it on his head himself.

In August 1944, at the thanksgiving ceremony for the Liberation of Paris, the new president, General Charles de Gaulle, was shot at during the Te Deum.

the giant glass-and-concrete **Opéra-Bastille** is a primary venue for opera and ballet. From the Port de l'Arsenal on the south side of the square, you can take a boat along the **Canal St-Martin** to La Villette further north (Canauxrama; www.canauxrama.com).

The Louvre

To the west of the Ile de la Cité and hugging the Seine on the Right Bank lies the **Musée du Louvre** ❶ (www.louvre.fr; Wed–Mon 9am–6pm, Wed and Fri until 10pm; charge), occupying a vast palace with I.M. Pei's modern pyramid providing a grand entrance to the world-famous galleries (see p.72–3).

Beside it is the **Jardin des Tuileries** ❶, dating from 1564 and so named as it was created out of a clay quarry for tiles. The park was redesigned 100

The Louvre's striking entrance is a glass pyramid

Opulent staircase at the Palais Garnier

Across the busy, arcaded rue de Rivoli from the Louvre stands the **Palais Royal**, built by Cardinal Richelieu in the 17th century. In the main courtyard are 250 black-and-white-striped columns, erected by artist Daniel Buren in 1986. The delightful **Jardin du Palais Royal**, once a meeting place for revolutionaries, is surrounded by arcades sheltering some eccentric old shops, top-end boutiques and fine restaurants, including **Le Grand Véfour**, which has fed the likes of Napoleon and Victor Hugo.

The Opéra, Montmartre and the Champs-Elysées

North of place de la Concorde, a system of tree-lined boulevards sustains the most luxurious shopping areas, as well as the less salubrious area of Pigalle and arty Montmartre (see p.76–7). Nothing is cheap along the vast avenue des Champs-Elysées, designed by André le Nôtre in 1667. To the south lies the Trocadéro and the Palais de Chaillot, with magnificent views of the Eiffel Tower.

The Opéra and Grands Boulevards

Rue Royale runs northwards out of the place de la Concorde and branches right into boulevard de la Madeleine at the Greek temple church of the same name, originally built by Napoleon as a temple of glory for his army. At the end stands the glorious **Palais Garnier ❶** (www.operadeparis.fr; daily 10am–5pm; charge). Designed by Charles Garnier and completed in 1875, this lavish emblem of the

years later by landscape artist André Le Nôtre, also responsible for the park at Versailles (see p.87). From the Louvre you have one of the longest architectural vistas in the world, through the Arc de Triomphe to the Grande Arche at La Défense, ghost-like in the distance.

At **place de la Concorde**, where Louis XVI was guillotined on 17 January 1793, the **Musée de l'Orangerie** (www.musee-orangerie.fr; Wed–Mon 9am–5.45pm; charge) contains Monet's unforgettable *Water Lilies* series (*Les Nymphéas*), and the tiny **Jeu de Paume** (www.jeudepaume.org; Tue noon–9pm, Wed–Fri noon–7pm, Sat–Sun 10am–7pm; charge) focuses on photography and film.

Paris and the Ile de France

⭐ THE LOUVRE

Kilometres of corridors, over 35,000 exhibits, art and artefacts from every part of the world up to the 19th century – the world's most visited museum can appear daunting, and the crowds around its star exhibits like the *Mona Lisa* unappealing. Nevertheless, take it without rushing, stop for regular breaks at the excellent cafés, focus on a few special areas of interest, and maybe drop by the celebrity paintings and sculptures when the hordes have thinned, and this magnificent treasure-house is richly, superbly enjoyable.

The Louvre owes its vast size to the fact that it was the main residence of France's kings until Louis XIV's departure for Versailles in 1682, and was added to by monarch after monarch. It became a public museum after the Revolution; in the 1980s, the *Grand Louvre* renovation project introduced the glass pyramid by I.M. Pei that now forms the main entrance.

From the giant lobby beneath it there is access to the three main wings: **Richelieu** to the north, **Sully** to the east and **Denon** to the south. However, the various collections, colour-coded on signs, are actually dispersed around all three, which can be confusing, so study the free maps to decide where to head for first.

To begin at the beginning, in the basement level of Sully is the medieval Louvre, with the foundations of the first Louvre fortress from the 1180s. Highlights of the ground floor are

The double-sided *David and Goliath* painted by Daniele da Volterra in the Grande Galerie

relics of the ancient world – a vast Egyptian collection, the astonishing Khorsabad human-headed winged bulls from ancient Iraq (Richelieu), and the armless *Venus de Milo* and other Greek and Roman treasures (Sully and Denon).

The most celebrated paintings are on the first floor, especially in Denon, where the magnificent Grande Galerie contains giant paintings like Delacroix's *Liberty Leading the People*, and the Salle des Etats hosts the *Mona Lisa*, often invisible behind bobbing heads.

It's also in the nature of the Louvre that you can wander along galleries that seem completely unmemorable, only to come upon masterpieces like Georges de la Tour's *Cheat with the Ace of Diamonds* (Sully, second floor) or Dürer's 1493 *Self-Portrait* (Richelieu, second floor), and oddities like Napoleon III's apartments (Richelieu, first floor).

Also on view are spectacular collections of decorative arts, from a 9th-century statuette of Charlemagne – or possibly his grandson – on horseback (Richelieu, first floor) to France's former Crown Jewels, in the sumptuously Baroque Galerie d'Apollon (Denon, first floor). Currently tucked away in the basement level of Richelieu are some stunning Islamic ceramics.

A ticket allows you to enter and re-enter as many times as you like on the same day, so you can head outside to relax in one of the restaurants nearby, such as the chic Café Marly in the Louvre arcades. Plus, there are also very high-standard souvenir shops.

Egyptian room

The Louvre

Venus de Milo, from around 100BC, depicts the Greek goddess of love and beauty

The magnificent Art Nouveau dome at Galeries Lafayette

Second Empire puts on opera and ballet in tandem with the Opéra-Bastille (see p.70). Inside, the grand ornate staircase is the ultimate celebrity catwalk.

The elegant avenues of the **Grands Boulevards** were built straight and wide to replace untidy, crowded slums as part of the city's 19th-century facelift under Baron Haussmann. The main axis was formed by four boulevards running into each other – Madeleine, Capucines, Italiens and Montmartre – and in a few years, the area was transformed into one of the most elegant parts of Paris.

Boulevard Haussmann, behind the Opéra, is dominated by the late 19th-century *grands magasins* (department stores) – **Galeries Lafayette** (famed for its Art Nouveau central hall and stained-glass dome) and **Printemps**. But for expensive jewellery go to **place Vendôme** ⓚ, to the east of the Madeleine, a 17th-century marvel of

opulence containing the **Hôtel Ritz**, once a haunt of Hemingway's. To the south of the square, fashionable rue St-Honoré runs west into rue du Faubourg Saint-Honoré, the city's most luxurious shopping street, and past the presidential **Palais de l'Elysée**.

Montmartre

The most popular excursion from central Paris is up the hill, or *Butte*, north to **Montmartre** ⓛ (see p.76–7), a picturesque former village a little set apart from the city, which manages to be a living community, a magnet for tourists and an artistic legend at the same time. Painters Toulouse-Lautrec and Utrillo, and later Picasso, poet Guillaume Apollinaire and pianist Erik Satie helped create the image of the freethinking hilltop.

The Etoile to the Trocadéro

The world's most famous avenue, the **Champs-Elysées** ⓜ leads you elegantly up to the Arc de Triomphe. Its reputation has ebbed and flowed through the centuries, but now it is filled with exclusive designer shops and is back to its former glory. At the eastern end stands the **Grand Palais**, holding the **Galeries Nationales** (www.grandpalais.fr; opening times according to exhibitions) and the **Palais de la Découverte** (Discovery Museum; www.palais-decouverte. fr; Tue–Sat 9.30am–6pm, Sun 10am–7pm; charge). Close by, the **Petit Palais** (www.petitpalais.paris.fr; Tue–Sun 10am–6pm) houses the Musée des Beaux-Arts.

The **Arc de Triomphe**  (www. arcdetriompheparis.com; daily, Apr–Sept 10am–11pm, Oct–Mar 10am–10.30pm; charge), in the centre of Etoile (so named because the streets radiate out like a star), was commissioned by Napoleon in 1806 to celebrate his victories. The arch can be reached by a tunnel, and a lift can take you to the top for one of the city's finest views.

From the top of the Arc de Triomphe are great views of the Champs-Elysées

Musée d'Art Moderne de la Ville de Paris

Avenue Kléber leads south from Etoile through the wealthy 16th *arrondissement* to **Trocadéro** and the austere **Palais de Chaillot** ◐. Dating from the 1937 World Exhibition, its curved wings hold the Théâtre National de Chaillot and the **Musée de l'Homme** (www.museedelhomme. fr; closed for renovation until autumn 2014), as well as the **Musée de la Marine** (www.musee-marine.fr; Mon, Wed, Thur 11am–6pm, Fri until 9.30pm, Sat–Sun until 7pm; charge), whose centrepiece is Napoleon's barge. A large central terrace, which draws the crowds, looks out over the Seine to the Eiffel Tower.

To the east in place d'Iéna, **Musée Guimet** ◐ (Musée National des Arts Asiatiques; www.guimet.fr; Wed–Mon 10am–6pm; charge) is one of the world's finest museums of Asian art and, close by, the **Palais de Tokyo** is another monumental vestige of the 1937 World Exhibition. The **Musée**

A hilltop village within Paris, Montmartre, or the *Butte*, provides a day's walk through narrow streets and squares that will reveal, under the tourist excesses, plenty to engage and surprise.

As you come out of the métro **Abbesses**, note the Art Nouveau canopy by Hector Guimard, one of only two remaining in the city. Opposite is another Art Nouveau structure, **St-Jean de Montmartre** (1897–1904). Walk eastwards down rue Yvonne le Tac to the funicular up to the basilica, looking in at the Chapelle du Martyr where, according to legend, St Denis, the first bishop of Paris, walked off with his head under his arm after being decapitated by the Romans in AD287.

At place St-Pierre, pop into the **Halle St-Pierre**, a 19th-century covered market hall housing a museum of brut and naïve artworks by artists from around the world, and an excellent café. Either walk up through the beautifully laid out terraces or take the funicular to the gleaming Sacré-Cœur; it's worth climbing the dome's 237 spiral steps for a wonderful view and a look at its huge bell, the Savoyarde.

Head west to the crowded **place du Tertre**, past St-Pierre de Montmartre, the second-oldest church in Paris, on the right, where on the opposite corner in stark contrast stands La Mère Catherine, reputedly Paris's first bistro. Walk southwards across the square to place du Calvaire, where in Espace Dalí you can see more than 300 works by the Surrealist artist.

Continue down rue Poulbot to rue des Saules and take the second right onto rue Cortot to the oldest house on

A stroll in Montmartre

Tips

- Distance: 3.5km (2¼ miles)
- Time: a full day
- Start at Abbesses métro and end in place Pigalle
- Montmartre's streets are very steep, so wear comfortable flat shoes
- A funicular runs up the hill to the basilica and costs one métro ticket
- The basilica's dome and crypt open at 9am, so get there early to avoid the crowds
- Avoid the restaurants on the place du Tertre, as they are pricey and crowded
- In early October, the grape harvest is celebrated with processions and street parties

the *Butte*, the **Musée de Montmartre**, for an in-depth view of the artists' quarter. Behind is a **vineyard** that was planted in 1933.

Across from rue Cortot, rue de l'Abreuvoir runs into the allée des Brouillards. Here, square Suzanne-Buisson occupies the former gardens of the **Château des Brouillards** opposite. The house was built in 1772 and takes its name from a windmill that could only be seen when the fog lifted. Renoir and the Symbolist poet Gérard de Nerval once lived here.

Turning south on rue Girardon, then right onto rue Lepic, you reach **Moulin de la Galette**, the windmill immortalised by Renoir in his 1866 painting. Back on rue Girardon, head downhill along rue d'Orchampt to place Emile Goudeau and **Le Bateau-Lavoir**, once a ramshackle wooden building where

Picasso painted *Les Demoiselles d'Avignon* (1907) and now a replica housing artists' studios. Turn right onto rue Garreau, then rue Durantin and left at the crossroads. Note the famous cinema, Studio 28, where, in 1930, Luis Buñuel's *L'Age d'Or* caused a riot due to its sexual content. At the end of rue Tholozé, turn right to join rue Lepic, the atmospheric market street, and up the hill is another bistro, A la Pomponette, and continuing on down rue Lepic you'll find the Café des Deux Moulins, immortalised in the film *Amélie*.

At the bottom, turn right on to boulevard de Clichy and the **Moulin Rouge** which is now more cheesy than sleazy. Turn back along Clichy and left up rue Germain-Pilon where Chez Toinette offers good, honest fare. End the tour at **place Pigalle**, or Pig Alley as the American soldiers called it in World War II.

Walking tour of Montmartre

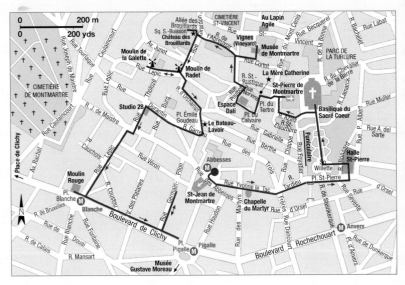

d'Art Moderne de la Ville de Paris
(www.mam.paris.fr; Tue–Sun 10am–
6pm, Thur until 10pm; charge) inside
houses Raoul Dufy's gigantic mural,
La Fée Electricité (Electricity Fairy), created for the Exhibition.

Eiffel Tower and the Invalides

Two Paris landmarks that cannot
be avoided are the Eiffel Tower and
Louis XIV's hospital, the Hôtel des
Invalides. A stone's throw away from
each other, they dominate the southwest bank of the Seine. In between
are smart mansions and elegant townhouses built by the nobility in the
18th century, such as the one housing
the Musée Rodin.

Around the Eiffel Tower

Visible from all over Paris and
beyond, the **Eiffel Tower ⊙** (www.

Enjoying the Eiffel Tower

Queues for the Eiffel Tower can be up
to two hours long in summer, so try to
get there early. The best, and certainly
most romantic, place to see the Eiffel
Tower is from the Trocadéro at night,
when it is gloriously lit up and in full
view across the Seine.

tour-eiffel.com; daily, mid-June–
Aug 9am–midnight, Sept–mid-June
9.30am–11pm; charge), the city's
trademark, was almost demolished
not long after it was built. Erected
for the Universal Exhibition of 1889,
the 300m (985ft) tower, designed
by Gustave Eiffel, was not meant to
be a permanent fixture. Eventually,
telegraphic communications saved
the tower, and it is still used as a radio
mast. The views, of course, are magnificent, especially an hour before sunset.

The Eiffel Tower from the Trocadéro

Musée du Quai Branly, designed by star architect Jean Nouvel

At the foot of the tower is the **Champ de Mars**, a beautifully laid-out park which for centuries was a market garden supplying vegetables to Parisians. When the **Ecole Militaire** was built at the other end in the middle of the 18th century, it became a parade ground holding up to 10,000 men.

Back on the Seine, the **Musée du Quai Branly** ❼ (www.quaibranly.fr; Tue–Wed, Sun 11am–7pm, Thur–Sat until 9pm; charge), which opened in 2006, features indigenous art and culture from Africa, Asia, Oceania and the Americas. The building itself – a striking, foliage-covered, maroon edifice by architect Jean Nouvel *(see p.51)* – stands in stark contrast to its grand neighbours.

At the Pont de l'Alma, the sewers – **Les Egoûts de Paris** (www.egouts. tenebres.eu; Sat–Wed, May–Sept 11am–5pm, Oct–Apr 11am–4pm; charge) – are the city's least likely-sounding tourist attraction *(see p.82–3)*.

Les Invalides

The **Hôtel des Invalides** ❺, with its gleaming dome, is a masterpiece of French Baroque architecture built by Louis XIV to care for retired and wounded soldiers. Napoleon, whose wars kept the hospital full, made the royal **Eglise du Dôme** a necropolis and re-gilded the dome; it now contains his tomb. Napoleon also established the **Musée de l'Armée** (www.invalides.org; daily, Apr–Sept 10am–6pm, Tue until 9pm, Nov–Mar until 5pm, closed first Mon of each month; charge includes Dôme), which illustrates all too vividly man's propensity to fight.

Stretching to the Seine, the grassy **Esplanade des Invalides** is much

Left Bank bookshops

The landmark English bookshop **Shakespeare and Company** (37 rue de la Bûcherie; www.shakespeareandcompany.com; tel: 01 43 25 40 93; Mon–Fri 10am–11pm, Sat–Sun 11am–11pm) was founded in 1919 by American Sylvia Beach but closed during World War II.

Later, another American, George Whitman, great-grandson of Walt Whitman, started his own bookshop on the Left Bank, taking on the name. It stocks a wide range of literature, from the Bard to the Beatniks, and famous expatriate writers such as William Burroughs and James Baldwin were once frequent visitors. Today, George's daughter Sylvia runs the shop, hosting a biennial literary festival.

Sandwiched between Café de Flore and Les Deux Magots is the sleek **La Hune**, a delightful bookshop crammed with literature and books on art, architecture and performing arts, in French and English. Open until midnight, it feels most 'St-Germain' after dark.

loved by strollers, joggers, dog walkers, roller bladers and players of *pétanque* or boules.

To the west is the **Musée Rodin** ❶ (www.musee-rodin.fr; Tue–Sun 10am–5.45pm; charge) housed in the Hôtel Biron, a fine 18th-century mansion where the sculptor lived and worked and which provides the ideal setting for his works.

Set in the charming garden of roses, trees and ponds are some of his most celebrated sculptures, including *The Thinker*, *The Kiss*, *The Gates of Hell* and *The Burghers of Calais*.

Musée d'Orsay

Back down on the riverbank lies the spectacular Belle Epoque **Musée d'Orsay** ❶ (www.musee-orsay.fr; Tue–Sun 9.30am–6pm, Thur until 9.45pm; charge). A former railway station built for the World Fair 1900, it became a museum in 1986 and is now a perfect setting for the finest art from 1848 to 1914. Its collection

The Musée d'Orsay is a perfect setting for the Impressionists and post-Impressionists

Shakespeare and Co. bookshop on the Left Bank

of Impressionist paintings hangs on the top floor bathed in soft light from the glass-vaulted roof. Here you'll find all the big names, including Monet, Degas, Cézanne, Renoir and Van Gogh.

St-Germain, the Latin Quarter and Montparnasse

The historic heart of literary Paris, the *quartier* of St-Germain-des-Prés stretches from Les Invalides in the west to boulevard St-Michel in the east, exuding elegance and power. In contrast, the neighbouring Quartier Latin (Latin Quarter) is a maze of ancient streets that have been the stamping ground for students for eight centuries. Today, with high fashion increasingly replacing high art, the two areas maintain their Left Bank charm. To the south, the ghosts of early 20th-century artists, writers and composers haunt the smartened-up streets of Montparnasse.

St-Germain-des-Prés

After World War II, **St-Germain-des-Prés** became a breeding ground for literature and ideas. Existentialists, inspired by Jean-Paul Sartre, Simone de Beauvoir and Albert Camus, gathered in cafés such as the **Café de Flore** and **Les Deux Magots**, on boulevard St-Germain. Opposite, the **Brasserie Lipp** has been the venue for famous politicians and journalists since 1880.

Close by, the 11th-century church of **St-Germain-des-Prés** ⑦, the oldest in Paris, was once one of the most powerful abbeys in the land. Today, the streets around here are lined with chic boutiques, modern art galleries, antiques and designer shops. Rue de Buci throngs with shoppers in its colourful daily market (except Mon), and in rue de l'Ancienne Comédie, **Le Procope**, the city's first café, has been going strong since 1686.

★ CEMETERIES, CATACOMBS AND SEWERS

Paris is far more than just grand architecture, great art, chic shopping and boulevard cafés – it also has a fascinating underbelly. The city's great cemeteries host thousands of famous and infamous inmates who have contributed to its long and complex history, and are among its most evocative monuments. Deeper into subterranean Paris there is the dark maze of Les Catacombes, where the dead of earlier centuries reside, and kilometres of dank, gloomy sewers.

The three great Parisian cemeteries are among the city's most atmospheric open spaces, ideal for a reflective picnic, and also places of pilgrimage. Graves, between tree-lined *allées*, are marked with neo-Baroque family vaults, ornate crosses, whimsical follies and sometimes striking modern sculpture. Maps available at the entrances give a guide to the residents, French and international.

Père Lachaise, east of the centre (with its own métro station), is the most visited cemetery in the world, in part because it contains the graves of Jim Morrison and Oscar Wilde. The Romantic era is well represented (Chopin, Delacroix, Balzac…), and

Bags are checked on leaving the catacombs to make sure no bones are removed

there are also the medieval lovers Abélard and Héloïse, re-interred here in 1817. There are so many famous names in Père Lachaise that you can spend hours exploring, wandering, say, from the dancer Jane Avril, painted by Toulouse-Lautrec, past Edith Piaf to German Surrealist Max Ernst.

The grave of Edith Piaf, French singer and cultural icon who sang *La Vie en Rose*

Montmartre cemetery has fine views from its hilltop location. Among its famous figures are Berlioz, Degas, Stendhal and the dancer Nijinsky. The Cimetière de Montparnasse, a wonderful oasis of peace, has the poet Baudelaire, and a large number of modern literary and artistic figures: Jean-Paul Sartre and Simone de Beauvoir, Man Ray, Samuel Beckett, Jean Seberg and Serge Gainsbourg.

There is nothing macabre about these cemeteries, but the grim and gruesome can be found in Les Catacombes, (Denfert-Rochereau métro). The major cemeteries were opened in the 19th century, because the old cemeteries of central Paris had been closed as health hazards, and their contents transferred to these former limestone quarries. The bones of Robespierre, Mme de Pompadour and thousands more are all bizarrely arranged along long, dark corridors (take your own torch).

Free of the dead but still dank and dark are Les Egouts de Paris, Paris's 2,100km (1,300 miles) of sewers, which have a visitors' entrance by the Pont de l'Alma, on the Left Bank. Paris's sewers are marked with signs that indicate the streets above, so you can play spot-the-underside of the boulevard you've just walked along.

Cemeteries, catacombs and sewers

Statue at Père Lachaise

Musicians busking on the Pont des Arts

Off rue Jacob is the **Musée Dela-croix** (www.musee-delacroix.fr; Wed–Mon 9.30am–5pm, Sat–Sun June–Aug until 5.30pm; charge), where the Romantic artist lived from 1857 while he painted murals in St-Sulpice close by. He was here until his death in 1863.

To the south, the **Jardin du Lux-embourg** Ⓦ is a haven of manicured greenery with a pond and fountain at its heart. On Wednesdays and week-ends (and every day during school holidays), the famous Guignol puppet show is performed in the **Théâtre des Marionettes**. The **Musée du Luxem-bourg** (www.museeduluxembourg. fr; daily 10am–8pm, Fri and Sat until 10pm; charge) puts on crowd-pulling major exhibitions.

Presiding over the gardens, the **Palais du Luxembourg**, built in the 17th century for Marie de Médicis after the murder of her husband, Henri IV, houses the French Senate.

In front of the **Institut de France**, where the French language is pre-served with gusto, is the pedestrian **Pont des Arts** linking St-Germain-des-Prés with the Louvre *(see p.72–3)*. It has always been a popular meeting place and continues to attract per-formers and artists today.

The Latin Quarter

Cross the river from the Ile de la Cité onto the Left Bank and you step into the Quartier Latin, so named because the university students used Latin as their working language until Napoleon stopped it after the Revolution. The vibrant streets are still full of students, served by innumerable small shops, bars, cafés and ethnic restaurants.

The tangle of narrow lanes harbour the medieval churches of **St-Séverin** and **St-Julien-le-Pauvre** (daily 9.30am–1pm, 3–6.30pm; free) on the riverbank. The Italian poet Dante is said to have prayed in this humble-looking church in 1304.

At the corner of boulevards St-Michel and St-Germain stands the **Musée National du Moyen Age/Thermes et Hôtel de Cluny**  (www.musee moyenage.fr; Wed–Mon 9.15am–5.45pm; charge), France's national repository of all things medieval. The core of the building is a 15th-century *hôtel*, one of the few medieval mansions remaining in Paris, but attached to this are the remnants of a Roman bath or frigidarium. The Musée de Cluny, as it's more commonly known, concentrates on the Romanesque and Gothic periods, with the highlight being a set of six extraordinary 15th-century tapestries known as *La Dame à la Licorne* (The Lady and the Unicorn).

Close by lies the **Sorbonne**, founded in 1253 as a college for 20

poor theological students, now one of the most celebrated and distinguished universities in the world. Cardinal Richelieu is buried in the university's chapel with his hat suspended above his tomb: it will fall, legend has it, when he is released from hell.

Uphill the neoclassical **Panthéon**  (www.pantheonparis.com; daily 10am–6pm; charge) sits atop Montagne Ste-Geneviève, the heart of the Roman city. Completed in 1789, its crypt is an honoured resting place of the most illustrious French citizens, including Victor Hugo, Voltaire, Rousseau, Zola and Resistance leader Jean Moulin.

Behind, **rue Mouffetard**, originally the road to Rome, is one of the oldest streets in Paris: narrow, crowded and full of cheap and cheerful places to

La Dame à la Licorne at the Musée de Cluny

eat. Place de la Contrescarpe is a lively place to sit and people-watch, and there is a market every day (except Mon) further down.

Montparnasse

The once-rural area southwest of the Jardin du Luxembourg was, in the early 20th century, a magnet for artists, composers and revolutionaries, including Chagall, Picasso, Modigliani, Lenin and Stravinsky. They gathered in cafés and brasseries on the boulevard du Montparnasse such as **Le Select** (No. 99), **La Coupole** (No. 102) and the **Closerie des Lilas** (No. 171). In the 1920s, writers such as Samuel Beckett and Henry Miller moved in.

Boulevard Edgar-Quinet, lined with cafés and a lively morning market on Wednesdays and Saturdays, leads eastwards from the ugly, 59-storey Tour Montparnasse to the **Cimetière du Montparnasse ②** (mid-Mar–mid-Nov Mon–Fri 8am–6pm, Sun 9am–6pm, mid-Nov–mid-Mar Mon–Fri until 5.30pm, Sun 9am–5.30pm; charge) and under the lion at place Denfert-Rochereau stretch **Les Catacombes** (Tue–Sun 10am–5pm; charge; *see p.82–3*).

Around Paris

While the Ile de France, surrounding the **Paris metropolis ①**, has forests and nature reserves, its countryside is pleasant rather than spectacular.

However, there are several attractions which are ideal for a day trip from the city, such as the palaces and châteaux of Versailles, Vaux-le-Vicomte and Fontainebleau – and the more modern attraction of Disneyland Resort Paris, which appeals to adults and children alike. The best way to see the region is on an assortment of day trips *(see map on p.88)*.

The château and gardens at Versailles

Main Street USA at Disneyland Resort Paris

Versailles

Just 21km (15 miles) to the west of central Paris stands the epitome of opulence, the **Château de Versailles** ❷ (www.chateauversailles.fr; Apr–Oct Tue–Sun 9am–6.30pm, Nov–Mar 9am–5.30pm; charge). Louis XIV (1643–1715) created the château in an unequalled expression of wealth, privilege and absolute monarchy. Highlights of the palace are the Grands Appartements, the King's Bedchamber and the Queen's Bedroom, where 19 royal children were born; the astonishing **Galerie des Glaces** (Hall of Mirrors) was constructed to catch the setting sun.

The elaborate park (daily, Apr–Oct 8am–8.30pm, Nov–Mar 8am–6pm) was designed by the landscape artist André Le Nôtre. From the palace steps, you can look down the length of the Grand Canal, which divides the park in two. On each side of the central path leading to the **Bassin d'Apollon** are statues, secret groves, goldfish ponds, fountains and flowerbeds. On Sunday afternoons from April to September, the fountains are switched on to music in Les Grandes Eaux Musicales.

On the northern side, Louis XIV built a smaller residence, the **Grand Trianon**, where he could escape from the stiff etiquette of the court. Louis XV added the **Petit Trianon**.

St-Denis

An easy visit from the centre is to **St-Denis** ❸, a formerly industrialised commune in the northern suburbs where the **Basilique St-Denis** (Apr–Sept Mon–Sat 10am–6.15pm, Sun noon–6.15pm, Oct–Mar Mon–Sat 10am–5.15pm, Sun noon–5.15pm; charge for royal tombs) is considered to be the first church built in Gothic style. It became the mausoleum of French kings and holds the tombs of most monarchs from Clovis (died 511) to Louis XVIII (died 1824).

To the northwest is **Auvers-sur-Oise** ❹, where Vincent Van Gogh spent his final days. He continued to paint – producing canvases of his doctor, Gachet, and Auvers church – but on 27 July 1890, when he was still only 37, the troubled artist walked into a field and shot himself, dying two days later in the Auberge Ravoux (Maison de Van Gogh; Mar–Oct Wed–Sun 10am–6pm; charge; *see p.39–40*).

Disneyland Paris

At least a whole day is needed for just a taster of **Disneyland Resort Paris** ❺ (tel: 08448 008 898; www.disneylandparis.co.uk; daily from 10am, closing times vary throughout the year) at Marne-la-Vallée, 32km (20 miles) east of the city. The fun park is divided into five themed areas: Main Street USA, Frontierland, Adventureland, Fantasyland for young children – containing Sleeping Beauty's Castle, the centrepiece of the park – and Discoveryland (high-tech wizardry). Alongside is Walt Disney Studios Park which produces daily eye-opening stunt shows.

It is best to get there early, as by midday queues at the most popular rides can be up to 45 minutes long. At the entrance in Main Street USA, City Hall, on the left, is the central information centre. Young children love the parade of Disney characters,

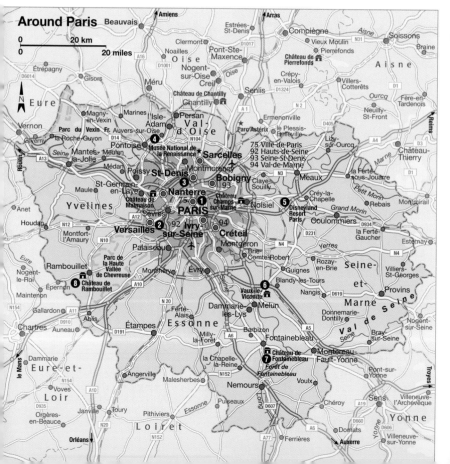

Château de Rambouillet, which you can visit when the president is not at home

which goes round both parks each afternoon, but the top thrills are on Big Thunder Mountain, Pirates of the Caribbean and Le Temple du Péril.

Châteaux

There are two châteaux worth visiting around Fontainebleau. Near the ancient town of Melun, on the northern edge of the Fontainebleau forest, 55km (35 miles) southeast of Paris, lies the extravagant **Château de Vaux-le-Vicomte** ❻ (www.vaux-le-vicomte.com; daily, mid-Mar–mid-Nov 10am–6pm, candlelit evenings May–Oct Sat 8pm–midnight, fireworks display 1st and 3rd Sat 10pm; charge), commissioned by Nicolas Fouquet, Louis XIV's finance minister. He used his privileged position to amass a fortune and called on the finest designers, architect Louis Le Vau and landscapist André Le Nôtre, to create his palace.

However, the king was not amused when it was completed in 1661 and

jailed Fouquet for life for embezzlement, while he built Versailles. On the eastern edge of the forest is **Barbizon**, known for its links to 19th-century artists (see p.36–7).

Another 15km (9 miles) from Melun stands the massive **Château de Fontainebleau** ❼ (www.musee-chateau-fontainebleau.fr; Apr–Sept Wed–Mon 9.30am–6pm, Oct–Mar until 5pm; charge). This first royal hunting palace was built in the 12th century, and every subsequent resident has left his mark on it. In 1814, Napoleon I fled here from Paris when his government collapsed.

Beyond Versailles is the ivy-clad **Château de Rambouillet** ❽ (guided visits only; Apr–Sept Wed–Mon 10am–4pm, closed during official residence; charge), the summer home of the president of France. Nearby, the **Fôret de Rambouillet** is one of the largest areas of woodland in central France, with a nature reserve (see p.33).

ACCOMMODATION

Paris has some of the grandest, most luxurious hotels in the world and ultra-chic modern boutique hotels, but also charmingly individual mid-range hotels and a growing number of bed-and-breakfast options. Frequent offers, especially online, can soften the high prices even in upscale hotels.

City-wide
Alcôve & Agapes
Tel: 01 44 85 06 05
www.bed-and-breakfast-in-paris.com
A reliable bed-and-breakfast booking agency with a wide range of attractive rooms across the city at reasonable prices. €–€€€

The heart of Paris
Hôtel de Crillon
10 place de la Concorde, 75008
Tel: 01 44 71 15 00
www.crillon.com
Built for Louis XV in the 1750s, dominating place de la Concorde, this is one of the world's truly grand hotels. The marble reception, tearoom, suites and two restaurants, Les Ambassadeurs and L'Obélisque, are all on a most luxurious scale. €€€€€

Hôtel Duo
11 rue du Temple, 75004
Tel: 01 42 72 72 22
www.duo-paris.com

Opulence at Hôtel de Crillon

Refined and calm, this very chic Marais establishment is one of the most attractive of Paris's boutique hotels. Fittings, from bathrooms to electronics, are state-of-the-art. €€€€

Hôtel du Jeu de Paume
54 rue Saint-Louis-en-l'Ile, 75004
Tel: 01 43 26 14 18
www.jeudepaumehotel.com
This 17th-century building on Ile St-Louis began life as a court for palm-tennis (forerunner of modern tennis), and now hosts a charming hotel combining exposed beams, contemporary art and a glass lift. €€€€

Murano Urban Resort
13 boulevard du Temple, 75003
Tel: 01 42 71 20 00
www.muranoresort.com
This hip, high-tech designer hotel on the edge of the Marais has novelties such as furry lifts, a restaurant with innovative cuisine and a spa. Two suites have their own outdoor pools on balconies. €€€€€

Hôtel de Nice
42bis rue de Rivoli, 75004
Tel: 01 42 78 55 29
www.hoteldenice.com
The delightful creation of collectors-turned-hoteliers, featuring period decor. Rooms are small, but have a wealth of charm and character. Rooms overlooking the courtyard are best. €€

Pavillon de la Reine
28 place des Vosges, 75003
Tel: 01 40 29 19 19

www.pavillon-de-la-reine.com
The most charming hotel in the Marais, a combination of a 17th-century mansion on the place des Vosges, antiques and discreetly stylish modern fittings, including a luxurious spa. €€€€€

Opéra, Montmartre, Champs-Elysées

Hôtel Chopin
10 boulevard Montmartre/46 passage Jouffroy, 75009
Tel: 01 47 70 58 10
www.hotel-chopin.com
A quiet, friendly hotel in an excellent location, in a 19th-century glass-and-steel-roofed arcade off the main shopping boulevards. Generous rates make it one of the city's best-value options. €€

Hôtel Plaza Athénée
25 avenue Montaigne, 75008
Tel: 01 53 67 66 65
www.plaza-athenee-paris.com
One of Paris's classic luxury hotels, sumptuously furnished in Second Empire style. Close to the Champs-Elysées, it's a favourite with celebrities and the fashion crowd. The five restaurants are under the supervision of Alain Ducasse. €€€€€

Eiffel Tower and Invalides
Grand Hôtel Lévêque
29 rue Cler, 75007
Tel: 01 47 05 49 15
www.hotel-leveque.com
Excellent-value hotel a short walk from the Eiffel Tower. Rooms have been attractively renovated, and some have balconies. Book well in advance. €€

St-Germain, Latin Quarter, Montparnasse
Hôtel d'Angleterre
10 rue Jacob, 75006
Tel: 01 42 60 34 72
www.hotel-dangleterre.com
Once the British Embassy (in the 1780s), this pleasant, classic hotel maintains a faintly British air. Centrally located in

Pavillon de la Reine

St-Germain, it has a very pretty courtyard garden. €€€€

Hôtel de Fleurie
32 rue Grégoire de Tours, 75006
Tel: 01 53 73 70 00
www.hoteldefleurieparis.com
A very popular, family-run St-Germain hotel which successfully combines elegance, cosiness and accessible prices. The sitting room has stone walls and exposed beams. €€€

Hôtel Lutetia
45 boulevard Raspail, 75006
Tel: 01 49 54 46 46
www.lutetia-paris.com
A classic, opulent hotel on the Left Bank, built in Art Nouveau style in 1910 but with exquisite Art Deco fittings from the 1930s. The bar is permanently fashionable. €€€€

Hôtel de Nesle
7 rue de Nesle, 75006
Tel: 01 43 54 62 41
www.hoteldenesleparis.com
A laid-back budget hotel with simple facilities but bargain prices: delightful bedrooms all have vibrant murals on various themes, and some overlook a garden. €–€€

Hôtel Saint-André-des-Arts
66 rue St-André-des-Arts, 75006
Tel: 01 43 26 96 16
www.france-hotel-guide.com

Listings

The bar at Hôtel Lutetia

A 16th-century building that is now one of Paris's most characterful budget hotels. Thin-walled bedrooms are basic, and there's no lift, but it's full of friendly Left Bank atmosphere. **€€**

Around Paris
La Demeure du Parc
6 rue d'Avon, 77300 Fontainebleau
Tel: 01 64 22 24 24
www.hotelfontainebleau.fr
A renovated 17th-century building in Fontainebleau town centre, with gardens and a swimming pool. Rooms are plain but spacious and well equipped. **€€**

Disneyland Hotels
77777 Marne-la-Vallée
Tel: 08 25 30 02 22
www.disneylandparis.com
There are seven hotels in the Disneyland resort, all designed on different American themes. A wide range of price packages is available. **€€€–€€€€€**

RESTAURANTS

Paris remains one of the world's great culinary capitals. Grand haute cuisine restaurants, atmospheric bistros and bustling Art Nouveau brasseries are still highlights of the scene, but around them there are plenty of inventive modern variations and international options.

Restaurant price categories

Prices are for a three-course meal for one (usually a set menu) with a drink. Eating à la carte will be more expensive.

€ = below €20
€€ = €20–45
€€€ = €45–90
€€€€ = over €90

The heart of Paris
Auberge Nicolas Flamel
51 rue de Montmorency, 75003
Tel: 01 79 97 30 98
www.auberge-nicolas-flamel.fr
Considered to be the oldest house in the city, formerly home to the eponymous 14th-century alchemist. Favourite dishes served in the charming dining room include sea bass grilled in Provençal herbs with aubergines. Closed Sun. **€€–€€€**

Berthillon
29–31 rue Saint-Louis-en-l'Île, 75004
Tel: 01 43 54 31 61
www.berthillon.fr
The fresh and frosty delights made in this celebrated ice-cream salon on the Île

St-Louis are a Parisian institution. Buy to take away, or enjoy them with coffee and cakes in the *salon de thé*. €

Brasserie Bofinger
5–7 rue de la Bastille, 75004
Tel: 01 42 72 87 82
www.bofingerparis.com
This historic brasserie has one of the finest Parisian Art Nouveau interiors, a monument to the Belle Epoque, and a huge menu. Reserve ahead to sit beneath the beautiful glass dome. €€€

Café Beaubourg
100 rue Saint-Martin, 75004
Tel: 01 48 87 63 96
A stylishly trendy café with spacious terrace beside the Centre Pompidou, popular with locals and tourists alike and with a menu including light, international dishes. €€

Café Marly
93 rue de Rivoli, 75001
Tel: 01 49 26 06 60
The most chic spot for coffee, a cocktail or lunch around the Louvre, with an arcaded terrace overlooking the pyramid. Ideal for relaxing after touring the galleries. €€–€€€

Au Chien qui Fume
33 rue du Pont-Neuf, 75001
Tel: 01 42 36 07 42
www.auchienquifume.com
Porcelain dogs and pictures of dogs decorate 'the smoking dog', a popular and friendly traditional restaurant founded in 1740. Cuisine is similarly traditional, with delicious seafood a speciality, and there's a terrace for outdoor dining. €€

Le Grand Véfour
Jardins du Palais-Royal, 17 rue de Beaujolais, 75001
Tel: 01 42 96 56 27
www.grand-vefour.com
One of the city's most historic restaurants, open since 1784. The dining room is magnificent, the cuisine of chef Guy Martin a gourmet delight. Closed Sat, Sun and Aug. €€€€

Au Pied de Cochon
4 rue de Coquillière, 75001
Tel: 01 40 13 77 00
www.pieddecochon.com
A temple to tradition, this Les Halles brasserie is open 24 hours every day of the year, for coffee, salads, onion soup, seafood and the speciality that gave it its name, grilled pigs' trotters. €€€

Le Train Bleu
Gare de Lyon, 75012
Tel: 01 43 43 09 06
www.le-train-bleu.com
The most magnificent 'station café' ever built, with 1900 gilded decor that gives a special class to the Gare de Lyon. A bit pricey, but for atmosphere it's hard to beat. €€€

Opéra, Montmartre, Champs-Elysées
Café de la Paix
5 place de l'Opéra, 75009
Tel: 01 40 07 36 36
www.cafedelapaix.fr
Another of Paris's restaurant-monuments, with glittering 1860s decor by Charles Garnier, and a terrace that has never been out of fashion. The restaurant enjoys a high reputation for luxurious classic cuisine. €€€–€€€€

Le Chalet des Iles
Lac Inférieur du Bois de Boulogne, Porte de la Muette, 75016

Café de la Paix

Le Chalet des Iles

Tel: 01 42 88 04 69
www.chalet-des-iles.com
A beautiful and secluded restaurant, inaugurated in 1880, on the edge of a lake in the Bois de Boulogne. The perfect location for a romantic summer evening. **€€–€€€**

Senderens
9 place de la Madeleine, 75008
Tel: 01 42 65 22 90
www.senderens.fr
The historic 1890s Lucas Carton restaurant is now the venue for the refined cooking of Alain Senderens, one of France's most innovative chefs. A gourmet adventure. **€€€€**

Eiffel Tower and Invalides
Jules Verne
Tour Eiffel, avenue Tour Eiffel, 75007
Tel: 01 45 55 61 44
www.lejulesverne-paris.com
Of the three dining options on the Eiffel Tower, this is the most special, with an adventurous Alain Ducasse menu and stunning views from the second level. A second-best is 58 Tour Eiffel (tel: 08 25 56 66 62; **€€**) on level 1. **€€€€**

Saint-Germain, Latin Quarter, Montparnasse
Café de la Nouvelle Mairie
19 rue des Fossés-Saint-Jacques, 75005
Tel: 01 44 07 04 41
This relaxed Latin Quarter bar is a wine-lover's delight, with a superb range from smaller winemakers around France, by the glass or bottle. To eat there's rich cuisine from the Aveyron in the Massif Central. Closed Sun. **€–€€**

Le Comptoir
Hôtel Relais Saint-Germain, 9 carrefour de l'Odéon, 75006
Tel: 01 44 27 07 97
www.hotel-paris-relais-saint-germain.com
Chef Yves Camdeborde has been hugely influential with this modern bistro, with light, original variations on classic cuisine at friendly prices. It's part of his equally chic hotel, which has a bar with delicious snacks. **€€**

La Coupole
102 boulevard Montparnasse, 75014
Tel: 01 43 20 14 20
www.flobrasseries.com/coupoleparis
The archetypal Art Deco brasserie first opened in 1927, and eating here still has a special buzz. The classic menu, with loads of choices, includes superb steaks, shellfish platters and Alsatian *choucroute*. **€€–€€€**

Le Dôme
108 boulevard Montparnasse, 75014
Tel: 01 43 35 25 81
La Coupole's great rival, the most opulent of Montparnasse's giant brasseries has a plush interior and broad terrace. The great specialities are superb seafood platters, all ideally fresh. **€€€**

Le Grenier de Notre-Dame
18 rue de la Bûcherie, 75005
Tel: 01 43 29 98 29
Vegetarian restaurants are fairly scarce in Paris, but this Latin Quarter favourite does its best to compensate with lively, imaginative dishes, and organic wines. **€–€€**

Le Restaurant – L'Hôtel
13 rue des Beaux-Arts, 75006
Tel: 01 44 41 99 00
www.l-hotel.com
The celebrated hotel where Oscar Wilde died in 1900 has had a lavish boutique

makeover, and its Michelin-starred restaurant offers inventive modern cooking. €€€–€€€€

Le Troquet
21 rue François Bonvin, 75015
Tel: 01 45 66 89 00
Creative modern bistro fare with a Basque accent in an animated, friendly setting, on the western edge of Montparnasse. Desserts are irresistible. Closed Sun and Mon. €€

Around Paris
Gordon Ramsay au Trianon
1 boulevard de la Reine, 78000 Versailles
Tel: 01 30 84 55 55
www.gordonramsay.com/grautrianon
The two-Michelin-starred celebrity chef directs this French venture in the heart of Versailles, bringing innovation and novelty to traditional French cooking.

Alongside it, La Veranda is a more casual, more economical alternative (tel: 01 30 84 55 56; €€€). €€€€

NIGHTLIFE AND ENTERTAINMENT

Paris' glitzy cabarets keep going, but there's a much hipper nightlife scene: the brightest areas are Pigalle, the Bastille and studenty République, and the Marais is the gay focus. There is also theatre, opera, concerts and dance for all tastes, and a choice of movies unrivalled in Europe. To find out what's on, check the weekly magazine *Pariscope*.

Cabarets
Moulin Rouge
82 boulevard de Clichy, 75018
Tel: 01 53 09 82 82
www.moulinrouge.fr
The classic cancan girls with lots of feathers in a show evoking Montmartre's glory days.

Nightclubs and music venues
Le Bataclan
50 boulevard Voltaire, 75011
Tel: 01 43 26 65 05
www.myspace.com/bataclanparis

Palais Garnier

Designed like a Chinese pagoda, this old theatre hosts all kinds of live music and DJs.

Caveau de la Huchette
5 rue de la Huchette, 75005
Tel: 01 43 26 65 05
www.caveaudelahuchette.fr
Famous jazz club with a funky contemporary programme that attracts big crowds.

New Morning
7–9 rue des Petites Ecuries, 75010
Tel: 01 45 23 51 41
www.newmorning.com
One of the world's foremost jazz venues, where the greats have played since the 1940s.

Theatre, opera, classical music, dance
Comédie Française
2 rue de Richelieu, 75001
Tel: 08 25 10 16 80
www.comedie-francaise.fr
The temple of French classical theatre, which has broadened its repertoire to appeal to a wider audience.

Opéra National de Paris
Opéra Bastille, 2bis place de la Bastille,
75012
Palais Garnier, place de l'Opéra, 75009
Tel: 08 92 89 90 90
www.operadeparis.fr
Larger productions are presented at the
modern Opéra Bastille; the glittering Palais
Garner mainly hosts more traditional operas
and ballet.

Théâtre du Châtelet
1 place du Châtelet, 75001

Tel: 01 40 28 28 00
www.chatelet-theatre.com
Leading theatre hosting musicals, opera,
dance and symphony concerts.

Cinema
Cinémathèque Française
51 rue de Bercy, 75012
Tel: 01 71 19 33 33
www.cinematheque.fr
France's national film theatre has a great
modern home in Bercy, with programmes
that cover the whole of world cinema.

TOURS

A fascinating variety of tours is available. For the full range, check at tourist
offices, or on www.parisinfo.com.

Art Process
52 rue Sedaine, 75011
Tel: 01 47 00 90 85
www.art-process.com
A chance to take a behind-the-scenes look
at studios and other centres for cutting-edge
art, fashion and design.

Batobus
Port de la Bourdonnais, 75007
Tel: 08 25 05 01 01
www.batobus.com
Hop-on, hop-off riverboat trips along the
Seine that allow you to see the city from a
different perspective.

Batobus, for a different perspective

Edible Paris
**www.edible-paris.com [initial contact is
online only]**
Personal, custom-designed itineraries
around every field of Parisian food culture,
from the best chocolates to gourmet chefs.

Paris-l'Open Tour
13 rue Auber, 75009
Tel: 01 42 66 56 56
www.parislopentour.com
User-friendly open-topped bus tours with
four routes around Paris; your ticket allows
you to get on and off as many times as you
like the same day.

Paris à Vélo c'est Sympa!
22 rue Alphonse Baudin, 75011
Tel: 01 48 87 60 01
www.parisvelosympa.com
Friendly small-group tours by bicycle, on
different themes.

Paris Walks
12 passage Meunier, 93200 Saint-Denis
Tel: 01 48 09 21 40
www.paris-walks.com
Fascinating walks with expert, English-
speaking Paris residents.

FESTIVALS AND EVENTS

Those listed below are only a selection of the events each year. For more on events at any time, check at tourist offices or on www.parisinfo.com.

April–June

Foire du Trône
Pelouse de Reuilly, 75012
www.foiredutrone.com
Early Apr–early June
France's biggest funfair takes over this park near Bercy every year.

Fête de la Musique
Venues throughout the city
www.fetedelamusique.fr
21 June
The day when, in every part of France, anyone who can play any instrument is encouraged to appear and play. Orchestras and major names also give free concerts.

Gay Pride
Montparnasse to the Bastille via St-Germain
www.inter-lgbt.org
Late June
An elaborate parade ending in a big party in place de la Bastille.

July–August

Bastille Day
Various venues
14 July

The official parade for France's *fête nationale* is on the Champs-Elysées, but there's a huge party in place de la Bastille the night before, and spectacular fireworks at the Eiffel Tower on the 14th.

Paris Quartier d'Eté
Various venues
www.quartierdete.com
14 July–mid-Aug
A lively summer arts festival.

October

Fête des Vendanges à Montmartre
Rue des Saules, 75018
www.fetedesvendangesdemontmartre. com
Early Oct
The wine harvest in Paris's only vineyard is the occasion for a very convivial, fun festival.

December

Nouvel An
Various venues
31 Dec
Crowds mass around the Champs-Elysées, the Trocadéro and the Eiffel Tower for midnight fireworks.

Fête de la Musique brings all kinds of musicians out onto the streets to celebrate

The north and east

A historical crossroads, France's northeast corner is not on the classic tourist trail and yet has much to offer: fascinating towns and cities, many with their medieval hearts intact; charming villages, seemingly untouched by time, and a wide and varied landscape, from beaches and broad wetlands to lush green mountains. The region also bears the traces of many wars, most notably World War I.

Lille and Strasbourg

Population: 228,300 (Lille); 274,800 (Strasbourg)

Local dialling codes: Lille: 03 20; Strasbourg: 03 88

Local tourist offices: Lille: Palais Rihour, place Rihour; tel: 08 91 56 20 04 (from France); www.lilletourism.com. Strasbourg: 17 place de la Cathédrale; tel: 03 88 52 28 28; www.otstrasbourg.fr

Main police stations: Lille: 19 rue de Marquillies; tel: 03 62 59 80 00. Strasbourg: Hôtel de Police, 34 route de l'Hôpital; tel: 03 90 23 17 17

Main post offices: Lille: 1 boulevard Carnot. Strasbourg: 5 place du Château

Hospitals: Lille: Hôpital CHRU, 2 rue Oscar Lambret; tel: 03 20 44 59 62. Strasbourg: Hôpitaux Universitaires de Strasbourg, 1 place de l'Hôpital; tel (for all six main hospitals in the region): 03 88 11 67 68

Local newspapers/listings magazines: Lille: *La Voix du Nord* (daily), *Liberté-Hebdo* (weekly). Strasbourg: *Dernières Nouvelles d'Alsace* (daily)

Often dismissed as places to be passed through, the northern and eastern areas of France offer something to appeal to everyone, from high coastal dunes and rolling farmland to picturesque mountains, forests and vineyards, dotted with pretty villages and historic towns. The villages of Flanders abound with flowers in the summer, while the region's larger towns – Lille, Arras and Amiens to the north, Reims in the centre, and Nancy and Strasbourg to the east – exude civic pride.

The evidence that this part of the world has been much fought over is clear to see. A line of fortifications was built at Calais, Dunkerque, Douai and Lille during Louis XIV's wars against the Netherlands in the 17th century. Flanders and the valleys of the Somme and Marne were major battlefields of World War I, marked by moving memorials and military cemeteries, while several coastal towns had to be rebuilt after the devastation of World War II.

The region is perhaps best known for Champagne, the most northerly wine-producing area of France – its principal city, Reims, is the centre for this 'wine of kings'. In Alsace, the rich farmland between the mountains of the Vosges and the Rhine produces its own delicious white wines.

Pas-de-Calais and the Nord

Many visitors arrive in France via the Channel coast only to head straight to the autoroutes going south, but the historic ports, towns and villages are linked by miles of sandy beaches, dunes and cliffs, with cafés and restaurants looking out to sea, and are definitely worth some time.

The Channel coast

The main gateway to France from Britain, **Calais** ❶ is a busy port that has seen many changes over the centuries.

Fishermen and ferry at Calais docks

Along the Côte d'Opale, Pas-de-Calais

Its medieval heart was bombed in 1940, destroying the architecture from the time when it was an English possession (1347 to 1558). The English siege of 1346–7 is commemorated by Rodin's magnificent statue *The Burghers of Calais*, commissioned by the city in 1885. More of Rodin's work is on show in the **Musée des Beaux-Arts** (Apr–Oct Tue–Sat 10am–noon, 2–6pm, Sun 2–6pm, Nov–Mar until 5pm; charge), and fine lace, a Calais speciality, is on show in the **Cité Internationale de la Dentelle** (Apr–Oct Wed–Mon 10am–6pm, Nov–Mar until 5pm; charge).

Dunkerque ❷, 48km (30 miles) to the north, also needed extensive reconstruction after 1945. A Flemish-speaking port, definitively part of France since 1662, it has a long maritime history, inventively recalled in the **Musée Portuaire** (www.museeportuaire.com; July–Aug daily 10am–6pm, Sept–June Wed–Mon 10am–12.45pm, 1.30–6pm; charge). The events of May–June 1940, when over 300,000 British and French troops were evacuated off the Dunkerque beaches to England, are

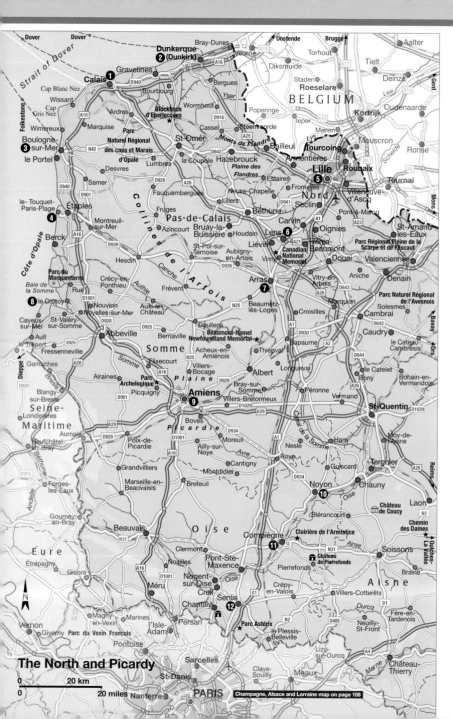

The North and Picardy

0 — 20 km
0 — 20 miles

Champagne, Alsace and Lorraine map on page 106

Street scene in Boulogne-sur-Mer

34km (21 miles) to the south, has an impressive main square, which holds an excellent market on Saturdays. A typical 18th-century town mansion houses the **Musée de l'Hôtel Sandelin** (Wed–Sun 10am–noon, 2–6pm; charge), with Louis XV furnishings and St-Omer faïence and Delftware.

Back on the coast, **Boulogne-sur-Mer ❸** has been a well-established port for over two millennia. It served as the launch pad for Julius Caesar's first invasion of Britain in 55BC, and the massive walls that still surround the *haute ville* on the hill date from the 1220s. **Place Dalton** below hosts the area's best traditional market on Wednesdays and Saturdays, and the town's seafood restaurants are renowned. Beside the busy harbour, the **Nausicaa** sealife centre (www.

commemorated in the **Mémorial du Souvenir** (www.dynamo-dunkerque. com; Apr–Sept daily 10am–noon, 2–5pm; charge), in a former bunker.

Prosperous from its textile industry since the Middle Ages, **St-Omer**,

The north and east

Lille transport

 Airports: Lille-Lesquin: tel: 08 91 67 32 10 (in France), +33 3 20 49 67 47 (from abroad); **www.lille.aeroport. fr**; 8km (5 miles) from the centre. Shuttle buses (Navette): tel: 03 20 49 67 47; every half-hour to city railway stations, 5.30am–10.15pm, journey time 20 minutes; €7 single

 Buses, trams and métro: Run by Transpole; tel: 0 820 42 40 40; **www.transpole.fr**. Two métro lines and a comprehensive bus and tram network serve the whole Lille conurbation. Tickets are valid for all systems and a Lille City Pass, available from the tourist office, gives unlimited travel and free admission to various attractions for 1 or 2 days

 Trains: SNCF: tel: 3635, **www.sncf.fr**. Lille-Europe (Eurostar and TGV) and Lille-Flandres (regional routes) within walking distance of each other in the city centre

 Taxis: Taxi Union: tel: 0 892 701 610; **www.taxi.fr/lille**. Gare Taxi (at the railway stations): tel: 03 20 06 64 00

 Car hire: Avis, 33 place de la Gare; tel: 03 28 36 55 66; **www.avis.co.uk**. National/Citer, 33 rue de Tournai; tel: 03 2 06 35 55, **www.citer.fr**

P **Parking:** There are eight Park and Rides, with free parking on the major roads that link up with public transport into the city

nausicaa.fr; daily, July–Aug 9.30am–7.30pm, Sept–June until 6.30pm; charge) is a hit with children.

The seaside resort of **Le Touquet** ❹, 22km (14 miles) to the south, became established at the end of the 19th century when swimming became popular for its health benefits, earning the soubriquet 'Paris-Plage'. It is still a popular resort, with long sandy beaches, some good restaurants and plenty to keep the children amused.

Inland, the walled town of **Montreuil-sur-Mer**, high above the valley of the River Canche, was a thriving port before the river silted up in the 1300s. Today it is a busy market town with cobbled streets and medieval alleyways. Victor Hugo used Montreuil as a setting for *Les Misérables,* and every summer a *son et lumière* performance is staged around the **Citadelle**.

Merchant towns of the north

French Flanders stretches eastwards from St-Omer, where place names – Zuytpeene, Godewaersvelde – indicate this is not conventional France. This is a corner that retains an engaging distinctness, with boisterous festivals, traditional games, very un-French cuisine, fine beer and quaint pub-like bars called *estaminets*. Many Flemish towns formed part of the Front Line in World War I, and there are several war cemeteries in the area.

At the centre of the fourth-largest urban area in France and a major high-speed train (TGV and Eurostar) hub, **Lille** ❺ was one of the great trading and weaving cities of medieval Flanders, reflected in its architecture. In the **Grand'Place**, home of the Braderie flea market *(see box, right)* every September as well as a Christmas

Relaxing on the beach at Le Touquet

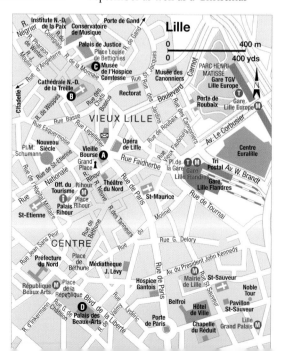

Lille

0   400 m
0   400 yds

Grand'Place, the main square in Lille, lined with elegant 18th-century townhouses

fair, stands the **Vieille Bourse** , its red and gold facades a classic of Flemish merchant Baroque, containing small shops and book stalls. The narrow streets of **Vieux Lille**, to the north, are lined with fashion, design and food shops: on rue des Chats Bossus, **A l'Huitrière**, with its 1928 Art Deco tiles, is a spectacular fishmonger and restaurant. Lille's cathedral, **Notre-Dame de la Treille** , is a strange anomaly of 19th-century vintage which had a much-criticised facelift in 1999, and on delightful rue de la Monnaie, the **Musée de l'Hospice Comtesse** (Wed–Sun 10am–12.30pm, 2–6pm, Mon 2–6pm; charge), in a former hospital (1237), displays art and craftwork from the 14th to the 17th century.

After 1667, and in the hands of Louis XIV, Lille was given a more French look and the **Citadelle** was built for protection. The **Palais des Beaux-Arts** (Wed–Sun 10am–12.30pm, 2–6pm, Mon 2–6pm; charge) features sumptuous Flemish and Dutch art, notably by Rubens, David, Courbet and Goya.

If you prefer modern art, head to Villeneuve d'Ascq, a few kilometres southeast of Lille, where the **Musée LAM**, a huge sculpture park and modern art museum, has recently

Lille's flea market

Lille's Braderie is the largest flea market in Europe, and is held on the first weekend of September. It dates back to at least the 13th century, and one of its roots is said to be a law that allowed servants to sell their masters' old clothes for a few days each year. It now attracts some 2 million visitors. There are food stands as well as junk stalls, and stopping for some *moules-frites* is part of the ritual.

been extended. Meanwhile **Lens** ❻, 28km (17 miles) to the southwest, once the capital of the mining district, has a new gem at its heart: the **Louvre-Lens** (www.louvrelens.fr), which is set to open at the start of 2013 in a cutting-edge, all-glass building on a former mining site, exhibiting some of the vast holdings of *the* Louvre not often shown.

Famous in the Middle Ages for its production of cloth and hanging tapestries, **Arras** ❼ has two of the most beautiful city squares in France. The town and surrounding countryside saw fierce fighting throughout World War I, and the **Boves** (Carrière Wellington; daily 10am–12.30pm, 1.30–6pm; charge), a labyrinth of chalk tunnels, gave shelter to Allied troops.

Lying 66km (41 miles) to the southeast of Arras, **Le Cateau-Cambrésis** is a plain little town where, in 1869, Henri Matisse was born. The **Musée Matisse** (Wed–Mon 10am–6pm; charge) has a large collection of the artist's work, including his 1951 *Woman in a Blue Gandourah*.

Picardy

Progressing further south, closer to Paris, Picardy is unmistakably French, as can be seen in the architecture of its great Gothic cathedrals, pillars of the historic heartland of France. The region is often remembered, however, for its more recent battlefields and the terrible bloodshed and destruction of the two World Wars (see p.42–7).

Amiens and the Somme

After entering Picardy in the west, along the Côte d'Opale, the coast opens up into the **Baie de la Somme**, a giant arc of sand flats, salt marsh and immense skies, a landscape ideal for walkers, cyclists and birdwatchers. Sand-yachters head for the beach at **Le Crotoy** ❽, a modest Belle Epoque seaside resort whose

Exploring the Hortillonages in Amiens by boat

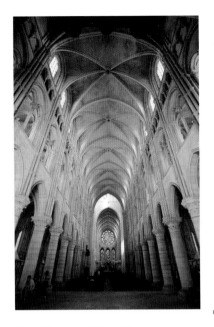

seafood restaurants are weekend favourites with locals.

William the Conqueror set sail for England in 1066 from **St-Valery-sur-Somme** across the bay. Today, this small fishing port with a walled upper town (*ville haute*) of half-timbered houses, is popular with weekending Parisians and holds the bay's best market on Wednesdays and Sundays. A steam train puffs up and down between Le Crotoy St-Valery and Cayeux from April to November.

The capital of Picardy, **Amiens** ➒, midway between Boulogne and Paris, is renowned for its monumental **Cathédrale Notre-Dame**, a 13th-century masterpiece of French Gothic architecture and the largest in the country. The canalside St-Leu quarter, the renovated millers' area, escaped damage in World War II and is now dotted with bars and brasseries. Another water feature is the marsh gardens (*Hortillonages*) which have been producing vegetables for the town since Roman times.

East of Amiens are the Somme battlefields of World War I, where thousands of British, Commonwealth, French and German troops died in 1916. The Franco-British Memorial at **Thiepval** (www.thiepval.org.uk; Mar–Oct 10am–6pm, Nov–Feb 9am–5pm; free) is the largest of many battlefield memorials and cemeteries. In Péronne, the **Historial de la Grande Guerre** (daily 10am–6pm, closed mid-Dec–mid-Jan; charge) is an impressive museum covering all aspects of the war (*see p.45*).

The Aisne and the Oise

The coronations of both Charlemagne, crowned king of the Franks in 768, and Hugues Capet, crowned king of France in 987, took place in the first cathedral at **Noyon** ➓ in eastern Picardy. Its replacement, **Notre-Dame de Noyon**, built from 1145, finely represents the transition from Romanesque to Gothic, with a soaring twin-towered facade. One of the first great masterpieces of true Gothic, the cathedral at **Laon** to the east, was built from around 1160 to 1230, the same time as Notre-Dame in Paris. The town's medieval streets are clustered on top of a high ridge and can be seen for miles.

Roughly 15km (9 miles) south, the **Chemin des Dames** (the Ladies' Road) – built for the daughters of Louis XV to get to their châteaux

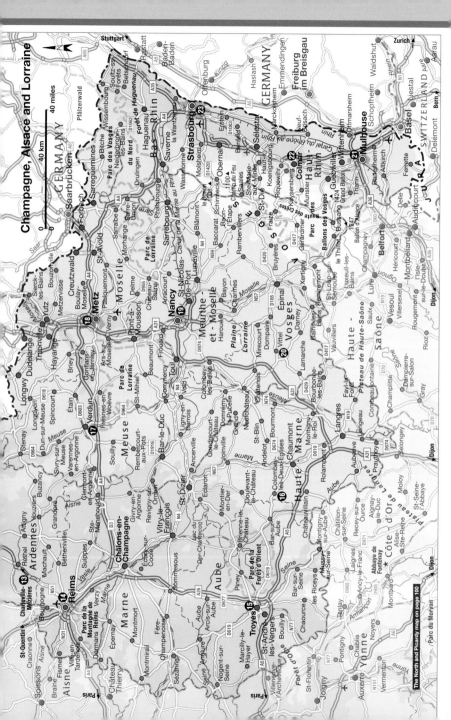

Champagne, Alsace and Lorraine

Stuttgart

Zurich

GERMANY

SWITZERLAND

The Château de Chantilly houses an excellent museum of French paintings

– runs along a ridge above the River Aisne. The scene of much World War I activity, it is marked with memorials and cemeteries. Deep caves (the Caverne du Dragon) house the **Musée du Chemin des Dames** (May–Sept daily 10am–6pm, Oct–Apr Tue–Sun 10am–6pm, closed Jan; charge), in **Oulches-La Vallée**.

In southern Picardy the town of **Compiègne ⓫** borders the **Fôret de Compiègne**, a magnificent oak and beech forest full of walks and cycle routes. On its north side is the **Clairière de l'Armistice** (Apr–mid-Oct Wed–Mon 9am–12.30pm, 2–6pm, mid-Oct–Mar 9am–noon, 2–5.30pm; charge), where the Armistice ending World War I was signed in November 1918, and where Hitler formalised the defeat of France in 1940. Napoleon III and his empress Eugénie made the **Château de Compiègne** (www.musee-chateau-compiegne.fr; Wed–Mon 10am–6pm; charge), in the town, their country seat, elaborately redecorating many of its 1,000 rooms. Napoleon's taste for extravagance was also expressed across the forest in the extraordinary **Château de Pierrefonds** (May–Aug daily 9.30am–6pm, Sept–Apr Tue–Sun 10am–1pm, 2–5.30pm; charge).

Closer to Paris, just off the A1, **Senlis ⓬** has retained its part-medieval walled town, and its cathedral, **Notre-Dame de Senlis**, is another early Gothic jewel. To the south, the lush woodland of the **Forêt de Chantilly**, once an aristocratic hunting reserve, embraces the beautiful 16th-century **Château de Chantilly**.

Champagne

Champagne needs no introduction for its chief export. Since the 17th century, this region has been cultivating grapes from its dry, chalky hillsides to produce the most prestigious of all sparkling wines and the one that others aspire to. Champagne's largest city, Reims, has a network of wine cellars running beneath it *(see p.110)*.

The Ardennes and the home of Champagne

The modern region of Champagne-Ardenne is divided between the

⭐ NOT-SO-FRENCH FRANCE

For all its regional diversity, overall the identity of France is so distinctive that it can appear homogeneous and solid. Nevertheless, on its northeastern and eastern borders France does not so much come to an end as fade into its neighbours. The 'natural borders' of French culture in these regions have never been clear, and the official borders were set by political decision, so that Frenchness here often comes diluted by an eccentric, sometimes disconcerting cultural mix.

East of St-Omer lies French Flanders, where village names such as Steenvorde or Bollezeele demonstrate its special cultural roots. The area became French only because it surrounds the Monts de Flandre, strategic points that Louis XIV's generals decided France had to have in the 1670s. The regional capital, Lille, was itself mostly Flemish when it was seized in 1667, but was then intensively Frenchified. In the villages, the Flemish language has largely been driven out by French education, but the people here are different, attached to raucous Carnival celebrations and traditional games. Most distinctive is their approach to food, naturally a fundamental in France. The centres of local culture are *estaminets*, cosy pubs unknown elsewhere in France, with great beer and hearty dishes like *potjevleesch*, a mix of cold meats with chips and mustard.

In Alsace, French again is firmly

Half-timbered houses in Strasbourg old town

Flemish architecture in Arras

in linguistic command, but the half-timbered villages and the lofty old towns of Colmar or Strasbourg look as if they came from a Germanic fairy tale by the Brothers Grimm. Cuisine, again, is archetypically Germanic: beer, Riesling-style white wines, and hefty platters like the signature dish *choucroute*, a gallicisation of *sauerkraut* – shredded, pickled cabbage with potatoes and several forms of pork.

Alsace had always been part of the German cultural sphere until the 1640s, after Cardinal Richelieu decided France should control the left bank of the Rhine. Strasbourg was one of the free, independent cities of Germany until 1681, when Louis XIV seized it. The region then became fairly well integrated into France – though most country people still spoke *Elsasserditsch*, their own south German dialect – until in 1871, after the Franco-Prussian War, Alsace became part of newly unified Germany.

France never accepted its loss, and over 100,000 Alsatians chose to leave rather than become German, introducing beer and brasseries (with *choucroute* on the menu) to Paris and other French cities. When France finally regained Alsace in 1918, though, its residents had been German for 47 years, and many hoped for autonomous status as a compromise. The embrace of the French state, however, came unconditionally, and schools clamped down fiercely on any use of standard German or *Elsasserditsch*. It is not surprising that Alsatians are such keen supporters of the European Union.

Not-so-French France

Choucroute, an Alsatian speciality

Champagne grapes are cultivated on the dry, chalky soil of Champagne

Champagne crayeuse, dry, chalky land just right for growing vines, and the *Champagne humide*, a much wetter area of farmland, hills, forests and lakes *(see p.23)*. In more recent times, though, it has been one big battlefield. Nudging up through to the Belgian border, the region was strategically important during each of the wars against invading German armies.

The thickly wooded hills of the **Ardennes** make up the north of the region, with the Meuse river wriggling through **Charleville-Mézières** ⑬, the home town of the poet Arthur Rimbaud, honoured in the **Musée Rimbaud**, an old watermill, and **La Maison des Ailleurs** (both museums: Tue–Sun 10am–noon, 2–6pm; charge), where he was born.

A centre of champagne production, **Reims** ⑭ is also where kings of France were crowned from the Middle Ages to the 19th century. The magnificently proportioned 13th-century **Cathédrale Notre-Dame** (daily 7.30am–7.30pm; free) was left a hollow shell in 1918, but it has been superbly restored and remains one of the country's greatest Gothic edifices. The originals of the cathedral's major sculptures are on display next

Champagne cellars of Reims

The city's champagne cellars comprise 250km (155 miles) of galleries quarried out of its chalk foundations in the days of Roman Gaul. Practically all the major champagne houses, such as Krug and Veuve Cliquot, offer tours of the cellars; the Office de Tourisme (beside the cathedral, at 2 rue Guillaume de Machault) is the best source of information. However, free samples are not always given at the end of visits, and the champagne houses may not be the cheapest places to buy supplies.

door in the **Palais du Tau** (May–Aug Tue–Sun 9.30am–6.30pm, Sept–Apr 9.30am–12.30pm, 2–5.30pm; charge). Altogether different is the **Musée de la Reddition** (Museum of the Surrender; Wed–Mon 10am–noon, 2–6pm; charge), behind the railway station, where a document of German surrender was signed on Monday 7 May 1945.

In **Epernay**, 26km (16 miles) south of Reims, Moët et Chandon, one of the largest and most famous houses, gives tours of its cellars with a tasting session (charge). Nearby, 6km (4 miles) to the north, is a replica of the monk Dom Pérignon's 17th-century cellar and laboratory in the abbey museum of **Hautvillers**, where he

worked on perfecting the quality of the local wine.

Although smaller than Reims, **Châlons-en-Champagne** is the capital of the region of Champagne-Ardenne, with a harmonious collection of preserved half-timbered houses best seen by boat on the canal.

Troyes and the lakes

The historic centre of **Troyes** ⓯, 81km (50 miles) to the south of Châlons, features nine Gothic churches, narrow winding streets with half-timbered houses and a major collection of modern art – including works by Matisse, Modigliani and Picasso – in the **Musée d'Art Moderne** (Tue–Sun 10am–1pm, 2–6pm; charge). Outside the town, the great lakes of the **Parc Naturel Régional de la Forêt d'Orient** attracts watersports and wildlife enthusiasts.

Further east is the village of **Colombey-les-Deux-Eglises** ⓰, where Charles de Gaulle is buried close to his country home, now a museum (Apr–Sept daily 10am–6.30pm, Oct–Mar Wed–Mon 10am–1pm, 2–5.30pm; charge). More impressive is the **Mémorial Charles de Gaulle** (May–Sept 9.30am–7pm, Oct–Apr 10am–5.30pm; charge), a visitor centre beneath the cross on a hill above the village, which has exhibitions about the man and his times.

Lorraine

Industrial towns contrast with unspoilt countryside in Lorraine, which hugs the slopes of the Vosges and extends north to the borders of Germany, Luxembourg and Belgium.

Sculpture at Musée d'Art Moderne, Troyes

Finally incorporated into the French Crown in 1788, Lorraine – along with neighbouring Alsace – was later claimed by Germany, which wanted its coal and iron ore, and the two regions shuttled backwards and forwards between the rival states from 1871 to 1944.

The north and Metz

More than any other battlefield, **Verdun** ⓱ represents the horrors of World War I for the French *(see p.43)* and a visit to the ossuary of **Douaumont** is a moving experience (www.verdun-douaumont.com; May–Aug 10am–6.30pm, Apr 10am–6pm, Feb–Mar and Oct–Dec 10am–5pm; charge). Today, Verdun styles itself as a *'ville de paix'*, a 'town of peace', and is home to the **Centre Mondial de la Paix** (World Centre for Peace; www.cmpaix.eu).

Verdun cemetery, memorial of World War I

Lorraine's regional capital, **Metz** ⓲, 63km (39 miles) to the east, stands near the confluence of the rivers Seille and Moselle. The city's most conspicuous monument is the **Cathédrale St-Etienne**, with the largest stained-glass windows in the world – some by Marc Chagall. Metz's cultural reputation has grown since the opening in 2010 of the **Centre Pompidou-Metz** (www.centrepompidou-metz.fr; Mon, Wed 11am–6pm, Thur, Fri 11am–8pm, Sat 10am–8pm, Sun 10am–6pm; charge), a branch of the famous cultural centre in Paris. Housed in a dramatic hexagonal building, the museum holds exhibitions of modern art.

Nancy to the Vosges

Much more appealing as a city is **Nancy** ⓳, 40km (25 miles) south of Metz, which owes its 18th-century elegance to the dukes of Lorraine, as seen in their residence, now part of the **Musée Lorrain** (Tue–Sun 10am–12.30pm, 2–6pm; charge). Today a modern university city, it is also notable for the Art Nouveau buildings created by the Ecole de Nancy.

About 50km (31 miles) southwest is **Domrémy-la-Pucelle**, where Joan of Arc, France's exemplary heroine, started life in 1412. Lorraine has several spas, and the best known is **Vittel** ⓴ to the southeast. Here, Lorraine is separated from Alsace by the **Massif des Vosges,** a range of low mountains rising gently through dark, green forests. **Epinal**, the main town, is synonymous with a distinctive kind of print produced by the **Imagerie d'Epinal** (www.imagerie-epinal.com) since the 18th century.

Colmar has a well-preserved old town, with buildings dating back to the 14th century

Alsace

Alsace may be France's smallest mainland region but it is crammed with sights and exquisite, flower-filled villages. A stay here is made all the more pleasant by the food, renowned wines (white and fruity) and beers. The influence of Germany, on the other side of the Rhine, is undeniable, as can be seen in the place names, architecture, cuisine and local patois.

Upper Alsace and the wine lands

The Vosges, bordering Alsace to the west, are a favourite place for walking with 18,000km (11,000 miles) of signposted footpaths. By car, the best way to get a flavour of the range is to follow the **Route des Crêtes** along a road built to facilitate troop movements during World War I. To the south, **Mulhouse ㉑** has reinvented

itself as a city of technological museums, such as the unique **Musée de l'Impression sur Etoffe** (www.musee-impression.com; Tue–Sun 10am–noon, 2–6pm; charge), devoted to the printed cloth, and the **Musée de l'Automobile** (www.collection-schlumpf.com; daily, Apr–Oct 10am–6pm, Nov–Mar until 5pm; charge), which has a collection of over 500 antique and rare cars.

Vineyards hug the gentle slopes between the Vosges and the Rhine along a single narrow 120km (75-mile) strip. The *Route du Vin* (*see p.23*) begins at **Colmar ㉒**, where wine professionals come for Alsace's fruity, sweet-smelling dry white wines. Delightful medieval and 16th-century villages and castles – such as **Haut-Koenigsbourg** (www.haut-koenigs bourg.fr; July–Aug 9.15am–6pm,

Strasbourg's city centre is a Unesco World Heritage Site

Apr–May, Sept until 5.15pm, Mar, Oct 9.30am–5pm, Nov–Feb 9.30am–noon, 1–4.30pm; charge), high up on an outcrop of rock – make it the prettiest vineyard tour in the country, especially in October.

Strasbourg and Lower Alsace

Strasbourg ㉓, the capital of Alsace, lies on the Rhine at a strategic intersection of trade routes. Its historic city centre is confined to the **Grande Île**, surrounded by a river transformed

---

Strasbourg's green transport

Strasbourg is a good city for cycling, with an efficient bike-hire scheme such as Vélhop (www.velhop.strasbourg.eu). There are around 500km (300 miles) of well-marked cycle tracks within the urban area, and many roads in the city centre are closed to cars but not to bikes. For more leisurely travel around the city, there are five tram lines, a mini-tram and riverboats.

---

into a series of basins and canals. Easy to explore on foot, the narrow streets are lined with an odd assortment of buildings and museums – such as the 18th-century **Palais des Rohan** (Mon and Wed–Fri noon–6pm, Sat–Sun 10am–6pm; charge) for fine art, decorative art and archaeology – which converge on the rosy Gothic **Cathédrale Notre-Dame**.

Modern Strasbourg is one of three non-capital cities in the world (along with New York and Geneva) to be the headquarters of major international institutions. The Euro-quarter contains the seats of the Council of Europe and European Court of Human Rights, and the European Parliament sits in the Palais de l'Europe.

To the north of Strasbourg is a land of ancestral forests and castles. The **Forêt de Haguenau** shelters hamlets of wooden houses, renowned for their colourful folk festivals, and **Betsch-dorf,** on the forest's northern edge, is famous for its blue and grey pottery.

ACCOMMODATION

While these regions do not have as much tourist traffic as other parts of France, they still have a range of attractive, individual hotels, many in historic buildings, and prices are much lower than elsewhere too.

Pas-de-Calais, Nord, Picardy

L'Hermitage Gantois
224 rue de Paris, 59000 Lille
Tel: 03 20 85 30 30
www.hotelhermitagegantois.com
One of Lille's classic Flemish buildings, a former hospital partly from the 1460s, has been beautifully converted into this original luxury hotel. The Hermitage restaurant and Estaminet Gantois bar are just as impressive. €€€€

Hotel Mercure Amiens Cathédrale
21–23 rue Flatters, 80000 Amiens
Tel: 03 22 80 60 60
www.mercure.com
Conveniently located near the cathedral and the Quartier St-Leu, this hotel has more character than many in the Mercure chain, but still has its good-value facilities. €€–€€€

Hôtel Les Tourelles
2–4 rue Pierre Guerlain, 80550 Le Crotoy
Tel: 03 22 27 16 33
www.lestourelles.com
The views across the Baie de la Somme from this charmingly modernised hotel are entrancing, and the seafood at the restaurant sets them off perfectly. Prices are a great bargain. €–€€

Hôtel Les Trois Luppars
49 Grand'Place, 62000 Arras
Tel: 03 21 60 02 03
www.hotel-les3luppars.com
The oldest house on Arras's Grand'Place, with a Flemish gable facade from 1467, is its most memorable hotel. Rooms are small, but those on the upper floors have fine views, and it's great value. €

Accommodation price categories

Prices are for one night's accommodation in a standard double room (unless otherwise specified).

€ = below €80
€€ = €80–130
€€€ = €130–200
€€€€ = €200–300
€€€€€ = over €300

Champagne

Le Clos Raymi
3 rue Joseph de Venoge, 51200 Epernay
Tel: 03 26 51 00 58
www.closraymi-hotel.com
Delightful hotel in an elegant 19th-century house, with seven bright and comfortable bedrooms decorated with great attention to detail. €€€

Grand Hôtel du Nord
75 place Drouet d'Erlon, 51100 Reims
Tel: 03 26 47 39 03
www.hotel-nord-reims.com
The pick of the hotels on this lively restaurant-lined Reims square offers bright rooms at low prices (those at the front are more spacious) and a helpful welcome. €–€€

Lorraine and Alsace

Best Western Hôtel Monopole-Métropole
16 rue Kuhn, 67000 Strasbourg
Tel: 03 88 14 39 14
www.bw-monopole.com

Best Western Hôtel Monopole-Métropole

Suite at Hostellerie Le Maréchal

One of Strasbourg's longest-established hotels, close to the Petite France area, which has been modernised with excellent facilities and comfortable rooms. €–€€

Hôtel de la Couronne
5 rue de la Couronne, 68340 Riquewhir
Tel: 03 89 49 03 03
www.hoteldelacouronne.com
A prettily restored 16th-century house in the middle of old Riquewihr, with a cobbled courtyard. Several rooms have beamed ceilings and hand-painted furniture. €

Les Jardins d'Adalric
rue du Maréchal Koenig, 67210 Obernai
Tel: 03 88 47 64 47
www.jardins-adalric.com
A distinctive *hotel de charme* in the heart of Obernai, with a swimming pool in a peaceful garden, and sober, stylish rooms. €€

Hostellerie Le Maréchal
Quartier Petite Venise, 4–6 place des Six Montagnes Noires, 68000 Colmar
Tel: 03 89 41 60 32
www.hotel-le-marechal.com
A classy small hotel in a 16th-century timber-frame building by the river in the romantic 'Little Venice' area of old Colmar. Rooms are decorated with antiques, and there's also a fine restaurant. €€–€€€

RESTAURANTS

Many restaurants in the north make fine use of local specialities – vegetables, fine meats, excellent seafood on the coast – and French Flanders and Alsace both have very distinctive cuisines which are strongly Germanic in flavour.

Restaurant price categories
Prices are for a three-course meal for one (usually a set menu) with a drink. Eating à la carte will be more expensive.

€ = below €20
€€ = €20–45
€€€ = €45–90
€€€€ = over €90

Pas-de-Calais, Nord, Picardy

L'Assiette du Marché
61 rue de la Monnaie, 59000 Lille
Tel: 03 20 06 83 61
www.assiettedumarche.com
In a distinguished 17th-century building in old Lille, this striking restaurant stands out for its chic modern decor, informal feel and light, varied menus ideally suited to contemporary tastes. It also offers exceptional value. €€

Chez Jules
8 place Dalton, 62200 Boulogne-sur-Mer
Tel: 03 21 31 54 12
www.chez-jules.fr
A perfect multipurpose town brasserie, on Boulogne's market square. Downstairs is the terrace, café and bustling brasserie, while above is a more comfortable dining room. The menu covers everything from small snacks like *croque-monsieurs* to magnificent traditional seafood platters. €–€€

La Faisanderie
45 Grand'Place, 62000 Arras
Tel: 03 21 48 20 76
www.restaurant-la-faisanderie.com
This lovely restaurant occupies one of the
Boves cellars beneath Arras's Grand'Place,
and feels like a snug refuge, far from any
urban bustle. Refined seasonal menus
make great use of local produce, and there's
a superior wine selection. **€€**

Het' Kasteelhof
8 rue St Nicolas, 59670 Cassel
Tel: 03 28 40 59 29
At the top of Mont Cassel, highest point
in Flanders, this is the model of a Flemish *estaminet* or pub, with knick-knacks
around the walls, fabulous beer, and hearty
food such as tartine open sandwiches,
potjev'leesch (mixed cold meats) or beef in
beer, with chips. Plus, superb views from the
main room or the outdoor terrace. Closed
Mon–Wed. **€**

Champagne
Les Crayères
64 boulevard Henry Vasnier, 51100 Reims
Tel: 03 26 24 90 00
www.lescrayeres.com
Haute cuisine in a luxurious château hotel
with an excellent selection of vintage cham-
pagnes to accompany the gourmet dishes.
For a slightly cheaper, less formal but still

very attractive option, there's also Le Jardin
brasserie (**€€**), in the château's beautiful garden. Restaurant closed Mon, Tue.
€€€–€€€€

Lorraine and Alsace
L'Acoustic
5 place du Marché Vert, 67600 Selestat
Tel: 03 88 92 29 40
www.restobiolacoustic.com
Only 100 percent organic food is served in
this restaurant beneath a brick vault in the
centre of Selestat. Half the menu choices
are vegetarian, and the wholemeal bread is
home-made. **€**

Au Cerf
5 rue de la Gare, 67250 Hunspach
Tel: 03 88 80 41 59
www.aucerf.fr
The best option for a meal when visiting
one of the prettiest villages of Alsace, in the
northern Vosges. Among the dishes on the
menu are a *feuilleté* of local Munster cheese
and *choucroute* with fish. **€–€€**

Maison Kammerzell
16 place de la Cathédrale,
67000 Strasbourg
Tel: 03 88 32 42 14
www.maison-kammerzell.com
Excellent food and wine in one of the oldest
houses in Strasbourg, next to the cathedral.

Listings

Haute cuisine at Les Crayères

The historic building, dating back to the Renaissance, is decorated with frescoes, a deserving backdrop to the exquisite versions of Alsatian dishes such as the signature *choucroute* with three different fish. €€–€€€

Au Trotthus
9 rue des Juifs, 68340 Riquewihr
Tel: 03 89 47 96 47
www.trotthus.com
Typical Alsatian cuisine, including fine

choucroute and a variety of *tartes flambées*, served in a pretty, friendly *winstüb* towards the top of one of the region's prettiest towns. €€

Winstüb Gilg
1 route du Vin, 67140 Mittelbergheim
Tel: 03 88 08 91 37
www.hotel-gilg.com
A classic half-timbered traditional *winstüb* tavern on the Alsace wine route, where you can complement wine tasting with a range of fish dishes. Closed Tue–Wed. €€–€€€

NIGHTLIFE AND ENTERTAINMENT

The larger cities all have prestigious cultural venues. For information on what's on in any part of France, check www.cityvox.fr (also in English).

Pas-de-Calais, Nord, Picardy
L'Aéronef
168 avenue Willy Brandt, 59777 Lille
Tel: 03 20 13 50 00
www.aeronef-spectacles.com
Big high-tech venue for the latest in live music.

Le Biplan
19 rue Colbert, 59000 Lille
Tel: 03 20 12 91 11
www.lebiplan.org
Fringe theatre and very eclectic live music.

Opéra de Lille
2 rue des Bons Enfants, 59800 Lille
Tel: 03 20 42 23 65
www.opera-lille.fr
Hosts adventurous opera and ballet, and orchestral concerts.

Alsace
Opéra National du Rhin
19 place de Broglie, 67008 Strasbourg
Tel: 03 88 75 48 00
www.operantionaldurhin.eu

Strasbourg nightlife

Prestigious centre for opera, dance and classical music, which also has venues in Colmar and Mulhouse.

Zénith Strasbourg
1 allée du Zénith, Eckbolsheim, 67034 Strasbourg
Tel: 03 88 10 50 50
www.zenith-strasbourg.fr
Giant modern live music venue on the edge of the city. There are also Zénith venues in several other French cities.

TOURS

Most local tourist offices offer an interesting variety of tours, especially in cities and wine regions. For battlefield tours, *see p.47.*

Horizons d'Alsace
28 rue du Général Dufleux,
68650 Lapoutroie
Tel: 03 89 78 35 20
www.horizons-alsace.com
A group of hotels in the Vosges mountains that jointly offer walking or cycle tours, with your baggage carried ahead of you.

Office du Tourisme d'Epernay
7 avenue de Champagne, 51201 Epernay
Tel: 03 26 53 33 00
www.ot-epernay.fr
Epernay tourist office organises tours of champagne cellars (with tastings) at weekends and holidays, as well as providing all kinds of other information.

FESTIVALS AND EVENTS

Northern and eastern France has a very distinctive mix of celebrations, fed by Flemish and Germanic traditions.

January–February
Carnaval
Dunkerque, Lille and French Flanders
www.tourisme-nord.fr
Late Jan–Feb
French Flanders enthusiastically celebrates Carnival with raucous parades of 'giants', mythical figures and other traditions. Dunkerque's celebrations continue until April.

June
Festival de Musique de Strasbourg
Various venues, Strasbourg
www.festival-strasbourg.com
Mainly focuses on classical music, with some jazz.

September
Braderie de Lille
Central Lille
www.lilletourism.com
1st weekend Sept
Europe's largest flea market, held for 700 years, and with plenty of food stands and entertainment too.

December
Christmas Markets
Amiens, Arras, Lille, Metz,
Strasbourg and other cities
www.noel-a-lille.com, http://noel.
tourisme-alsace.com
Late Nov–Dec or early Jan
Cities across northern France, especially Lille and Strasbourg, all host beautiful markets in the run-up to Christmas, selling seasonal gifts and plenty of warming food and drinks.

Christmas markets like this one in Strasbourg are popular in the north

Normandy and Brittany

The green Atlantic seaboard is a place of enchanting extremes, from the long, sandy beaches of Normandy, dotted with old seaside resorts, to the spectacular coastline of Brittany, sheltering tiny coves and fishing villages. Inland, the rich green landscape gives way to ancient towns and cities and a wilder countryside.

Rouen, St-Malo, Rennes

Population: 112,800 (Rouen); 50,700 (St-Malo); 209,400 (Rennes)

Local dialling codes: Rouen: 02 35; St Malo: 02 99; Rennes: 02 99

Local tourist offices: Normandy: tel: 02 32 33 79 00; www.normandy-tourism.org. Brittany: 11 rue St-Yves, Rennes; tel: 02 99 36 15 15; www.tourismebretagne.com

Main police stations: Rouen: rue Brisout de Barneville; tel: 02 35 88 40 88. St-Malo: place Bouvet; tel: 02 99 81 72 51

Main post offices: Rouen: 67 rue Orbe. St-Malo: 4 place des Frères Lamennais; Rennes: 1 rue Pré Botté

Main hospitals: CHU-Hopitaux de Rouen, 1 rue Germont; tel: 02 32 88 89 90; www.chu-rouen.fr. CHU-Rennes, 2 rue Henri le Guilloux; tel: 02 99 28 43 21; www.chu-rennes.fr

Local newspapers/listings magazines: Normandy: *Paris Normandie* (daily). Brittany: *Ouest-France* (daily) with weekly *Guide* (what's on)

The western coast of France is given its characteristic shape by two peninsulas. The smaller and more northerly of them is the Cotentin of Normandy, a land of mellow fruitfulness, producing cider apples and well-known cheeses such as Camembert, with timber-framed houses, ruined abbeys and the inspirational city of Rouen, beyond. The sea has always played an important role in the history of this region, bringing the Viking warriors in their longships who established Normandy – the land of the 'northmen' – in the 9th century, and permitting the Normans' own invasion of England 200 years later. More recently came the Allied landings of 1944.

The effect of the sea has been even greater in the larger peninsula of Brittany, a dramatic granite spur buffeted by the Atlantic, and part-populated by descendants of Celts who arrived from Wales and Cornwall fleeing Anglo-Saxon invasions.

A region rich in Celtic traditions and prehistoric relics, its magnificent coastal scenery shelters fishing ports and popular seaside resorts.

Rouen and Upper Normandy

The Seine meanders slowly to the sea dividing Normandy in two. Upper (Haute) Normandy to the northeast is edged by the brilliant white cliffs of the Côte d'Albâtre (Alabaster Coast) with the major ports of Dieppe and Le Havre. Midway down the river to Paris, Rouen was an important Roman city, founded at a natural crossing point, and abbeys proliferated on the banks. On the other side of the city, the river passes by rich pastures and forests to Giverny and Monet's inspirational garden.

Boats on Yport beach, near Fécamp

Rouen to the sea

Rouen ❶ is the historic centre of Normandy and the place of Joan of Arc's martyrdom – a national symbol of resistance to tyranny. The region's capital suffered devastating damage in World War II, and many buildings have since been restored or reconstructed, such as the beautiful medieval and Renaissance centre around the **Cathédrale Notre-Dame** (Mon–Sat 8am–7pm, Sun 8am–6pm). Its towers and spires famously attracted Monet to paint it at different times of the day in different light, producing more than 30 canvases. The historic **place du Vieux Marché**, where Joan of Arc was burnt at the stake in 1431, is now buzzing with cafés.

Over 100km (62 miles) from the sea, Rouen is the last point upriver on the Seine open to ocean-going shipping. Alongside the D982 is the start of the **Route des Abbayes**, which meanders around the medieval Norman abbeys at St-Martin-de-Boscherville, St-Wandrille and Le Bec-Hellouin, including the impressive 7th-century ruins at **Jumièges**.

The Gros-Horloge (Big Clock) in Rouen

Normandy and Brittany

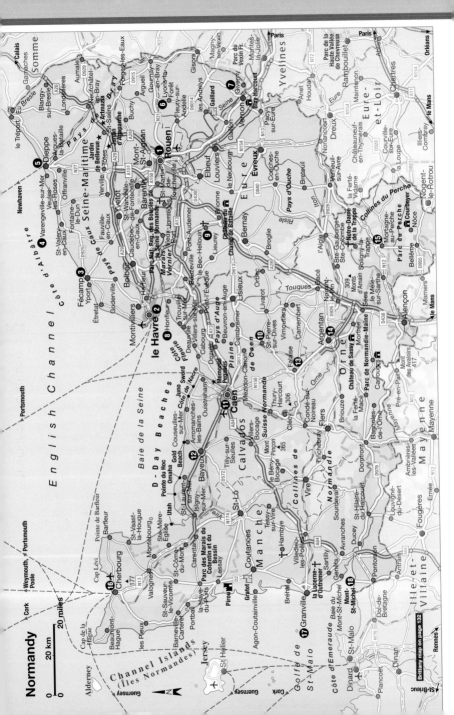

The cliffs at Etretat, part of the Alabaster Coast

At the mouth of the Seine stands **Le Havre** , France's largest Atlantic port, and a delight for lovers of modern architecture. Brutally bombed in 1944, Raoul Dufy's home town was 'recreated' with massive concrete edifices and radical creations such as Brazilian architect Oscar Niemeyer's 1970s Espace Niemeyer cultural centre.

The Côte d'Albâtre

A near-continuous line of white chalk cliffs runs northeast from Le Havre to Normandy's border at the River Bresle. Called the Côte d'Albâtre, or Alabaster Coast, its limpid light was treasured by the Impressionist painters, especially Monet. The most often painted cliffs are at **Etretat**, sitting in a deep, protected coastal cleft, unmissable towards sunset.

Fécamp , 15km (9 miles) east, with a harbour mouth between towering cliffs, has a history of deep-sea fishing and 19th-century holidaymaking. Its unique feature is the neo-Gothic

---

Rennes transport

 Airport: Aéroport de Rennes; tel: 02 99 29 60 00; www.rennes.aeroport. fr; 10km (6 miles) southeast of city centre, 67km (42 miles) from St-Malo. Buses (No. 57) from airport to city centre take 20 minutes. Taxis 10–15 minutes; €12–15

Trains: Gare de Rennes, boulevard Solférino; tel: 02 99 67 31 12. The TGV takes 2 hours from Paris. TER Bretagne; tel: 0 800 880 562; www. ter-sncf.com, is a regional network

 Buses and métro: Star: 02 99 79 37 37; InfoSTAR: 08 11 55 55 35; www. star.fr. Rennes has sixty bus routes and one métro line. Single ticket €1.20, valid across network. Bicycle rental (véloStar) at 83 outlets

Car hire: SIXT, Gare de Rennes; tel: 02 99 53 89 65

 Taxis: Taxis Rennais; tel: 02 99 30 79 79. AATT; tel: 02 99 30 12 40 or at taxi ranks in the city centre

wonderland of the **Palais Bénédictine** (tours daily July–Aug 10am–7pm, Apr–June, Sept–Oct 10am–1pm, 2–6.30pm, Feb–Mar, Nov–Dec 10.30am–12.45pm, 2–6pm; charge), the home of Bénédictine liqueur.

The coast rises to discreetly lovely **Varengeville-sur-Mer** ❹, where villas spread among the woods. Cubist artist Georges Braque lived here, designing exquisite stained glass for the 12th-century clifftop church, where he is buried. The **Manoir d'Ango** (www. manoirdango.fr; Apr–Sept daily 10am–12.30pm, 2–6pm, Oct Sat–Sun only; charge), built in the 1530s, is a curious mix of rustic manor and Renaissance château.

France's oldest seaside resort, **Dieppe** ❺, a few kilometres away, is both a Channel ferry port and a fishing port with a pretty seafront. For great-value seafood restaurants, go to the fishing port and weekend seaside town of **Le Tréport**, 30km (19 miles) further northeast. Just inland, in the attractive town of **Eu**, the **Château-Musée Louis-Philippe** (www.

Monet's garden at Giverny

> **On the wings of a dove**
>
> Colombiers, dovecotes or pigeon lofts, were a major status symbol in medieval and Renaissance Normandy, since only aristocrats were allowed to have this important source of meat and fertiliser. They became increasingly elaborate as lords showed off their wealth, and it was no surprise that the non-noble ex-pirate Jehan d'Ango, being permitted to have one, built the largest in France at his Manoir d'Ango.

louis-philippe.eu; Mar–Oct Wed–Thur, Sat–Mon 10am–noon, 2–6pm, Fri 2–6pm; charge), is a delightful Renaissance château where Queen Victoria and Prince Albert were entertained in 1843 and 1845.

Fields, forests and Monet's garden

The countryside behind Dieppe and Eu is deeply, unalterably rural. The **Pays de Bray** is where Neufchâtel, the oldest and, to some, finest of Normandy cheeses comes from (see p.24). At Beaumont-le-Hareng, the **Jardins de Bellevue** (daily 10am–6pm; charge) grows exotic plants from around the world, while **Artmazia** (May–Aug daily and Sept Sat–Sun 2.30–6.30pm; charge), outside Massy, is a garden and 'art maze' created by British artist Geoff Troll.

To the south the beech trees become denser as you head into the Forêt de Lyons, once a hunting reserve of the Norman dukes. At its heart is another of France's great beauties, **Lyons-la-Forêt** ❻, with a famous village square of contrasting

The harbour at the old port of Honfleur

black and white Norman half-timbering and delightful places to stay and eat.

Back on the Seine, above **Les Andelys**, stands Richard the Lionheart's ruined 12th-century **Château Gaillard** (Mar–Nov Wed–Mon 10am–1pm, 2–6pm; charge; grounds free; *see p.43*). Below it, the charming riverside quarter of **Le Petit Andely** has restaurant terraces with beautiful views.

A road beside the river leads to the most renowned of all Normandy's gardens at **Giverny** ❼, Claude Monet's family home. It is beautifully maintained as the **Fondation Claude Monet** (www.fondation-monet.fr; Apr–Oct daily 9.30am–6pm; charge), where his love of light and nature is apparent throughout (*see p.37*).

Classic Normandy

Of all the idyllic green landscapes in Normandy, nowhere are the leaves more lush, the valleys more softly curving or the cows more contented-looking than on the fertile plains of the region between the Seine and the Orne rivers. Edged by the Côte Fleurie (Flower Coast), the delightful little ports make way for the wide beaches of the D-Day landings, on to the wilder, more remote Cotentin Peninsula, while southern Normandy was the stamping ground of William the Conqueror.

Côte Fleurie and Pays d'Auge

A different Normandy appears in the Côte Fleurie, Parisians' favourite quick seaside escape for over 150 years. At its eastern end is **Honfleur** ❽, an old port whose inhabitants founded Quebec in 1608, which has always been a magnet for artists and is popular with weekenders. Behind the quay stands an extraordinary half-timbered wooden 'cathedral', built in the 1460s by local shipwrights.

★ BRITTANY'S CELTIC ROOTS

An extraordinary number of prehistoric menhirs and standing stones testify to the long history of human occupation in Brittany, an area never entirely conquered by the Romans. Its Celtic culture was reinforced in AD400–600, as migrants arrived from Wales and Cornwall, escaping Anglo-Saxon invasions. This heritage has populated Brittany with myths and legends, and left traditions in culture, language and music that, with the wild Atlantic landscape, give it a very special character.

Brittany has much in common with Celtic parts of the British Isles, including many figures of Celtic mythology. Stories of King Arthur are a major part of Breton folklore, and the mythical forest of Brocéliande, said to be the Paimpont forest in east-central Brittany, is Arthur and Merlin's Breton home.

Some features of Brittany's ancient culture, such as the spiral patterns carved on the Neolithic standing stones of Carnac or the giant cairn-tomb of Barnenez near Roscoff, all over 3,000 years old, even seem to have been inherited from its pre-Celtic inhabitants. In the 9th century AD, with the population swelled by Welsh and Cornish migrants, the chieftain Nominoe forced the Frankish kings to recognise Brittany as an independent duchy and, despite being torn between both sides in the Hundred

The *Pardon* of Ste-Anne-la-Palud, Finistère

Years War, its dukes retained their independence until 1532.

Brittany's distinctiveness remained in other ways, such as its religiosity and its architecture, especially the extraordinary parish-close churches of Finistère, where you can see figures of Breton myth such as the skeleton-like Ankou, the collector of the dead, alongside Catholic imagery. Rural Brittany's most traditional festivals are the *Pardons*, processions in traditional dress to a shrine of a saint, followed by music, dances, food and traditional games. The *Pardons* of St Yves in Tréguier (third Sunday in May) and Notre Dame in Le Folgoët (first Sunday in September) are particularly well observed.

France and its schools have traditionally stamped on regional languages, and Breton has declined severely since the 1900s, when most of western Brittany spoke it. Even today, despite some concessions such as bilingual road signs, there is minimal support for Breton education. However, this has not prevented a vigorous Breton cultural revival, begun in the 1970s and sparked by master-harpist Alan Stivell. Towns and villages host *Fest-noz*, local dance and music sessions, where music is played on traditional instruments like the harp, the Breton bagpipe (*biniou*) and oboe-like *bombarde*. Many music and culture festivals are held each year (see www.gouelioubreizh.com), but the best traditional and contemporary music events are the Kann ar Loar in Landerneau and Festival de Cornouailles in Quimper (both July), and the Interceltique Festival in Lorient, in August.

Alan Stivell is credited with popularising Celtic music

Ankou, the collector of the dead, is part of Breton mythology

Hôtel Normandy in Deauville, a very upmarket seaside town popular with Parisians

A tree-shrouded corniche road leads to the long beaches of Trouville and Deauville, separated by a bridge across the River Touques. **Trouville** on the right bank is bohemian and arty, with a fabulous market (Wed and Sun). **Deauville** is neat and luxurious, with a casino, two horse-racing tracks and the **Festival du Cinéma Américain** (see p.143).

The Risle river meets the Seine at its mouth. The *pièce de résistance* of this historic valley is the one-time intellectual hub of the Norman Empire, the abbey of **Le Bec-Hellouin** ❾ (www.abbayedubec.com), where the Benedictine community welcomes visitors.

Marked by pretty villages of half-timbered houses (see p.49), the sumptuous **Pays d'Auge**, due south of the Côte Fleurie, is the only area with *appellations contrôlées* for both its calvados and ciders (see p.24). Three of the great Norman cheeses also hail

from here – Pont l'Evêque, Livarot and Camembert – centring around **Cambremer**, the district's main town. The Auge's agricultural hub is **St-Pierre-sur-Dives** ❿, where the Monday market has been held since medieval times.

Caen and the invasion beaches

The favourite city of William the Conqueror, **Caen** ⓫ was a battlefield for over a month in 1944 (see p.45–6), and as a result much of it has the typically bland, grey appearance of post-war reconstruction. The events are described in the **Mémorial de Caen** (Feb–Oct daily 9am–7pm, Nov–Jan Tue–Sun 9.30am–6pm; charge) and in the **Musée-Mémorial de la Bataille de Normandie** (daily, May–Sept 9.30am–6.30pm, Oct–Dec and Mar–Apr 10am–12.30pm, 2–6pm; charge) in Bayeux. The abbey churches – **St-Etienne** and **La Trinité** – jewels of Norman Romanesque architecture and part of the giant abbeys endowed by William and his wife, Matilda, both survived the onslaught. **Bayeux** ⑫, 22km (14 miles) to the west, fell to British troops early, so its medieval and 18th-century houses emerged near-unscathed. Its unique treasure, of course, is the Bayeux Tapestry, superbly presented in the **Centre Guillaume-le-Conquérant** (May–Aug 9am–7pm, Mar–Apr, Sept–Nov 9am–6.30pm, Dec–Feb 9.30am–12.30pm, 2–6pm; charge). On the south side of town lies the largest **British War Cemetery** in Normandy.

The D-Day landing beaches (see p.45–6) stretch 95km (60 miles) west from the small port of Ouistreham. One striking site is at Pegasus Bridge over the Caen Canal, where the **Mémorial Pegasus** (May–Aug 9.30am–6.30pm, Feb–Apr, Oct–Nov 10am–5pm; charge) commemorates the British paratroopers who took the bridge on the night of 5–6 June 1944. The coast is interrupted by the **Marais du Cotentin**, a protected expanse of bird-filled marsh and wetland with the **Ponts d'Ouve** visitor centre

---

All about Camembert

There is plenty to learn about cheese at the quaint **Musée du Camembert** (Apr–Oct Thur–Mon 2–5.30pm; charge) in pretty **Vimoutiers**, and even more at the hard-sell **Maison du Camembert** (www.maisonducamembert.com; May–Aug daily 10am–6pm, Mar–Apr, Sept–Oct Wed–Sun 10am–6pm; charge) in the idyllic hilltop village of **Camembert** in the Pays d'Auge.

(Easter–Sept daily 9.30am–7pm, Oct–Easter closed Mon; free) at St-Côme-du-Mont near Carentan. Beyond are the long dunes of Utah Beach. Just inland, on the church tower of **Ste-Mère-Eglise**, a dummy of a US paratrooper hanging by a parachute commemorates Private John Steele, who was caught on the tower for most of D-Day, while the Germans thought he was dead.

Southern Normandy

William the Conqueror was born in **Falaise** ⑬, 35km (22 miles) south of Caen, in 1028. His existence was the

Normandy and Brittany

A section of the Bayeux Tapestry, which tells the story of the Norman invasion of England

result of a liaison between Robert, second son of the duke of Normandy, and a 17-year-old tanner's daughter, Herleva (or, traditionally, Arlette), and until his conquering success he was known as 'William the Bastard'. His home, the **Château Guillaume-le-Conquérant** (www.chateau-guillaume-leconquerant.fr; July–Aug 10am–7pm, Sept–June 10am–6pm; charge), sits dramatically atop a rocky crag.

Argentan ⑭, 22km (14 miles) to the south, retains much of its historic centre, including the flamboyant Gothic-Renaissance church of St-Germain. The Orne Valley around it is celebrated horse country; the hills rise southwards into the **Perche** with a more remote feel than the Auge. **Mortagne-au-Perche** ⑮, the main

Market day in Granville

town, has a backwater tranquillity, with a fascinating accumulation of historic buildings. This is also Normandy's capital of *boudin noir* (black pudding), and its *charcuteries* (delicatessens) are impressive.

The Cotentin Peninsula

The Cotentin Peninsula is wilder and more isolated than much of Normandy, with granite cliffs or windswept dunes along the coast, punctuated by austere villages of grey stone. In its northeast corner, tiny **Barfleur**, amazingly, was once the chief port for the Anglo-Norman Empire, but is now a placid fishing and leisure port.

Anyone fascinated by ships will enjoy **Cherbourg** ⑯, which grew up as a navy port under the *ancien régime* and Napoleon, and saw plenty of action in 1944. To the west are the spectacularly rugged cliffs of the **Cap de la Hague**, a granite spur that's at its most dramatic when the Atlantic winds are up. On the west coast, **Barneville-Carteret**, a combination of country town, fishing port and easy-going beach resort, makes an excellent base in the area.

The *bocage* – small fields enclosed by impenetrable hedgerows – is at its densest in the southern Cotentin, and getting lost among the hills and green-tunnel lanes is part of the enjoyment. On the west coast, the old town of **Granville** ⑰ occupies a rocky headland, with some good seafood restaurants along the harbour. It was the location of the couturier Christian Dior's childhood holiday home, which is now the **Musée Christian**

The medieval abbey of Mont St-Michel stands on a rock rising out of a vast tidal bay

Dior (May–mid-Sept daily 10am–6.30pm; charge).

The vast Baie du Mont St-Michel, where the sea disappears for 15km (9 miles) at low tide, seems expressly designed around its magical, medieval abbey (May–Aug 9am–7pm, Sept–Apr 9.30am–6pm; charge) atop the islet of **Mont St-Michel** ⑱. At nearby Genêts you can book a guide to take you across the bay – the sight of the mount and its spire glimpsed from the sands hasn't changed since medieval times when pilgrims crossed the sands.

Northern Brittany

A chunky finger pointing out into the fierce Atlantic, Brittany (see map on p.132) possesses France's most spectacular coastline, while inland lies a deep-green rural world of lonely hills, forests and idiosyncratic little towns. With its isolation, Celtic traditions and folklore, Brittany is quite unlike the rest of France; the architecture of its lofty old townhouses and multi-spired churches strays from the usual styles recognised further east. All this makes the region a distinctive, appealing place to explore.

The Emerald Coast

St-Malo ⑲ on the Côte d'Emeraude (Emerald Coast) is steeped in seafaring history – its sailors left its name as far afield as the Falkland Islands (Les Malouines) – and today it remains a busy fishing port, ferry

A break on the walls

At every point around St-Malo's ramparts there are superb views over ever-changing seascapes and the Rance river, as well as inland over narrow, winding streets. A great place to stop for a break on the terrace is at the Corps de Garde crêperie (see p.141), next to the Tour Notre-Dame.

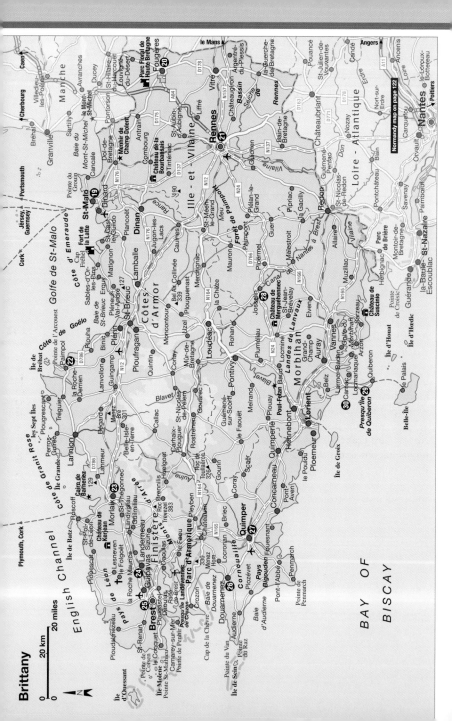

The golden sand of St-Malo's beaches

terminal and yacht harbour. St-Malo suffered severe damage during World War II, but the old town, surrounded on three sides by the sea, has been tastefully restored. In the **Musée d'Histoire de la Ville** (Apr–Sept daily, Oct–Mar Tue–Sun 10am–noon, 2–6pm; charge), in the castle keep, the town's naval history is told through the lives of its great navigators and pirates.

Like many French seaside resorts, **Dinard**, across the Rance estuary, was a 'discovery' of the British in the 19th century, as it has a particularly mild microclimate – palms, fig trees, tamarisk and camellias all flourish here. Arrival in **Dinan**, at the start of the estuary, gives an immediate introduction to the sheer oddity of Brittany's historic towns, while a walk around its medieval ramparts gives beautiful views over the Rance Gorge.

To the west, the pink sandstone cliffs at **Cap Fréhel**, 70m (230ft) high, look out across the Grande and Petite Fauconnière bird sanctuaries. In prime position looms the most spectacular of all Brittany's castles, the

14th-century **Fort de la Latte** (www. castlelalatte.com; daily, early July–Aug 10am–7pm, Apr–early July, Sept until 6pm, Oct–Mar Sat–Sun, holidays 1.30–5.30pm; charge) with enough battlements and winding staircases to fire anyone's imagination.

The Breton borders

The most dramatic fortifications are at **Fougères** ❷⓪, on Brittany's eastern border, which from around 900 to the 1530s was the eastern bastion of independent Brittany. Built, unusually, almost in a ravine, to guarantee its water supply, the **Château de Fougères** (www.chateau-fougeres. com; July–Aug daily 10am–7pm, May–June, Sept daily 10am–1pm, 2–7pm, Oct–Apr Tue–Sun 10am–12.30pm, 2–5.30pm; charge) is one of the largest medieval castles in Europe.

Given the rural or coastal feel of most of Brittany, the urbanity of its capital, **Rennes** ❷①, 32km (20 miles) west, can be a shock. One of France's fastest-growing cities, Rennes was once an important Roman city; in the Middle Ages it became a residence of

Half-timbered buildings in Dinan

the dukes of Brittany, who surrounded it with fortifications. Surviving squares and narrow lanes of multi-coloured, timber-frame buildings in old Rennes house restaurants and clubs, and the **place des Lices** holds one of France's largest food markets every Saturday morning.

The Pink Granite Coast

Brittany's most celebrated coastline is the **Côte de Granit Rose**, so called because its rocks have a distinctive pinkish hue. Often immense, battered over centuries into weird shapes, they lie along the coast like giant abstract sculptures. All human habitation has been built around and between them, from prehistoric shelters to neat Art Deco villas.

Paimpol **㉒** was famous as a hardy deep-sea fishing port and still has an inshore fishing fleet. From tiny L'Arcouest, north of Paimpol, boats run to the popular **Ile de Bréhat**, a 10-minute crossing that can be a bit of an adventure when the wind is up. Some of the craziest rock formations can be seen along the coastal footpath

from **Perros-Guirec**, a mix of fishing-and-leisure port and old-fashioned resort, with a popular surfing beach.

Finistère

Considered by the French as the end of the earth (hence the name), the wild, windy and battered region of Finistère has long, empty beaches backed by rocks and grassy dunes, and strange-looking churches. Natural harbours shelter marinas full of yachts, and the ancient mountains behind provide perfect hiking and biking. This region maintains a strong Celtic identity, having been the first port of call for Celts fleeing Cornwall across the Channel in the 6th century.

The wild northwest

Morlaix ㉓ sits in a gorge-like valley at the head of an estuary that made it an excellent refuge from enemies and storms, and today is one of Brittany's best-equipped yacht harbours. On the east bank is the **Cairn de Barnenez** (May–Aug daily 10am–6.30pm, Sept–Apr Tue–Sun 10am–12.30pm, 2–5.30pm; charge),

Perros-Guirec is perfect for watersports from March to October

Ile d'Ouessant is a stopping-off place for migrating birds in mid-October and April

one of the largest Neolithic stone burial mounds in Europe, dating from 4500–3900BC. **Roscoff**, to the west, a rugged little granite sea town, was once surprisingly prominent in cross-Channel affairs, even before it became a port for British and Irish ferries. In 1548 Mary, Queen of Scots, landed here aged six on her way to marry the French Dauphin. Further west, boats leave Le Conquet for the **Ile d'Ouessant**, feared for its storms and terrifying rocks but nowadays a great place for biking.

Rural Brittany reasserts itself inland, and here and there are the *enclos paroissiaux*, the church closes containing grandiose religious buildings, constructed with religious fervour between the 16th and 18th centuries. Just 18km (11 miles) west of Morlaix, there are three examples of these *enclos*, with the one at **St-Thégonnec** being one of the largest and most extravagantly Baroque.

Further west, **Landerneau** 24 spreads across the 1510 Pont de Rohan over the River Elorn, one of the few inhabited bridges left in Europe, and the location for one of the largest Breton culture festivals every July *(see p.143)*.

A ridge of ancient mountains, the **Monts d'Arrée**, forms the backbone of Finistère, crisscrossed with walking trails. Drop down into one of the sheltered clefts to the **Ecomusée**

Johnny Onion men

In the 19th century, Roscoff became the main port of departure for the Breton 'Johnny Onion' men who for decades left every year for a short period, attired in striped shirts and berets, with their bikes to sell their famous onions around Britain. The **Maison des Johnnies** (tours June–Sept Mon–Sat 11am, 3pm, 5pm, Oct–Dec, Feb–May Tue, Thur, Fri 3pm; charge), tells their story.

des Monts d'Arrée (July–Aug daily 11am–7pm, Mar–June, Sept–Oct Mon–Sat 10am–6pm, Sun 2–6pm; charge), which occupies a 1610 mill and recalls the life of the hill villages.

Brest and its bays

Below Le Conquet, the coast turns sharply eastwards into the **Rade de Brest**, a natural harbour that became one of France's main naval ports in the 17th century. Hidden away, **Brest** ㉕ suffered terribly in the siege of 1944. Afterwards, it was rebuilt as an entirely modern city, a slice of contemporary France with tower blocks and edgy suburbs.

South of Brest, two giant spurs dart out into the ocean, the **Crozon Peninsula** and **Cap Sizun**. On Crozon (parts of which are military reserves), snug inlets and tree-shrouded beaches lead out to majestic seascapes at the peninsula's end. On the northern shore stands the **Abbaye de Landévennec**, an atmospheric ruin with a museum on monastic life and early Breton history.

Across the bay on Cap Sizun lies the beautiful town of **Douarnenez** ㉖. Its bay is said to be the site of the mythical city of Ys. From the 19th century it was France's foremost sardine fishing and canning port. Just inland is **Locronan**, one of Brittany's most celebrated beauty spots.

Pointe du Raz, at the end of Cap Sizun, can seem further west than Pointe de Corsen to the north as it's so much more spectacular. The massive blade of granite cliffs looks magnificent from **Pointe du Van** across the wide expanse of beach in between.

Cornouaille and Pont Aven

Southern Finistère is known as Cornouaille, or Cornwall, since it was populated by migrants from across the Channel in the 5th and 6th centuries. Its southwest corner, the **Pays Bigouden**, is famed for its Breton culture and tradition. In **Pont-l'Abbé**, the **Musée Bigouden** (June–Sept daily 10am–12.30pm, 2–6pm, Apr–May Tue–Sun 2–6pm; charge) covers the area's language, dress and culture.

Said to have been founded by legendary Breton king Gradlon, **Quimper** ㉗ is a Breton cultural centre. Its heart is still a medieval fairy-town of massive houses jutting out over narrow streets. On the more gentle southern coast, **Concarneau's** walled old town

Josselin's riverside château

Megalithic stone monuments in Carnac

stands picturesquely on a rocky island in the harbour. Just to the east is the artists' town of **Pont-Aven** (*see p.37–8*).

Brittany's softer south

Brittany's southern coast has a much softer quality than the ocean-battered north and west. Village architecture has a more varied – and more conventionally French – look, and creek-sized estuaries form delightful little harbours, flanked by beach villages. Inland, lush landscapes give way to dense woodland, awash with Arthurian legends, and a magnificent array of prehistoric standing stones.

The inland forests

Towards the middle of Brittany, little **Josselin** ㉘ is perhaps the prettiest of all the region's fairytale towns, its riverside château having enough tall towers for any fairy story, and a dolls' museum inside. The **Fôret de Paim-pont**, east of Josselin is, British visitors may be surprised to learn, the Breton home of King Arthur, and finding the legendary sites (maps from the Paim-pont tourist office) adds to the enjoyment of some beautiful walks.

Beaches and megaliths

The rocky spike of the **Presqu'île de Quiberon** ㉙ is linked to the mainland by a long neck of sand. Benign beaches spread along its east side down to Quiberon harbour, and the windier west side attracts surfers and windsurfers. You can take a ferry to **Belle-Île**, the largest of Brittany's islands, which offers superb walks around its coast, once painted by Monet. Around the corner, the busy resort of **Carnac** ㉚ is the centre of the densest concentration of megalithic stone monuments in Europe, and the **Carnac Alignments**, awe-inspiring parallel lines of over 3,000 standing stones, extend like a great barrier for over 4km (2½ miles) behind the town. The **Maison des Mégalithes** (daily, May–Aug 9am–7pm, Sept–Apr 10am–5pm; charge) has a lively explanatory exhibition, and provides guided tours. To the east, the coast opens into the **Golfe du Morbihan** or 'little sea' in Breton, a shallow, sheltered inland sea over 20km (12 miles) wide, dotted with islands and idyllic for gentle boating.

ACCOMMODATION

The half-timbered and granite-towered architecture of Normandy and Brittany provides locations for utterly charming, distinctive hotels, many in delightful locations on the coast or in green countryside.

Accommodation price categories

Prices are for one night's accommodation in a standard double room (unless otherwise specified).

€ = below €80
€€ = €80–130
€€€ = €130–200
€€€€ = €200–300
€€€€€ = over €300

Rouen and Upper Normandy

Domaine St Clair-Le Donjon
Chemin de St Clair, 76790 Etretat
Tel: 02 35 27 08 23
www.hoteletretat.com
Eccentric architecture is characteristic of Belle Epoque Etretat, and this luxury hotel occupies 'The Keep', an 1860s mock-medieval château above the cliffs. Rooms, and the elegant restaurant, are plushly comfortable. **€€–€€€**

Le Moulin des Chennevières
34 chemin du Roy, 27620 Giverny
Tel: 06 81 13 77 72
www.givernymoulin.com
A magnificent 17th-century mill a short walk from the Monet house in Giverny, with four magnificent B&B rooms and a spectacular suite in a tower. **€€**

Le Vieux Carré
34 rue Ganterie, 76000 Rouen
Tel: 02 35 71 67 70
www.vieux-carre.fr
An informal modern hotel with small but comfortable rooms in a half-timbered building. The breakfast room is also a popular *salon de thé*, and serves delicious light lunches. Exceptional value. **€**

Classic Normandy

Hôtel d'Argouges
21 rue St-Patrice, 14400 Bayeux
Tel: 02 31 92 88 86
www.hotel-dargouges.com
An elegant option in the heart of Bayeux, this Louis XV-style town mansion has a garden and antique furnishings, but retains a very relaxed feel. **€€**

Hôtel des Isles
9 boulevard Maritime, 50270 Barneville-Carteret
Tel: 02 33 04 90 76
www.hoteldesisles.com
A fresh approach to the French seaside hotel, situated right above Barneville beach, and attractively renovated to make the most of the wonderful coastal light. The restaurant is just as enjoyable. **€€**

Hôtel des Loges
18 rue Brûlée, 14600 Honfleur
Tel: 02 31 89 38 26
www.hoteldesloges.com
Chic and charming, this is the most appealing of Honfleur's boutique hotels, skilfully inserted in a historic building. Fruit-filled breakfasts are delicious. **€€–€€€**

Manoir de la Roche-Torin
La Roche Torin, 50220 Courtils
Tel: 02 33 70 96 55
www.manoir-rochetorin.com
A superior option near Mont St-Michel, this ivy-shrouded old house is on the south side

At Hôtel des Isles

of the bay, with hypnotic views of the mount. The best rooms have garden terraces. **€€–€€€**

Aux Trois Damoiselles
Place Michel Vermughen, 14430 Beuvron-en-Auge
Tel: 02 31 39 61 38
www.auxtroisdamoiselles.com
This inn is only a few years old, but built in harmony with Beuvron's celebrated square, a symbol of the Pays d'Auge, using traditional techniques. Excellent value, and ideal for cider and calvados hunters. **€–€€**

Northern Brittany
Hôtel Castel Beau Site
Plage de St-Guirec, 22700 Ploumanac'h
Tel: 02 96 91 40 87
www.castelbeausite.com
Located on the most beautiful cove of the Pink Granite Coast, this hotel has been given a very smart makeover, and the restaurant is similarly stylish. The views are ravishing. **€€–€€€**

Hôtel Elizabeth
2 rue des Cordiers, 35400 St-Malo
Tel: 02 99 56 24 98
www.st-malo-hotel-elizabeth.com
Occupying two of the oldest houses in St-Malo, next to the ramparts, with a stone cellar where breakfast is served. Bedrooms are spread over the two buildings, and the best are in 'Les Armateurs'. **€–€€**

Villa Reine Hortense
19 rue de la Malouine, 35800 Dinard
Tel: 02 99 46 54 31
www.villa-reine-hortense.com
Ideal for appreciating Dinard's Belle Epoque atmosphere, this elegant villa has opulent rooms and gorgeous sea views. Closed Nov–Mar. **€€€**

Finistère and southern Brittany
Les Ajoncs d'Or
1 place de l'Hôtel de Ville, 29930 Pont-Aven
Tel: 02 98 06 02 06
www.ajoncsdor-pontaven.com

Hôtel Castel Beau Site

The hotel where Gauguin and other artists stayed retains its Belle Epoque character – as well as a family feel and low prices. The pretty restaurant serves excellent classic fare. **€**

Hôtel Europa
Port-Haliguen, 56173 Quiberon
Tel: 02 97 50 25 00
www.europa-quiberon.com
A large beach hotel with excellent facilities, including a spa and indoor pool, imaginatively modernised rooms and lovely terrace restaurant. Closed mid-Nov–Mar. **€€–€€€**

Hôtel Les Sables Blancs
Plages des Sables-Blancs, 29900 Concarneau
Tel: 02 98 50 10 12
www.hotel-les-sables-blancs.com
Chic hotel with delightful views in an Art Deco building on a beach outside Concarneau, with an excellent seafood-based restaurant. Guests can walk from the hotel to the Pointe du Raz, the westernmost point of Continental Europe. **€€€**

Hôtel Ty Mad
Plage St Jean, Tréboul, 29100 Douarnenez
Tel: 02 98 74 00 53
www.hoteltymad.com
In a beautiful location above Tréboul beach outside Douarnenez, the Ty Mad ('Good House' in Breton) has been refurbished in a bright boutique style, with a great restaurant. Sunset views are stunning. **€€**

Listings

RESTAURANTS

Norman restaurants make great use of the region's products – apples, cheese and cream. In Brittany every town has a few crêperies, a great alternative to larger French meals for kids.

Rouen and Upper Normandy

Ancien Hôtel Baudy
81 rue Claude Monet, 27620 Giverny
Tel: 02 32 21 10 03
The hotel-restaurant where Cézanne and others stayed when visiting Monet no longer has rooms, but in high season it's open for breakfasts and great-value meals. Closed Nov–late Mar. €

Brasserie Paul
1 place de la Cathédrale, 76000 Rouen
Tel: 02 35 71 86 07
www.brasserie-paul.com
Simone de Beauvoir, Marcel Duchamp and many other Rouen residents have been regulars at this classic brasserie. It's right opposite the cathedral, and the menu has something for everyone. €–€€

A la Marmite Dieppoise
8 rue St Jean, 76200 Dieppe
Tel: 02 35 84 24 26
A culinary institution in Dieppe renowned for its eponymous speciality, the *marmite dieppoise*. A rich seafood stew of sole, scallops and other ingredients in a Norman cider and cream sauce, this is a dish to take time over. Alternatively, there are other fresh fish choices and some meats. Closed Sun evening and Mon. €€

Classic Normandy

L'Absinthe
10 quai de la Quarantaine, 14600 Honfleur
Tel: 02 31 89 39 00
www.absinthe.fr
A lovely restaurant with pretty quayside terrace, impeccable service and innovative modern cuisine in the oldest part of Honfleur. The owners also have an attractive hotel. €€–€€€

Oysters in Cancale, Brittany

Manoir de la Drôme
129 rue des Forges, 14490 Balleroy
Tel: 02 31 21 60 94
www.manoir-de-la-drome.com
In an old mill outside Balleroy west of Bayeux, this is one of Normandy's finest gourmet restaurants, where chef Denis Leclerc creates superbly delicate flavours. Closed Sun evening, Mon, Tue midday and Wed. €€€

Au Marquis de Tombelaine
7 route des Falaises, 50530 Champeaux
Tel: 02 33 61 85 94
www.aumarquisdetombelaine.com
High on the cliffs at Champeaux, this traditional restaurant has magical views of Mont St-Michel. Closed Tue evening and Wed. €€

Le Moderne
Place du Général de Gaulle, 50760 Barfleur
Tel: 02 33 23 12 44
www.hotel-restaurant-moderne-barfleur.com
Serves every kind of fish and seafood,

superbly fresh and beautifully presented.
Service is charming, and the atmosphere,
like the little harbour of Barfleur, relaxed. **€€**

Les Vapeurs
160–162 quai Fernand Moureaux, 14360
Trouville-sur-Mer
Tel: 02 31 88 15 24
www.lesvapeurs.fr
The definitive French harbourside brasserie,
an unbeatable place to savour a bowl of
mussels with frites and ice-cold Muscadet.
Many more choices, too. **€€**

Northern Brittany
Le Corps de Garde
3 montée de Notre Dame, 35400 St-Malo
Tel: 02 99 40 91 46
www.le-corps-de-garde.com
This budget crêperie has a special attraction
– it's the only restaurant on the walls of old
St-Malo, so you can enjoy glorious sea views
while enjoying crêpes or savoury *galettes*. **€**

Au Plaisir des Sens
54 rue d'Antrain, 35000 Rennes
Tel: 02 99 38 67 51
www.auplaisirdessens.com
A very comfortable restaurant, where chef-
owner Philippe Faget produces notably
original dishes. The lunchtime menu is an
amazing bargain. Closed Sun evening, Mon
and Sat midday. **€–€€**

Les Triagoz
Plage Coz Pors, 22730 Trégastel
Tel: 02 96 15 34 10
It's hard to be closer to the sea than at this
modern beach bistro on the Pink Granite
Coast. Space is at a premium around sunset.
Closed Wed lunch and Oct–Easter. **€€**

La Vieille Tour
13 rue de l'Eglise, 22500 Paimpol
Tel: 02 96 20 83 18
This traditional restaurant has many fans
for its homely service and excellent Breton
and classic French cuisine. Sept–June
closed Sun evening, Wed evening and Mon.
€€–€€€

Finistère and southern Brittany
L'Estaminet
73 rue St Cornély, 56340 Carnac
Tel: 02 97 52 19 41
Charming small restaurant with a garden
terrace and great-value menus. Sept–May
closed Sun evening and Mon. **€–€€**

Hôtel de la Plage
29550 Ste-Anne-la-Palud
Tel: 02 98 92 50 12
www.plage.com
Gourmet seafood and other succulent
dishes in a magnificent location above the
beach in a village just north of Douarnenez,
with a superb view across the waves. Also a
luxury hotel. Closed Nov–Mar. **€€€**

Le Moulin de Rosmadec
Venelle de Rosmadec, 29930 Pont-Aven
Tel: 02 98 06 00 22
www.moulinderosmadec.com
A sumptuous gourmet restaurant in one of
the mills in Pont-Aven painted by Gauguin.
Serves superb grilled lobster. Sept–June
closed Sun evening and Thur. **€€–€€€**

Le Temps de Vivre
17 place Lacaze Duthiers, 29680 Roscoff
Tel: 02 98 61 27 28
www.letempsdevivre.net
Out-of-the-way Roscoff has a gourmet
restaurant, where Jean-Yves Crenn makes
spectacular use of local seafood. There's
also a chic hotel. Restaurant closed Sun
evening, Mon, Tue midday. **€€–€€€**

Traditional Breton crêpe

Listings

NIGHTLIFE AND ENTERTAINMENT

Côté Rouen and *Côté Caen* are free weekly what's-on magazines for their respective cities. Also check out www.cityvox.fr (includes an English version).

Hangar 23
Boulevard Emile Duchemin, 76000 Rouen
Tel: 02 32 18 28 25
Ticket office: 16 rue Jeanne d'Arc, 76000
Rouen; tel: 02 32 18 28 10
www.hangar23.fr
'Music and dance cultures of the world' is this hip centre's motto; programmes cover an inspiringly huge range.

Opéra de Rouen Haute-Normandie
7 rue du Docteur Rambert, 76000 Rouen
Tel: 08 10 81 11 16

www.operaderouen.fr
The company performs at the Théâtre des Arts, Normandy's most prestigious cultural venue, which also hosts dance and orchestral concerts.

Ubu
1 rue Saint-Hélier, 35000 Rennes
Tel: 02 99 31 12 10
www.ubu-rennes.com
A cutting-edge range of gigs and DJ nights at this live music venue, which is often one of the stop-off points for touring indie bands.

SPORTS AND ACTIVITIES

Western Normandy and Brittany form one of the best areas in Europe for sailing, windsurfing, kayaking and other ocean sports; for more on this, see *On the water*, *p.55–7*. Normandy is famous horse country, and both regions are also great for hiking, particularly around the coast. The Manche *département* and Brittany have extensive networks of *Voie Vertes* or 'green ways', trails for walkers, cyclists or horse riders. For information, see *Exploring the landscape, p.32*, and www.brittanytourism.com or www.manchetourisme.com.

Centre Nautique Pleneuf-Val André
22370 Pleneuf-Val André
Tel: 02 96 72 95 28
www.cnpva.com
Well-equipped and friendly sailing and

watersports centre on the Côte d'Emeraude with sail training and trips for all ages. Sand-yachting on the area's broad beaches is another option.

Golf Barrière de Deauville
Mont Canisy-Saint-Arnoult, 14803 Deauville
Tel: 01 31 14 24 24
www.lucienbarriere.com
Deauville is a major golf centre, and this is the most luxuriant of five courses around the town.

Ride in France
2 place Charles de Gaulle, 38200 Vienne
Tel: 04 37 02 20 00
www.rideinfrance.com
Horseback-tourism specialists providing tours of Mont St-Michel Bay and elsewhere.

Sailing school in Treffiagat, Finistère

TOURS

Many tours are available from tourist offices. For tours in the bay of Mont St-Michel, see *Exploring the landscape, p.31–2*. For D-Day battlefield tours, see *Marks of war, p.47*.

FESTIVALS AND EVENTS

Normandy's food is the focus of many events, while Brittany's distinctive music and other Celtic traditions give it a rich festival calendar (see also *Brittany's Celtic Roots, p.126–7*).

May
Fête de la Bretagne
All over Brittany
www.fetedelabretagne.com
One week mid-May
The week around 19 May, the day of Brittany's native patron saint Yves (or Ives), has been declared a *fête* for the whole region, with varied events held all around Brittany, France and in other countries.

July–August
Kann al Loar
Landerneau, Finistère
www.kann-al-loar.com
One week mid-July
The festival entirely takes over this beautiful small town with six days of Breton concerts, dances, parades and other events.

Festival de Cornouaille
Quimper, Finistère
www.festival-cornouaille.com
One week late July
Following after Landerneau, this is one of the largest Breton festivals.

Foire aux Fromages
Livarot
www.paysdelivarot.fr
End July or early Aug
Two-day celebration of cheeses and AOC

Festival de Cornouaille

(appellation d'origine contrôlée) Norman produce, with various entertainment.

Festival Interceltique de Lorient
Lorient
www.festival-interceltique.com
One week early Aug
Big festival that features performers from other Celtic countries and eclectic modern styles, as well as traditional Breton arts.

September
Festival du Cinéma Américain
Deauville, Calvados
www.festival-deauville.com
Ten days early Sept
Hollywood stars provide extra shine to Deauville's usual glitz.

October
Foire de la Pomme
Vimoutiers
www.vimoutiers.net
Third weekend Oct
A celebration of apples, cider and everything to do with them.

Listings

The Loire Valley

The wealth and beauty of the lush Loire Valley was once the setting of the royal court and only accessible to a privileged few, but today the many magnificent châteaux are open to all, and the whole region has been listed as a Unesco World Heritage Site. In between the palaces, you can enjoy the quiet pleasures of a little-changed landscape, and the river that defines it.

Tours, Orléans, Nantes

 Population: 141,620 (Tours); 124,150 (Orléans); 277,300 (Nantes)

 Local dialling codes: Orléans: 02 38; Nantes: 02 40; Tours: 02 47

 Local tourist offices: Orléans: 2 place de l'Etape; tel: 02 38 24 05 05; www.tourisme-orleans.com. Nantes: 2 place St-Pierre; tel: 08 92 46 40 44; www.nantes-tourisme.com. Tours: 78–82 rue Bernard Palissy; tel: 02 47 70 37 37; www.ligeris.com

 Main police station: Tours: 72 rue Marceau; tel: 02 47 39 09 31. Nantes: 6 place Waldeck Rousseau; tel: 02 40 37 21 21.

Orléans: rue du Faubourg St-Jean; tel: 02 38 24 30 00

 Main post office: Orléans: 2 rue Bresil. Nantes: 2 place Bretagne. Tours: 67 rue de la Victoire

 Hospitals: Tours: Hôpital Bretonneau, 2 boulevard Tonnelle; tel: 02 47 47 47 47. Nantes: Hôtel-Dieu, 1 place Alexis–Ricordeau; tel: 02 40 08 33 33. Orléans: 1 rue Porte Madeleine; tel: 02 38 51 44 44

 Local newspapers/listings magazines: Tours: *La Nouvelle République du Centre Ouest* (daily). Nantes: *Metro France Ouest* (daily). Orléans: *La République du Centre* (daily)

The name 'Loire Valley' is often used to refer to a short stretch of the river between Orléans and Angers, named 'the Valley of the Kings' because of its extraordinary Renaissance châteaux built by royalty and courtiers.

However, at 1,012km (630 miles), the Loire, France's longest river, rises in the Ardèche, on the eastern edge of the Massif Central *(see p.172)* and flows through 12 *départements*, draining a fifth of the land surface of France before meeting the Atlantic Ocean at St-Nazaire. A broader definition of the valley, therefore, takes in much of the area covered by the modern regions of Centre and Pays de la Loire, with the lower reaches extending into the Atlantic region of Poitou-Charente. In between the many tributaries that flow into the mighty river, the countryside is attractively varied, earning its moniker the 'garden of France' for its mixture of lush, fertile farmland characterised by sunflowers, wheat fields and vineyards, as well as extensive areas of woodland, marsh and bleak plateaux.

Apart from the great châteaux there are many other places to see, including castles built for defence rather than pleasure, great cathedrals, historic cities, monasteries, nature reserves, viewpoints and innumerable quaint towns and villages.

Chartres and Orléans

Just south of Paris, the Loire's northern journey takes a westward turn at the historic city of Orléans and joins up with its far more tranquil tributary, the Loir, flowing slowly through a landscape of meadows and lines of poplars. Not far away, the city of Chartres can be seen across the plain.

The soaring Gothic arches inside Chartres Cathedral

Loire countryside

North of the Loire

Chartres ❶ is close enough to Paris (97km/60 miles) to make it a popular day trip from the capital. The first glimpse of the lofty spires of the **cathedral** (8.30am–7.30pm; charge for tower) rising above the plain – exactly as 13th-century pilgrims must have seen them – is magical. Get closer and you'll see the incontestable glory of its 176 **stained-glass windows**, the world's most remarkable ensemble. In the **Centre International du Vitrail** (International Stained-Glass Centre; Mon–Fri 9.30am–12.30pm, 1.30–6.30pm, Sat 10am–12.30pm, 2.30–6pm, Sun 2.30–6pm; charge), you can see how it is done.

Chartres is the capital of the *département* of Eure-et-Loir, which, as its name implies, has two principal rivers. The Loir (without the e) flows south and eventually joins its near-namesake at Angers. The Eure is a tributary of the Seine. Between the two towns lies the medieval town of **Le Mans**, famous for its 24-hour endurance car race.

Eastwards across the valley, the Loir flows into **Vendôme ❷**, a

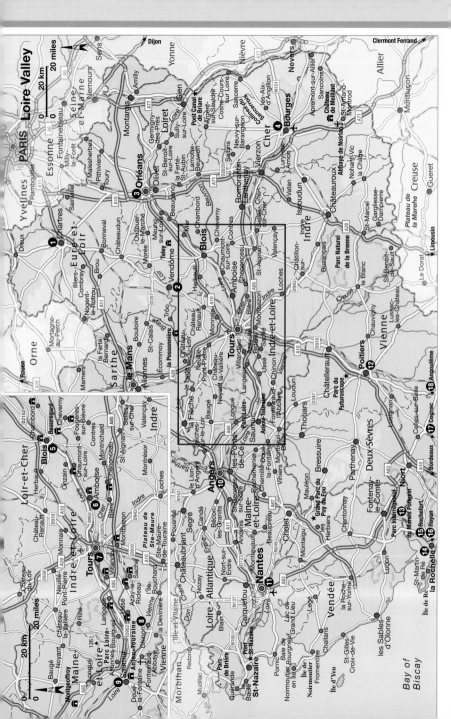

sophisticated and attractive old town full of elegant shops and restaurants, with a flamboyant Gothic abbey church as its centrepiece. Here the prettiest part of the Loir begins, with the village of **Trôo**'s maze of cave dwellings 24km (15 miles) downriver.

Orléans and Berry

At the northernmost point of the Loire's meandering course stands **Orléans** ❸, a modern city whose heart was bombed out during World War II. Its soul, however, lives on in the cult of Joan of Arc; it was here that she successfully resisted the English army before being burnt at the stake at Rouen. The site where she stayed in 1429 is now the **Maison Jeanne d'Arc** (3 place de Gaulle; www.jeannedarc.com.fr; May–Oct Tue–Sun 10am–12.30pm, 1.30–6.30pm, Nov–Apr 1.30–6pm; charge).

A little way upriver is the church of **St-Benoît-sur-Loire**, one of the finest Romanesque buildings in France. Seemingly afloat with the ducks and swans, the château of **Sully-sur-Loire**

Joan of Arc led the French to several victories during the Hundred Years War

The Loire Valley

Tours transport

 Airport: Tours Val de Loire; tel: 02 47 49 37 00; **www.tours.aeroport. fr**; 7km (4 miles) from city centre; Fil Bleu shuttle departs 20 minutes after arrival of Ryanair flights, about 20 minutes to city centre. Taxi takes about 20 minutes; from €15

 Trains: Gare de Tours, place du Général Leclerc; tel: 08 36 35 35 35

 Buses: Fil Bleu, 9 rue Michelet; tel: 02 47 66 70 70; **www.filbleu.fr**; tickets from €1.30

 Taxis: Tours City Taxis; tel: 02 47 20 30 40; **www.taxis-tours.fr**

 Car hire: Avis: tel: 02 47 49 21 49; **www.avis.co.uk**. National Citer: tel: 02 47 44 80 04; **www.nationalciter. fr**. Also at the Gare de Tours

 Parking: Fil Bleu runs Parkings Relais (park and ride), a convenient 8-minute bus ride from the city centre. Car park €2.10 for the day, €0.85 per person for an all-day bus ticket

(Tue–Sun 10am–noon, 2–5pm; closed Jan; charge), a few kilometres southeast, is a rare example of both medieval fortress and Renaissance pleasure palace in one.

The Loire flows down to Orléans between Burgundy to the east and the ancient province of Berry to the west. Across the fertile landscape, the 13th-century **Cathédrale de St-Etienne**, one of the finest Gothic buildings in France, stands at the heart of **Bourges ❹**. Close to the geographical centre of France, this venerable city has some lovely Renaissance domestic architecture.

Along the royal river

Magnificent Renaissance palaces stand almost cheek by jowl along the Valley of the Kings, either side of the Loire between Orléans and Angers. Once the setting for the French court, the Loire Valley attracted counts and courtiers who wanted easy access to the king, so they built their grandiose homes close to the royal palaces. Other castles were built for defence such as at Angers, Chinon and Loches.

Blois and the great châteaux

Just 18km (11 miles) downriver from Orléans lies quiet **Beaugency**, where an 11th-century bridge provides a view of the river and the medieval streets. Market days, with local produce and handicrafts, are particularly atmospheric. The 15th-century **Château de Dunois** has certainly remained unchanged, except for slight damage sustained during the French Revolution.

On the southern side of the river is the **Fôret de Chambord**, surrounded by the longest wall in France. Deer, wild boar and other animals roam

Detail of the Château de Blois

Château de Chaumont, once owned by Catherine de' Medici

The château's monumental octagonal staircase and its sculpted balconies are superb examples of early French Renaissance design *(see p.150–1)*.

At nearby **Chaumont**, the Loire is particularly wide, and the round towers of the **Château de Chaumont** (www.domaine-chaumont.fr; Apr–Oct 10am–6.30pm, Nov–Mar 10am–5pm, closing times may vary; charge) look down upon it from the top of a wooded hill *(see p.151)*, where it hosts the **International Garden Festival** each summer.

Continuing downriver, the town of **Amboise** ❻ nestles around its impressive château (www.chateau-amboise.fr; Mar–mid-Nov daily 9am–5.30–7pm, rest of the year 9am–12.30pm, 2–5.30pm, closing times vary; charge). Rich in history, Amboise belonged to the counts of Anjou and Berry before becoming the property of the French Crown in 1434. One of the Loire's busiest small towns, Amboise has a line of very enjoyable terrace restaurants along the street below the château, all with lovely views. Leonardo da Vinci is buried in the **Chapelle St-Hubert**.

the national game reserve freely, and observation towers have been set up for the public. In the middle stands the **Château de Chambord** (www.chambord.org; daily, Apr–Sept 9am–6pm, Oct–Dec 10am–5pm; charge), the largest château on the Loire *(see p.150–1)*. Inside, its most striking feature is a double-spiralled staircase.

Back on the Loire, the town of **Blois** ❺ was a central stage for courtly intrigue, with assassinations, subterfuge and power play going on in the **Château de Blois** (July–Aug 9am–7pm, Apr–June, Sept closes 6.30pm, Oct closes 6pm, Jan–Mar and Nov–Dec 9am–12.30pm, 1.30–5.30pm; charge). In the clear light of day, Blois is a pleasant place.

The end of Charles VIII

Some kings die for their country, others for beliefs. Unfortunately, on the eve of Palm Sunday 1498, Charles VIII hit his head on a door in Amboise while trying to get to the lavatory. He died nine hours later where he fell, no one having dared to move him.

★ CHATEAUX COUNTRY

The Loire Valley is where France's identification with luxury began. Emerging victorious from the Hundred Years War, French kings were keen to show off their wealth and supremacy over lesser mortals. Castles were no longer needed as fortresses, and the soft, sensual landscape of the valley began to fill with sumptuous pleasure-palaces surrounded by elegant formal gardens, a fit setting for the glittering, ever more lavish life of the court and its followers.

The Loire had long been a centre of power, with plenty of belligerent, fighting castles, such as the massive Chinon, built for Henry II of Normandy and England. Easy to reach from Paris, the region was full of royal hunting estates, hunting being an obsession for most French kings.

Pleasure-building began in the 1490s, when King Charles VIII rebuilt much of the old castle at Amboise, and commissioned the first French formal garden. His successor Louis XII moved his court to the Loire for long periods, preferring Blois over potentially rebellious Paris. The château of Blois is a remarkable box of styles: Louis XII's wing is a masterpiece of Flamboyant Gothic, but there is also a Renaissance wing added by François I, and a classical Baroque one contributed in the 1630s by Louis XIII's brother Gaston d'Orléans.

It was from 1515 under François I, raised at Amboise, that châteaux-

Chambord, the largest château in the Loire Valley

building reached its height. An enthusiast for the Renaissance, François replaced late Gothic with French Renaissance, with its more precise proportions and restrained Italianate decoration, as the de rigueur mansion style. He made additions to Amboise and Blois, and created his own giant monument at Chambord, deliberately on a larger scale than anything seen before it.

Royal ministers and great merchants followed the royal lead with their own residences, and great houses proliferated across the valley. Châteaux converted from military castles, as at Ussé – said to have inspired the story of Sleeping Beauty – were joined by almost entirely new ones such as Azay-le-Rideau, built for the royal treasurer Gilles Berthelot.

Châteaux primarily served as showcases for powerful men, but they did the same for several women, none more so than Chenonceau, the classic image of a Loire château. It is for ever associated with Diane de Poitiers, mistress of King Henri II, who virtually held her own court there. This was bitterly resented by the queen, Catherine de' Medici, who on Henri's death in 1559 seized Chenonceau for herself, and 'exiled' Diane to the plainer (but still huge) château of Chaumont.

The grandeur of the Loire was relatively short-lived, for the Bourbon monarchs tended to stay closer to Paris. Louis XIV visited Chambord to hunt, but preferred to spend his time in his own display case, the Château de Versailles.

Azay-Le-Rideau, a masterpiece of French Renaissance architecture

Ornate fireplace at the 15th-century Château de Chaumont

The Renaissance gardens at Villandry with low box hedges creating geometric patterns

A short walk away is **Clos Lucé** (www.vinci-closluce.com; July–Aug daily 9am–8pm, Feb–June and Sept–Oct 9am–7pm, Nov–Jan 10am–6pm; charge), the red-brick manor house where Leonardo spent the last three years of his life as a member of François I's royal court; the park outside is dotted with life-size interactive maquettes of his inventions.

Following the Cher, the Loire's southern tributary, takes you to the **Château de Chenonceau** (www.chenonceau.com; July–Aug daily 9am–8pm, the rest of the year times vary; charge). This is perhaps the most elegant of all the Loire Valley jewels, renowned for the arches that carry it across the water.

Tours to Nantes

The prime stretch of the Loire Valley is dominated by the city of **Tours** ❼, a Gallo-Roman settlement, which later grew rich on the manufacture of silk. Nowadays, it's a handsome university city and the fulcrum of the Loire wine region, portrayed in the **Musée des Vins de Touraine** (Fri–Sun 9am–noon, 2–6pm; charge), in the cellars of the 13th-century Abbaye Saint-Julien.

> ### Gardens at Villandry
>
> Planted with low boxwood and yew hedges, the flowerbeds at Villandry represent the four faces of love on one side, music on the other. The kitchen gardens and herb garden were designed according to documents preserved by medieval monks, and look like something from *Alice Through the Looking Glass*: each square describes a different geometric design in contrasting colours that change from year to year. The standard red roses represent the monks tending the vegetable plots.

Just by the confluence of the Cher and the Loire, 19km (12 miles) west of Tours, stands the **Château de Villandry** and its famous 16th-century **gardens** (www.chateauvillandry.fr; daily, July–Aug 9am–6.30pm, Sept–June from 9am, closing times vary; charge). The three tiers of the garden (the pond, the decorative gardens and the kitchen garden) can be viewed at once from the high terrace of the château *(see box, left)*.

A few kilometres to the south is **Azay-le-Rideau**, a small château of exquisite proportions (daily, July–Aug 9.30am–7pm, Apr–June, Sept daily 9.30am–6pm, Oct–Mar 10am–12.30pm, 2–5.30pm; charge). The River Indre forms a wide moat around this epitome of Renaissance grace and perfection *(see p.151)*. On

the other side, the D751 cuts straight through the forest for 18km (11 miles) to the well-preserved, historic town of **Chinon** ❽, on the River Vienne, another tributary. On the top of a steep ridge above the river stands an imposing, largely ruined, 12th-century **château fort** (www.forteresse chinon.fr; Apr–Sept daily 9am–7pm, Oct–Mar 9.30am–5pm; charge).

Another 14km (9 miles) back towards the banks of the Loire is the **Abbaye de Fontevraud** (www.abbayedefontevraud.com; daily, July–Aug 9.30am–7.30pm, Apr–May, Sept–Oct 9.30am–6.30pm, rest of the year times vary; charge), one of the largest surviving medieval abbeys and where Eleanor of Aquitaine, widow of Henri II, spent her final years.

The route from Fontevraud to **Saumur** ❾ (D947) sums up the Loire Valley. Besides the numerous châteaux perched above the majestic river, prehistoric dolmens and Roman remnants testify to a long history of human community in this region. Saumur is mainly known for its Renaissance **château** (July–Aug Tue–Sun 10am–6pm, Apr–June, Sept–Oct 10am–1pm, 2.30–5.30pm; charge) and its massive network of troglodyte caves nearby, some of which are inhabited, or used as restaurants, bars and shops.

Another 44km (27 miles) west along the Loire lies **Angers** ❿, the ancient capital of Anjou and fiefdom of the Plantagenets. The **château** (May–Aug 9.30am–6.30pm, Sept–Apr

The Loire Valley

The cloisters at the Abbaye de Fontevraud, founded in the 12th century

10am–5.30pm; charge) took 100 years to build. Inside is the world's largest tapestry at 107m (350ft), the **Apocalypse of St John**. Outside the town is a new botanical theme park, **Terra Botanica** (www.terrabotanica.fr; July–Aug daily 10am–7pm, Apr–June, Sept–Nov 9am–6pm, times may vary; charge), where all the activities are related to plant life.

Around 75km (47 miles) further west is the river port of **Nantes** ⓫, which was part of Brittany until 1972. Nantes made its fortune in the 18th century from the proceeds of sugar and slavery, and its most conspicuous expression of this wealth is the **Château des Ducs de Bretagne** (www.chateau-nantes.fr; July–Aug daily 10am–7pm, Sept–June Tue–Sun until 6pm; charge), where the Edict of Nantes was issued in 1598, ending the Wars of Religion. Close by is the beautiful, austere **Cathédrale de St-Pierre,** built of the same pale stone as Canterbury Cathedral.

South of the Loire is the Vendée, one of the less well-known regions of France. Along its coast are several modest-sized resorts and two interesting islands, **Noirmoutier,** a tidal island at the mouth of the Baie de Bourgneuf, and the **Ile d'Yeu,** accessed by ferry from Fromentine, Saint-Giles-Croix-de-Vie and Les Sables-d'Olonne in summer. To the east, near Les Epesses, is one of France's largest theme parks, the **Grand Parc du Puy du Fou** (www.puydufou.com; Apr–Sept 10am–7pm, closing times vary; charge).

Poitou and the Charentes

Islands and oysters, cognac, coastal wetlands and little-known country churches, the rural region of Poitou-Charentes on the southern edges of the Loire valley is almost where north meets south. Midway up the Atlantic

Château de Saumur, one of the few Loire châteaux built for defensive purposes

St Martin, capital of the Ile de Ré, has lovely backstreets lined with whitewashed houses

The Loire Valley

coast, and bordered to the east by the Massif Central, this region is the sunniest part of the country outside the Mediterranean.

Poitiers and its wetlands

The capital of the Poitou-Charentes region and one of the oldest cities in France, **Poitiers** ⓬, dating from the 8th century, is rich in architecture, with a fine Romanesque cathedral and a church with seven naves. Just to the north is the extraordinary **Parc du Futuroscope** (www.futuroscope.com; mid-Feb–mid-Sept daily 10am–10pm, mid-Sept–mid-Feb times vary, closed Jan; charge), an exciting futuristic theme park.

The beautiful marshlands of the **Marais Poitevin** ⓭ that extend across the southern reaches of the Vendée were tamed by 12th-century monks, who created 1,450km (900 miles) of waterways. These can be explored by traditional flat-bottomed boat, by bicycle, on horseback or on foot from **Arçais** and **Coulon** (www.maraispoitevin.com or www.parc-maraispoitevin.fr).

Just to the south lies one of the most handsome of France's ports, La Rochelle ⓮, careful to preserve its quiet charm and dignity. La Rochelle was one of the first towns in France to introduce a pedestrian-only zone, and today free bicycles are available for visitors. Surrounded by lively cafés, the Vieux Port still serves the fishing fleet and small sailing boats. Its entrance is guarded by two 14th-century towers remaining from the town's fortifications. Boats leave from here to the gleaming white villas and smart little hotels of fashionable Ile de Ré just off the coast, which has a sunny microclimate, beautiful pine-shaded beaches and succulent oysters and mussels. It is also accessible via a toll road bridge (which costs a hefty €16.50 in the summer months).

The home of cognac

Beguiling **Rochefort** ⓯, 28km (17 miles) south of La Rochelle, was created as a military port to defend the coast against the marauding English by Louis XIV's naval minister Colbert, and was laid out according to

Comic-book mural in Angoulême

a geometrical grid plan. Across the bay, reached by a road bridge, is the **Ile d'Oléron**, popular for its oysters, mussels and sandy beaches.

Further south, ferries cross the Gironde from the busy family resort of **Royan** ⑯ to the Médoc Peninsula. The harbour town suffered badly in World War II, losing most of its old architecture, but it has plenty to keep children amused, and some pleasant sandy bays. La Palmyre zoo further up the coast is home to more than 1,600 animals and operates a conservation programme. Running north of Royan, the River Seudre feeds the extensive oyster beds around Marennes.

The beaches north of Royan are part of La Côte Sauvage; aptly named as the Atlantic waves which roll in can be fierce. Body-boarding is popular here, but be warned – the undertow is very strong.

Back towards the centre of the region is brandy country, where **Cognac** ⑰ is the obvious place to enjoy a glass of it or two *(see p.25–6)*. To the east, **Angoulême** ⑱ was once famous for paper manufacturing but is now the centre for *bande dessinée* (BD) or comic strip books, revealed in the Cité International de la Bande Dessinée et de l'Image. It's a pleasant city with a fine cathedral and characterful old backstreets.

Ageing cognac

Cognac is produced from distilling the wine made from grapes from the Charente region, and is aged in oak barrels for at least two years. The age of a cognac is determined by a series of highly regulated ageing 'codes': Trois Etoiles is aged from 2½ to four years; VSOP (Very Superior Old Pale) from four to 10 years; XO, Napoléon, or Royal for over 10 years.

ACCOMMODATION

Befitting its status as a symbol of pleasure and luxury, the Loire has plenty of beautiful hotels in small châteaux, many with lovely restaurants.

Chartres and Orléans

Hôtel de Bourbon
Boulevard de la République, 18000 Bourges
Tel: 02 48 70 70 00
www.hoteldebourbon.fr
Pleasant hotel in a 17th-century former abbey in central Bourges, with well-modernised rooms. The Abbaye Saint-Ambroix restaurant occupies a spectacular former chapel. **€€€**

Hôtel Châtelet
6–8 avenue Jehan de Beauce, 28000 Chartres
Tel: 02 37 21 78 00
www.hotelchatelet.com
Comfortable, good-value hotel in central Chartres with a view of the cathedral from some rooms. **€€**

Hôtel Saint-Georges
14 rue Poterie, 41100 Vendôme
Tel: 02 54 67 42 10
www.hotel-saint-georges-vendome.com
In the heart of old Vendôme, the Saint-Georges has been very attractively reno-vated in modern colours, and the restaurant is a local favourite. **€€**

Along the royal river

Château du Breuil
23 route de Fougères, 41700 Cheverny
Tel: 02 54 44 20 20
www.chateau-du-breuil.fr
A true Loire experience: opulent rooms in an imposing château amid magnificent grounds near Chambord. The many comforts include a pool and delightful restaurant. **€€€–€€€€**

Le Choiseul
36 quai Charles Guinot, 37400 Amboise
Tel: 02 47 30 45 45

www.le-choiseul.com
Beautifully refurbished 18th-century mansion overlooking the river, with a delightful garden and pool, and restaurant in similar style. Closed mid-Dec–mid-Jan. **€€€**

Le Grand Monarque
3 place de la République, 37190 Azay-le-Rideau
Tel: 02 47 45 40 08
www.legrandmonarque.com
Close to the château, this hotel has been charmingly renovated, and the fine restau-rant opens on to a pretty courtyard. Closed Dec–mid-Feb. **€€**

Hôtel du Mail
8 rue des Ursules, 49100 Angers
Tel: 02 41 25 05 25
www.hotel-du-mail.com
A charming hotel in a 17th-century house, in a central yet quiet location. The brightly modernised rooms are very good value. **€–€€**

Mansion and garden at Le Choiseul

Listings

Manoir de Restigné
15 route de Tours, 37140 Restigné
Tel: 02 47 97 00 06
www.manoirderestigne.com
Magnificent château hotel in lovely gardens, with a pool, in the heart of Loire wine country near Tours. The fine restaurant naturally has a superb wine list. €€€€

Poitou and the Charentes
Hostellerie des Pigeons Blancs
110 rue Jules Brisson, 16100 Cognac
Tel: 05 45 82 16 36
www.pigeons-blancs.com
A family-run small hotel and restaurant in a prettily renovated 17th-century inn. Only six bedrooms, but all furnished with care, and the food is delicious. €€

Hôtel Le Sénéchal
6 rue Gambetta, 17590 Ars-en-Ré, Ile de Ré

At Hostellerie des Pigeons Blancs

Tel: 05 46 29 40 42
www.hotel-le-senechal.com
An old village hotel on the Ile de Ré transformed into a discreetly chic destination. Bedrooms come in different sizes (and prices), and the plant-filled courtyard has a tiny pool. €€–€€€€

RESTAURANTS

Loire restaurants pride themselves on their selections of local wines and cheeses. This is the home of Muscadet, Sancerre, Pouilly-Fumé, Saumur, Bourgeuil and Chinon, and soft goats' cheeses are a speciality.

Restaurant price categories
Prices are for a three-course meal for one (usually a set menu) with a drink.

€ = below €20
€€ = €20–45
€€€ = €45–90
€€€€ = over €90

Chartres and Orléans
Bistrot de la Cathédrale
1 cloître Notre Dame, 28000 Chartres
Tel: 02 37 36 59 60
The terrace at this friendly restaurant is ideal for surveying the great facade of Chartres cathedral. The *menu terroir* includes local specialities such as *pâté de Chartres*. €€

Le Lift
Place de la Loire, 45000 Orléans
Tel: 02 38 53 63 48
www.restaurant-le-lift.com
Chic, imaginative modern restaurant with a splendid terrace with views of the city and the Loire. There are bargain set menus and a gourmet tasting menu. €–€€

Along the royal river
L'Ardoise
42 rue Rabelais, 37500 Chinon
Tel: 02 47 58 48 78
www.lardoise-chinon.com
In his restaurant in the centre of Chinon, chef Stephane Perrot prepares high-quality, creative cuisine such as a millefeuille of salmon and langoustines. €€–€€€

Château de Noizay
Promenade de Waulsort, 37210 Noizay
Tel: 02 47 52 11 01
www.chateaudenoizay.com
A 16th-century château between Amboise and Tours – now a luxury hotel, with a superb restaurant in an exquisite setting. €€€–€€€€

Chez Bruno
40 place Michel Debré, 37400 Amboise
Tel: 02 47 57 73 49
The best of several terrace restaurants with great views below the château in Amboise, with enjoyable bistro menus and an excellent pick of local wines. €

La Cigale
4 place Graslin, 44000 Nantes
Tel: 02 51 84 94 94
www.lacigale.com
This historic Nantes brasserie is decorated in exuberant Belle Epoque style and serves excellent fish, seafood and other dishes; it is a favourite spot with locals for breakfast.
€–€€

Côté Loire-Auberge Ligérienne
2 place de la Grève, 41000 Blois
Tel: 02 54 78 07 86
www.coteloire.com
Continually changing menus making the best of regional market-fresh produce have

won this charming restaurant a great reputation. It's also a great-value small hotel.
€–€€

Poitou and the Charentes
Le Comptoir des Iles
Place Colbert,
17300 Rochefort
Tel: 05 46 87 44 81
Good-value brasserie in the town centre, with a terrace and a big menu including good seafood and salads. €

L'Entracte
35 rue saint Jean du Pérot,
17000 La Rochelle
Tel: 05 46 52 26 69
www.lentracte.net
One of three La Rochelle restaurants run by star chef Grégory Coutanceau, serving more traditional classics of French cuisine. Les Flots has more experimental cuisine, and Le Comptoir des Voyages is more globally influenced. €€–€€€

NIGHTLIFE AND ENTERTAINMENT

Orléans, Tours and Nantes are the three cities with the liveliest nightlife and most cultural events. Tourist offices *(see p.144)* have information on current events and programmes.

Angers-Nantes Opéra
Théâtre Graslin, place Graslin,
44000 Nantes
Tel: 02 40 69 77 18
Grand Théâtre, place du Ralliement, and Le Quai Forum, 49000 Angers
Tel: 02 41 24 16 40/02 41 22 20 20
www.angers-nantes-opera.com
Opera and classical music, presented in two venues in Angers and one in Nantes.

L'Astrolabe
1 rue Alexandre Avisse,
45000 Orléans
Tel: 02 38 54 20 06
www.lastrolabe.net
Eclectic live music and other events.

Le Hangar à Bananes
21 quai des Antilles, 44200 Nantes
www.hangarabananes.com
The hub of Nantes nightlife is this former

Nantes Opéra

banana warehouse, containing several bars, clubs, music venues and more.

Opéra de Tours
Grand Théâtre de Tours, 34 rue de la Scellerie, 37000 Tours
Tel: 02 47 60 20 00
www.operadetours.fr
Opera, ballet and symphony and chamber concerts.

SPORTS AND ACTIVITIES

Interconnecting cycle routes run all the way along the Loire to the sea, and the gentle countryside is ideal for cycling; www.loireavelo.fr has details and lists bike-rental facilities. There are also many horse-riding schools, and more operators offering canoeing or other boating trips on the Loire and its tributaries – generally more leisurely than the main river. Local tourist offices have details. For the Marais Poitevin marshlands, see *Exploring the landscape, p.32*; for watersports on the coast, see *On the water, p.55–7*. Overall guides to activities are on www.loirevalleytourism.com and www.westernloire.com.

Canopée Enchantée
Bois Farrault, 37230 Fondettes
Tel: 02 47 42 08 90
www.canopee-enchantee.com
Older children and more daring adults love this – rope-climbing along the tree canopy to get a different view of the Loire's forests.

Chinon Loisirs-Activités Nature
Quai Danton, 37500 Chinon
Tel: 06 23 82 96 33
www.loisirs-nature.fr
Canoe, kayak and bike hire, and guided canoe trips, from Chinon on the River Vienne.

TOURS

Loire tours available from Paris are often quite rushed. Many tourist offices coordinate local tours, and have full information. Comprehensive information in English on the Loire's wines and vineyards is on www.vinsvaldeloire.fr.

Loire Cruises – St-Martin-de-Tours
Quai de la Loire, 37210 Rochecorbon
Tel: 02 47 52 68 88
www.naviloire.com
Leisurely boat trips on the St-Martin-de-Tours boat, from just outside Tours.

Loire Wine Tours
Manoir de Gourin, 2 route de Puy, 49260 St-Macaire-du-Bois
Tel: (France) 02 41 59 31 21, (UK) 01303 226 692
www.loirewinetours.fr
Tours with expert guides, from half a day to several days.

RiverLoire
26 rue de la Concorde, 37400 Amboise
Tel: 02 34 37 01 70
www.riverloire.com
Small tour company offering individual, personal service, including special-interest and bespoke tours.

Routes François 1er
250 boulevard Raspail, 75014 Paris
Tel: 01 43 29 48 44
www.routesfrancois1.com
Château tours with expert, informative guides for those who really want to know their history.

FESTIVALS AND EVENTS

Many Loire châteaux have *son et lumière* displays on summer nights. For information, check with local tourist offices.

January–February

Festival International de la Bande Dessinée (Comics)
Angoulême
www.bdangouleme.com
Late Jan
Every January Angoulême becomes the global centre of comics with this hugely popular festival.

La Folle Journée de Nantes
Nantes
www.follejournee.fr
Early Feb
Popular festival that seeks to take classical music out of conventional venues.

April–September

Festival des Jardins de Chaumont-sur-Loire
Château de Chaumont-sur-Loire
www.domaine-chaumont.fr
Late Apr–Oct
Each year the grounds of the palace at Chaumont are turned over to different garden designers and artists, who are invited to create often stunning gardens on various themes.

Chartres en Lumières
Chartres
www.chartres-tourisme.com
Late May–mid-Sept
Every summer night Chartres Cathedral and other historic buildings are vividly illuminated in colours, in one of the most spectacular of France's *son et lumière* displays.

24 Heures du Mans
Circuit des 24 Heures, Le Mans
www.lemans.org
Mid-June
The celebrated 24-hour sports-car race is still Le Mans's biggest event.

Festival International d'Orgue de Chartres
Chartres
http://orgue.chartres.free.fr
July–Aug
The great organ of Chartres Cathedral is played to the full in these Sunday concerts, with prestigious organists.

Garden festival at Chaumont-sur-Loire

Burgundy to the Alps

The heart of gastronomic France, Burgundy and the central regions are awash with wines and exceptional restaurants. The watery landscape and slopes of the Alps are perfect for outdoor activities. The less well-known Auvergne is strung with volcanoes and crater lakes – and Limousin's meadows provide rich grazing for its famous cattle.

Dijon, Lyon, Grenoble

 Population: 150,000 (Dijon), 472,300 (Lyon), 158,550 (Grenoble)

 Local dialling codes: Dijon: 03 80; Lyon: 04 72/8; Grenoble: 04 76

i **Local tourist offices:** Dijon: 11 rue des Forges; tel: 08 92 70 05 58; **www.visitdijon.com**. Lyon: place Bellecour; tel: 04 72 77 69 69; **www. lyon-france.com**. Grenoble: 14 rue de la République; tel: 04 76 42 41 41; **www.grenoble-tourism.com**

 Main police stations: Dijon: 2 place du Suquet; tel: 03 80 44 55 00. Lyon: 3 rue de la Terrasse; tel: 04 72 07 40 50. Grenoble: 36 boulevard du Maréchal Leclerc; tel: 04 76 60 40 40

 Main post offices: Dijon: 3 place de la Libération. Lyon: 3 rue Président Edouard Herriot. Grenoble: 38 avenue Marèchal Randon

 Main hospitals: Lyon: Centre Hospitalier Lyon-Sud, chemin du Grand Revoyet; tel: 08 20 08 20 69. Grenoble: Centre Hospitalier Universitaire de Grenoble, 19 avenue de Kimberley; tel: 04 76 76 75 75

 Local media: Dijon: *Bien Public* (daily). Lyon: *Lyon Poche* magazine (weekly listings), *Metro Rhone* (daily)

Vineyards sweep up and down the rolling countryside of Burgundy, producing the world-famous wines of the region. This central core of France is unquestionably the land of wine and food, and in medieval times under its great dukes it became one of the foremost powers of of Europe. The vineyards continue south into the Rhône Valley, with Lyon, the gastronomic capital of France, where food is almost a religion. To the east of Burgundy, the region of Franche-Comté rises up from the Saône river towards the forested Jura mountains of the Franco-Swiss frontier, with plenty to do for those with a love of the great outdoors. The slopes of the French Alps, ideal in the ski season, are just as beguiling when carpeted with wild flowers in summer, providing beautiful walks with exhilarating views. In the Massif Central, the extraordinary volcanic landscape of the Auvergne is neighbour to the untouched towns, spas and gentle countryside of Limousin.

Burgundy and the Franche-Comté

Not only the heart but the stomach of France, the opulent province of Burgundy is also blessed with glorious architecture, vineyards as far as the eye can see, and the tranquil Canal de Bourgogne. Franche-Comté offers cross-country skiing, walking trails and crystal-clear waters in lakes, rivers and cascading waterfalls.

Sens to Dijon

Until 1622, the Archbishop of **Sens** ❶ lorded over an area extending

Vineyards in Burgundy

all the way to Paris. Next to the Gothic **Cathédrale St-Etienne**, his palatial lodgings house two museums (June–Sept daily 10am–6pm, Oct–May Wed, Sat and Sun 10am–noon, 2–6pm, Mon, Thur and Fri pm only; charge), while the **Trésor de la Cathédrale St-Etienne** has some rare liturgical garments. About 48km (30 miles) south along the Yonne lies **Auxerre** ❷, one of the oldest cities in France, where Renaissance houses follow a semicircular pattern around the 15th-century Tour de l'Horloge that not only tells the time but tracks the movement of the sun and stars. To the southwest, the spires of **Château de St-Fargeau** (Mar–Nov 10am–noon, 2–6pm, July and Aug until 7pm; charge) appear like minarets out of the rural beauty of **La Puisaye**, a gentle and watery region perfect for exploring by bicycle or on foot. This is where the Grande Mademoiselle, Louis XIV's sister, once lived. Dating from the 15th century, the château was renovated in the mid-17th century by Le Vau, the architect of Versailles. The area's most celebrated native

Burgundy to the Alps

The Tour de l'Horloge in Auxerre

daughter is the author Colette (1873–1953), whose writings remain popular in France and abroad. Her birthplace can be seen in rue des Vignes in the centre of the little town of St-Sauveur-en-Puisaye. The **Musée Colette** (Apr–Oct Wed–Mon 10am–6pm, Nov–Mar Sat–Sun 2–6pm; charge), housed in a beautifully furnished château, is dedicated to her life and work.

The Serein (Serene) River Valley, east of Auxerre, is a quiet haven that merits its name. Around the small town of **Chablis ❸**, world-famous vineyards cover the hills like patchwork quilts. And 26km (16 miles) upstream, cradled in a bend of the river, the little town of **Noyers** has preserved all the charm of its medieval history, with a rampart wall guarded by no fewer than 16 towers.

Not far away, at the bottom of a small valley near Montbard, is the **Abbaye de Fontenay** (www. abbayedefontenay.com; Apr–Oct 10am–6pm, Nov–Mar 10am–noon, 2–5pm; charge), founded by St Bernard in 1118 and Burgundy's most complete surviving medieval monastery, which shows the Cistercian ideal of simplicity. The church is often the setting for classical music concerts during the summer.

Gaul 'died and France was born' in the battle of Alesia, to the south, when the Gauls under Vercingetorix were defeated by Julius Caesar in 52BC. The battle is said to have taken place on Mont Auxois, above the village of **Alise-Ste Reine ❹**, and there are some fascinating archaeological finds in the new interactive **Alésia MuséoParc** (www.alesia.

Epoisses de Bourgogne cheese

com; Apr–Aug 9am–7pm, Oct–Mar 10am–5pm, Sept until 6pm; charge). Close by stands the **Château de Bussy-Rabutin** (mid-May–mid-Sept Tue–Sun 9.15am–1pm, 2–6pm, mid-Sept–mid-May until 5pm; charge), Burgundy's most absorbing stately home. Twelve kilometres (7 miles) on the other side of the medieval fortress town **Semur-en-Auxois**, to the west, lies **Epoisses**, less known for its medieval château (www.chateaudepoisses.com; July–Aug Wed–Mon 10am–noon, 3–6pm; charge) and Renaissance houses than for its delicious, creamy, pungent cheese.

Occupying a prominent hilltop to the southwest, **Vézelay** ❺ is one of the principal shrines of France and a departure point for an important

Lyon transport

 Airport: Aéroport de Lyon St-Exupéry; tel: 08 26 80 08 26; **www.lyonaeroports.com**; 25km (15½ miles) east of Lyon city centre. The Rhônexpress tram (tel: 08 26 00 17 18; **www.rhonexpress.fr**) runs every 15 minutes, costs €13 and takes 30 minutes from the airport. Taxis take 34 minutes and cost from €40. Altibus (tel: 08 20 32 03 68; **www.altibus.com**) operates shuttles from the airport to 34 mountain destinations

 Trains: Gare de Part-Dieu, boulevard Vivier-Merle; tel: 08 92 35 35 35, and Gare de Perrache, cours de Verdun; tel: 08 00 10 20 04. TGV (**www.raileurope.co.uk**), which takes 2 hours from Paris, and the regional TER Bourgogne (**www.ter-sncf.com**) serve these stations

 Buses, métro and tramway: TCL; tel: 08 20 42 70 00; **www.tcl.fr**, **www.multitud.org**; operates 4 métro lines, 2 funiculars (la Ficelle), 2 tram lines and 100 bus routes, from €1.60. A Lyoncitycard gives access to all public transport with reductions for tourist attractions. 1–3-day tickets range from €21–41

 Taxis: Taxi Lyon: tel: 04 72 10 86 86; **www.taxilyon.com**. Télé Taxi Banlieu: tel: 04 78 28 13 14; **www.tele-taxi-lyon.fr**; Cyclopolitain (electric tricycle taxis); tel: 06 80 60 58 04; **www.lyon.cyclopolitain**

 Car hire: Giraffe Car Hire, place des Terreaux; tel: 04 81 68 01 02; **www.giraffecarrentals.com**. Europcar Part-Dieu, 40 rue de la Villette; tel: 04 72 68 84 60

Bird's-eye view of Vézelay, one of France's most important shrines

pilgrimage route to Santiago de Compostela in Spain. The possession of Mary Magdalene's supposed relics made Vézelay itself a pilgrimage destination in the Middle Ages.

The landscape to the south changes dramatically as it meets the first spurs of the Massif Central *(see p.177)* in the **Parc Naturel Régional de Morvan**.

In eastern Burgundy, the capital **Dijon** ❻ is both a handsome and functional city. There are many old buildings in the centre, but none so great as the massive **Palais des Ducs** (guided tours arranged by tourist office, *see p.162*), on the semicircular place de la Libération. Once the seat of power of the dukes of Burgundy and now the city hall, the palace contains one of the finest fine art museums in France, the **Musée des Beaux-Arts** (Wed–Mon, May–Oct 9.30am–6pm, Nov–Apr 10am–5pm; charge).

The Burgundy wine country

The hills of the Côte d'Or *(see p.26)* are beautiful and the wines excellent. On the D974 that runs from Dijon southwards through Beaune, the names of the towns evoke the great Burgundian wines. Approaching **Beaune** ❼, the jewel-like roof of the **Hôtel-Dieu**

Messing about on the canal

Beyond the Chablis vineyards is the Canal de Bourgogne, which connects the River Saône with the Yonne, forming part of a network of inland waterways that joins the Mediterranean to the Atlantic. Today, the canals are increasingly used for holidays *(see p.58)*. Once on a canal, the rest of the world ceases to exist and one can drift down the tranquil waters visiting châteaux, markets and restaurants from Tonnerre to Bussy-Rabutin. There is an informative visitor centre at Pouilly-en-Auxois.

(Apr–Nov 9.30am–6pm, Dec–Mar 9–11.30am, 2–5.30pm; charge), made of multicoloured tiles, can be seen glimmering in the distance. Since the 18th century, Beaune has been the centre of the Burgundian wine trade, and its production is covered from ancient times to the present day in the **Musée du Vin de Bourgogne** (Apr–Nov daily 9.30am–6pm, Dec–Mar Wed–Mon until 5pm; charge) in the Hôtels des Ducs de Bourgogne. The region is also famous for its golden Dijon mustard, and **La Moutarderie Fallot** (www.fallot.com; guided tours only; charge) is the last independent manufacturer left in Burgundy.

Remainder of Cluny's abbey church

Just 23km (14 miles) south of Beaune, **Châlon-sur-Saône** ❽ sits in the middle of the Saône Valley amid scattered vineyards. Although Châlon is an industrial centre today, half-timbered houses still crowd around the Cathédrale St-Vincent in the old quarter of town. Châlon is also the birthplace of Nicéphore Niépce, who made the first photographic image with a camera obscura. The **Musée Nicéphore Niépce** (www.museeniepce.com; July–Aug daily 10am–6pm, Sept–June Wed–Mon 9.30–11.45am, 2–5.45pm; charge) is dedicated to him and to the history of photography. Deeper into the valley, one of Burgundy's greatest Romanesque churches can be found at **Tournus**, at its best when seen from the bridge over the river.

During the Middle Ages Burgundy gave birth to two great monastic orders, whose fervour and organisational zeal revived the spiritual life of Europe while also contributing to its political and economic development. The first and greatest of these orders were the Benedictines at an **abbey** (daily, May–Aug 9.30am–6pm, Sept–Apr 9.30am–noon, 1.30–5pm; charge) founded in 910 in **Cluny** ❾. Only a small part remains of its once immense church, for five centuries the largest in all Christendom.

Another 27km (17 miles) south along the Saône, the transition between Burgundy and the Lyonnais can be seen at **Mâcon** where northern pointed roofs of slate meet the southern, red, rounded Roman tile, and where the Romantic poet Lamartine was born in 1790.

Burgundy to the Alps

Franche-Comté

To the east of Burgundy, the Franche-Comté (free county) is an ancient province that survived the Revolution's determination to make a break with the past. Dominated by the Jura mountains, which straddle the border with Switzerland, the region is perfect for outdoor types, with plenty of forests, rivers, lakes and waterfalls to explore. The most spectacular waterfalls are in the **Vallée du Doubs** and are at their most impressive in spring (*see p.33–4*).

The region's capital, **Besançon ⑩**, in the crook of the Doubs river, developed into a major town because of its position on the Rhine–Rhône trade route. Formally a religious centre, and later a military stronghold, today it is reputed to be France's leading watch- and clock-making town. The **Musée du Temps** (Tue–Sat 9.15am–noon, 2–6pm, Sun 10am–6pm; charge), in the Renaissance Palais Granvelle, exhibits an impressive collection of timepieces. Another tribute to the trade is in the belltower of the

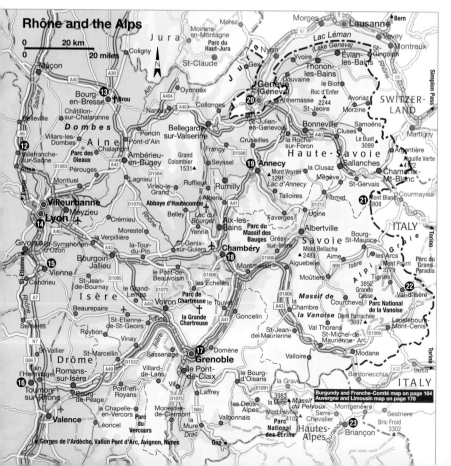

Rhône and the Alps

Burgundy and Franche-Comté map on page 164
Auvergne and Limousin map on page 178

Chapelle Notre-Dame-du-Haut

Cathédrale St-Jean – the Horloge Astronomique, a magnificent astronomical clock with 57 faces and 62 dials which gives the time in 16 places in the world.

In the northeast of the region, the frontier military town of **Belfort** ⓫, with a mountain-top citadel, is an ideal base for visiting the splendid **Chapelle Notre-Dame-du-Haut** at the former mining town of **Ronchamp**. Designed by Le Corbusier and completed in 1955, this building of curved white walls and vast swell of concrete roof is a masterpiece of contemporary architecture.

Lyon and the Rhône Valley

From its source high in the Swiss Alps, the mighty Rhône flows south to the Mediterranean, passing through Lyon, France's vibrant third city and a modern metropolis with a long history. The fertile Rhône Valley, a central artery between north and south, not only produces more of the world's most wonderful wines but is also home to other fine produce such as poultry from Bresse, fish from the Dombes, Charolais beef, and fruit from the orchards.

Beaujolais to Lyon

Once an ancient province, the Beaujolais region stretches from the Saône to the Loire, with **Villefranche-sur-Saône** ⓬ as its capital, producing excellent wines and the famous Beaujolais Nouveau (*see p.27*). On the eastern bank of the Saône is Bresse, a land of solid farm traditions in breeding and fattening its famous chickens, reputedly the best in the world. At the weekly poultry market in **Bourg-en-Bresse** ⓭, thousands of birds are snapped up by professional buyers.

A marshy plateau called the **Dombes**, with more than 100 (mostly artificial) lakes, spreads to the south, providing the perfect environment for birdwatchers and anglers. At **Villars-les-Dombes** is

Gastronomic capital

Lyon is stuffed with fine restaurants and bistros that the Lyonnais call *bouchons*, after the bunches of straw once used as bottle-stoppers. Regional specialities abound: *rosette* and *Jésus* salamis, pâté cooked in pastry, *quenelles de brochet* (poached mousse of pike), *poulet de Bresse* and freshwater crayfish. The daily rhythm of life revolves around meal times: the mid-morning *mâchon*, specifically Lyonnais, is no snack but a meal of charcuterie, which might include sausages and salamis as well as stuffed hocks and hams, and can be bought at the daily market on the riverside.

the **Parc des Oiseaux**, the largest ornithological park in France (www.parcdesoiseaux.com; daily Mar–Nov; charge). To the south, **Pérouges** is a medieval town metaphorically preserved in aspic.

Located at the crossroads between north and south and on both the Saône and Rhône rivers, **Lyon** ⓮ was the ideal choice as the Roman capital of Gaul. The silk trade played a large role in Lyon's expansion in the 16th century, and France's third city remains a prosperous centre with an important cultural heritage, a lively arts scene and a wealth of museums, including the **Musées des Tissus et des Arts Décoratifs** Ⓐ (34 rue de la Charité; www.musees-des-tissus.com; Tue–Sun 10am–5.30pm; charge), in the 18th-century Hôtel Lacroix-Laval, with some of the

rarest and most beautiful materials ever made. The **Musée d'Art Contemporain** Ⓑ (www.mac-lyon.com; Wed–Sun noon–7pm; charge) is fittingly housed in Renzo Piano's Cité Internationale; another futuristic construction of steel and glass is due to open as a cultural and scientific centre in 2014.

Along the Saône, a tree-lined quay gives a view over the wide water, with some bridges painted red. On the opposite bank lies the city's oldest quarter, **Vieux Lyon**. Typically, the Renaissance houses were constructed around a courtyard, which was reached from the street through a vaulted passage beneath a house. In each street a few courtyards had another vaulted passage at the back leading into the next street. These public passages, still in use, are called

Discover regional specialities at a *bouchon* (bistro) in Lyon

traboules. Up on **Fourvière Hill**, reachable by funicular, towers the rococo **Notre-Dame de Fourvière** , with a terrace overlooking the city, while on the southern slope are the remains of the original Roman city.

Vienne to the Ardèche

The Rhône Valley is best seen off the main routes in places such as **Vienne** , 20km (12 miles) south of Lyon, and full of Roman relics. Across the river, at **St Romain-en-Gal**, a Roman suburb of Vienne has been excavated, and its murals and mosaics can be seen in the museum (Tue–Sun 10am–6pm; charge).

Staying on the right bank of the river, moving south, the traffic-laden D86 passes **Condrieu**'s neatly trained vines on steep granite terraces that produce some of the best Northern

Rhône wines: rich, spicy, red Côte Rôtie and delicately perfumed Condrieu – delicious with the local goats' cheese, Rigotte de Condrieu.

Continuing south, the landscape develops a Mediterranean feel with vast orchards of apricot, cherry and peach trees. **Tournon-sur-Rhône** , a lively little town, especially on Saturday mornings when the market is in full flow, has an imposing 11th- to 16th-century château, which in the summer is the setting for Shakespeare plays – in French. Across the river, **Tain l'Hermitage** is not only famous for its Hermitage wines but for **Valrhona**, one of the finest chocolate manufacturers in France.

The scenery changes abruptly to the west of the Rhône, in the Ardèche region which marks the southern edge of central France. The Ardèche river, a

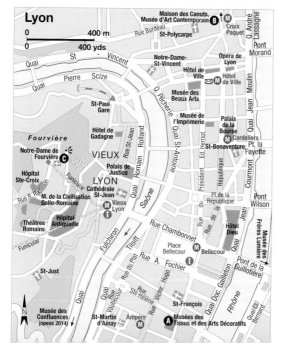

Kayaking along the gorges at Vallon Pont d'Arc

tributary of the Rhône, has carved its way through the limestone to create a towering, rugged landscape riddled with caves and tunnels containing the oldest cave paintings in the world (*see p.198–9*). Canoeing, kayaking and white-water rafting are popular in the **Gorges de l'Ardèche**, especially near **Vallon Pont d'Arc** where the gorges are particularly spectacular.

The French Alps

The high, snow-capped mountains, pristine lakes and the elegant spa towns of Savoie are not just for skiers and snowboarders. Vast fields of wild flowers welcome the spring visitor, and in summer horse riding, mountain biking, tennis, rafting, hang-gliding and paragliding now join the more traditional activities of climbing and hiking – all lorded over by the magnificent Mont Blanc, Europe's highest mountain.

Grenoble and mountain spas

Grenoble ⓱, the main city of the French Alps, lies in a wonderful mountain setting where the River Drac joins the Isère. The Winter Olympic Games of 1968 gave the town a push into the modern age and changed it for ever. At **Fort de la Bastille**, a cable-car ride away, there is a superb view of the city and surrounding mountains. The Chartreuse mountain chain to the north gave its name to the Carthusian Order of monks, who built their famous **Monastère de La Grande Chartreuse** there, far removed from human habitation. To this day the monks of the monastery distil their well-known liqueur.

Chambéry ⓲, 67km (42 miles) north of Grenoble, was the capital city of the dukes of Savoy in 1232 and remains defended by its fortress. Its best-known monument is the **Fontaine des Eléphants**, built in 1838 as

Take the cable car from Grenoble for spectacular views

Palais d'Isle (Island Palace) in the Thiou river, Annecy

Burgundy to the Alps

a memorial to a town benefactor. Lac le Bourget points northwards from Chambéry like a finger, and 6km (4 miles) along its eastern bank lies the elegant spa town of **Aix-les-Bains**, which has offered cures for rheumatism and other ailments since Roman times. Plenty of watersports are available on the lake, and cruise boats cross to the neo-Gothic Abbaye de Hautecombe.

Another lake to the east, **Lac d'Annecy**, also offers boat trips, some of which include a cable-car ride to the top of **Mont Veyrier** (1,291m/4,235ft) for its spectacular panorama of the Alps. The lovely old town of **Annecy** ⑲ is picture-perfect with its triangular-shaped, 12th-century Palais de l'Isle in the middle of the Thiou river.

About 40km (25 miles) further north, **Geneva** ⑳ – which is not in France – is the main air hub to the French Alps, and both France and Switzerland share **Lake Geneva** (Lac Léman in French) on which the city stands. The largest inland body of water in Europe at 70km (45 miles) long, the lake has two famous spas on its French shore. **Thonon-les-Bains**, a chic little town on a cliff overlooking

Alpine flowers

Spring and summer in the Alps are a prime time to discover the hundreds of plant species on the mountain slopes. Above the tree line Alpine juniper flourishes on south-facing slopes, while swathes of crocuses cover the ground in May. Richly coloured blue and yellow gentians, bellflowers, glacier buttercups and saxifrage thrive on the steep meadows, whose grasses are thick with flowers in June.

⭐ WILDLIFE

Thanks to its many different climates and huge areas of forest and mountain, France contains an extremely varied mix of wildlife, with over 100 different mammals and more than 500 species of birds having been recorded in different parts of the country. The Alps in particular are home to some of France's most emblematic animals. Their numbers have been under pressure, but with a bit of human assistance nature is now regaining ground.

One of the most treasured but also the most threatened of mountain creatures is the Alpine ibex or *bouquetin*, the large, long-horned mountain goat – indeed, both the Gran Paradiso park in Italy and the Parc National de la Vanoise, France's oldest national park, south of Val d'Isère, were established expressly in order to preserve it.

In France it had been hunted almost to extinction, but since the park was created in the 1960s numbers have revived, and there are now around 500 in the French Alps. They live at heights above 2,000m (6,500ft), so seeing one is especially rewarding. Much more common – but still at high altitudes – are the Alpine marmot, a burrowing rodent, and the smaller chamois goats, also found in the Pyrenees and the Jura. Controversially, small numbers of wolves, once extinct in France, have been reintroduced to the Parc du Mercantour in the southern Alps.

Male ibex in the French Alps

One of the sights of the Alps is the number of birds of prey, soaring or circling high overhead in search of potential prey. Golden eagles, lammergeier vultures, buzzards, a range of falcons and kites can all be spotted fairly easily, and closer to ground there are black grouse, rock partridges and colourful wallcreepers.

Below the mountains, large forests such as the Forêt des Bertranges in northern Burgundy also contain plenty of animal life, notably red deer, roe deer and the more elusive wild boar (*sanglier*). All are hunted and are a seasonal feature of local cuisine, but their numbers have actually been increasing across France, and deer in particular are easy to spot.

The wild, empty spaces of the Massif Central and Cévennes form another area that is welcoming to wildlife. Hardy mouflon sheep, the males with imposing spiral-horns, are relatively common, and you can also see more birds of prey such as the protected griffon vulture and, in the fast-flowing rivers, otters and other river mammals.

The Pyrenees are, with the Alps, the other great mountain habitat, with chamois, vultures and a reintroduced population of lynx managing to live relatively undisturbed by humans.

Things finally seem to have come to an end, though, for the Pyrenean brown bear. The last native French bear was shot by a hunter in 2004, and after protests from farmers the government has now abandoned attempts to re-establish the population with bears from Eastern Europe.

An Alpine marmot, living at high altitudes in the Parc National de la Vanoise

Wolves have been reintroduced to the Parc du Mercantour

Climbers tackle the slopes around Mont Blanc, Europe's highest mountain

the lake, has a funicular that links the upper town to the harbour where boats can be hired. The spa waters have a high mineral content, and you can fill up your water bottles with it free at the Fontaine de la Versoie in the Parc Thermal.

Much of the construction along the lakeside in elegant **Evian-les-Bains**, including the casino, dates from 1865, when the city fathers shrewdly decided to develop 'Evian water' and turn the small fortified city into a spa. Lake Geneva paddlewheel steamers carry tourists to the towns all around the lake.

The high mountains

Regarded from any viewpoint **Mont Blanc ㉑**, the highest mountain in Europe at 4,808m (15,780ft), is quite magnificent. Around it, the great chains of the Alps, stretching from Italy to Austria, seem like tiny mountain ridges below. At the foot of the mountain, the Bossons Glacier sweeps down to the border resort town of **Chamonix-Mont-Blanc** and the 11.5km (7-mile) Mont Blanc Tunnel linking France to Italy. To the west, the perennially fashionable resort of **Megève** is particularly popular for family skiing holidays as well as summer hikes, with cable cars to carry you to the higher ridges.

Val-d'Isère ㉒ is one of the finest ski areas in Europe, together with the more recently developed **Tignes**. Called Espace Killy after Jean-Claude Killy, world champion skier in the 1960s, the vast ski area has runs that go up to 3,750m (12,300ft) and, as in Chamonix, skiing is possible all year round. In summer, nature-lovers flock to the **Parc National de la Vanoise**, one of the more important reserves

Salers

Perched above a scenic valley, west of the Puy Mary in the Auvergne, is the striking little town of **Salers**, which has given its name to a breed of cow, a cheese and an aperitif made from the wild gentian that grows on the surrounding mountains. The lovely houses, notable for their *bartizans* (turrets), spiral staircases and stone window sashes, reflect the prestige the town gained by becoming the chief bailiwick of the high mountains of Auvergne in the 15th century.

of Alpine flora and fauna, with a network of hiking trails, making it well worth the cable-car trip up to Mont Bochor (2,070m/6,650ft) *(see p.174–5)*.

Further south, at 1,320m (4,334ft), **Briançon** 🈪 is the highest town in Europe, with the old town remaining much as it was in the time of Louis XI. It is also the gateway to the valley of La Vallouise and the **Parc National des Ecrins**.

The Auvergne

The Massif Central is the remote core of France, a huge, rugged plateau of granite and rock with rivers fanning out like fingers to develop into mighty waterways that snake their way to the Atlantic and the Mediterranean. It embraces the Auvergne, whose volcanic landscape is dramatic yet serenely peaceful. For centuries this region was largely cut off from the rest of France. Today, visitors are drawn to the Auvergne for its isolation and serenity, its rugged environment, its wildlife and its spas.

Clermont and the Puy de Dôme

Clermont-Ferrand 🈪, the regional capital, originally consisted of two rival towns, Clermont and Montferrand, which merged in the 18th century. The **Basilique de Notre-Dame-du-Port** is one of a group of Auvergnat Romanesque churches that are the pride of the Puy-de-Dôme *département*. To the southwest, the church of **St-Nectaire** stands majestically above the sleepy town of the same name. Its nutty-flavoured eponymous cheese is renowned all over France, and the mineral water from the town's 40 springs was appreciated by the Gauls and the Romans, who built baths at the ancient **Grottes du Cornadore** (tel: 04 73 88 57 97; www.grottes-de-cornadore.com; Feb–Oct daily, times vary; charge).

Volcano in the Auvergne region

Not far to the west is the highest point in the Massif Central, the **Puy de Sancy** (1,885m/6,184ft), where the River Dordogne rises. In winter, skiers from the nearby resorts of **Le Mont-Dore** and **La Bourboule** have an exhilarating time on its slopes, while in summer the summit offers unparalleled views of the Monts du Cantal and the Puy de Dôme, accessible by cable car.

In the heart of the **Parc des Volcans** ㉕ *(see p.34)*, a major leisure park, **Vulcania** (www.vulcania.com;

daily July–Aug 10am–7pm, Apr–June until 6pm, Sept–mid-Nov times vary; charge) simulates volcanic activity in a state-of-the-art underground museum. A spectacular drive through mountainous terrain leads to **Orcival**, where the 12th-century Basilique de Notre-Dame is another fine example of Auvergnat Romanesque.

For centuries **Riom**, 10km (8 miles) north of Clermont, was the city's fierce rival as capital of the region. Its erstwhile importance can be judged from its numerous Renaissance townhouses

The St Michel d'Aiguilhe chapel in Le Puy-en-Velay

of volcanic rock rising above its roofs – a stop for pilgrims on their way to Santiago de Compostela and a centre for lace-making. Perched on top of the largest lava pillar is Chapelle St Michel d'Aiguilhe, reached by climbing 268 steps.

The **Cantal mountains** in the southwest of the Auvergne formed the oldest and largest volcano in Europe, with a diameter of 70km (45 miles). At the southern edge lies **Aurillac** ㉘, whose **Musée des Volcans** (mid-June– mid-Sept Mon–Sat 10am–6.30pm, Sun 2–6.30pm, mid-Sept–mid-June Tue–Sat 2–6pm; charge) is an excellent source of information about the area's geological history.

The Limousin

The Limousin is a centre for the arts of fire – porcelain and enamel – and a land of water – rain and lakes. Still relatively unexplored by visitors, the unspoilt verdant landscape is rich with history and tradition, with pretty medieval villages, ancient churches and *bastides* (country houses).

Limoges and the Creuse

Many a bridal trousseau has been graced by delicate china from **Limoges** ㉙. In this quiet, half-timbered country town there are more than 30 porcelain workshops, many offering guided tours. The **Musée National Adrien Dubouché** (www.musee-adriandubouche.fr; Wed–Mon 10am–12.25pm, 2–5.40pm; charge) has a collection of 10,000 pieces from all periods since 1771. In

built of dark volcanic stone. To the northeast, **Vichy** ㉖ came to prominence when it was chosen as the seat of the government that collaborated with the Nazi occupation forces. Today it is a pleasant spa town that has kept up with the times.

Southern Auvergne and the Cantal

The road southeast through the Auvergne, towards Le Puy-en-Velay, climbs through colonnades of pine forest to **La Chaise-Dieu**, the remote and rugged site of a grand 11th-century monastery, and the venue of a prestigious classical music festival in August. **Le Puy-en-Velay** ㉗ is a spectacular sight, with two huge pillars

Burgundy to the Alps

Strolling through the country town of Limoges

the summer the city hosts porcelain and enamel exhibitions.

A 20-minute drive northwest of Limoges will bring you to **Oradour-sur-Glane** ③⓪, also known as the *Village Martyre*, or 'martyred village'. On 10 June 1944, just four days after the D-Day landings, the Germans massacred 642 villagers, and then set fire to the village. It has remained untouched since, with rusty carcasses of 1930s cars and crumbling facades of burnt-out buildings bearing testimony to the destruction. The **Centre de la Mémoire** (www.oradour.org; daily mid-May–mid-Sept 9am–7pm, mid-Sept–Oct, Mar–mid-May until 6pm, Nov–mid-Dec, Feb until 5pm; charge) recalls the fateful day.

Lying about 86km (54 miles) to the east, **Aubusson** ③① is to tapestry what Limoges is to porcelain. The industry grew here because of the clean waters of the Creuse region, and there are several places around town to see exhibitions of contemporary and traditional tapestry work.

The Corrèze

Sheltered under impressive grey slate roofs and towers, **Uzerche** ③② is set high up on a crag above a loop in the River Vézère in the southern Corrèze region, crowned by the Romanesque church of **St-Pierre**. Accordions are manufactured in **Tulle**, about 15km (9 miles) to the south, and visitors can watch them being made (Mon–Thur, by reservation only) at the Maugein Factory. They can also hear them played at the Nuits de Nacre festival in mid-September.

Perched on a rocky spur rising from the River Dordogne is picturesque **Turenne** ③③, just south of **Brive-la-Gaillarde**, the centre of the Resistance during World War II. Two towers, a guard room and crumbling ramparts remain of the once imposing château dominating this hilltop village. Nearby, **Collonges-la-Rouge** is a striking village with an ancient covered market and a communal bread oven that is still used each August during the Marché d'Antan (traditional market).

ACCOMMODATION

Places to stay in these regions range from indulgent set-ups in historic buildings in the Burgundy winelands to rustic Auvergne inns and ultra-modern ski hotels in the Alps.

Burgundy and Franche-Comté

Auberge sur la Roche
Le Chauffaud, 25130 Villers-le-Lac
Tel: 03 81 68 08 94
www.auberge-surlaroche.com
An 18th-century farmhouse 1,150m (3,773ft) up, not far from the Saut du Doubs waterfall, in the depths of the Jura mountains. There are double rooms and dormitories, and wonderful opportunities for cycling, hiking and canoeing nearby. **€**

Hostellerie de Bourgogne
Place de l'Abbaye, 71250 Cluny
Tel: 03 85 59 00 58
www.hotel-cluny.com
This stone *hôtel particulier* stands next to the famous abbey ruins. Rooms are simply and traditionally furnished, and there's a cosy lounge, pretty garden and a fine wine selection in the restaurant. Closed Dec–Feb. **€€–€€€**

Hôtel Le Cep
27 rue Jean-François Maufoux, 21200 Beaune
Tel: 03 80 22 35 48
www.hotel-cep-beaune.com

The lobby of Hôtel Le Cep

One of Burgundy's classic hotels, in a historic building in the heart of old Beaune, with plush furnishings, impeccable service, a gourmet restaurant and wine tastings from a magnificent cellar. **€€€–€€€€**

Hostellerie des Clos
18 rue Jules Rathier, 89800 Chablis
Tel: 03 86 42 10 63
www.hostellerie-des-clos.fr
A welcoming Logis de France (chain of independent hotel-restaurants) hotel, in a historic hospice, with comfortable rooms and an excellent, relaxed restaurant. Closed mid-Dec–mid-Jan. **€€**

Hostellerie la Gentilhommière
13 vallée de la Serrée,
21700 Nuits-St-Georges
Tel: 03 80 61 12 06
www.lagentilhommiere.fr
This lovely 16th-century former hunting lodge stands in large riverside grounds in this famous Côte d'Or wine village. Rooms have been stylishly modernised, especially the suites, and all have garden views. Outside, there's a great pool and tennis courts, and the restaurant is just as attractive. Closed mid-Dec–Jan. **€€–€€€**

Hôtel Le Jacquemart
32 rue Verrerie, 21000 Dijon
Tel: 03 80 60 09 60
www.hotel-lejacquemart.fr
A friendly hotel in an 18th-century building in the old quarter of Dijon, with simple but bright rooms with all the essential facilities. All rooms except the economy ones come with private bathrooms. **€**

Lyon lies on both the Saône and Rhône rivers

Hôtel de Vougeot
18 rue du Vieux Château, 21640 Vougeot
Tel: 03 80 62 01 15
www.hotel-vougeot.com
This is a simple hotel in a wine village between Dijon and Beaune, ideal for vineyard-visiting. The 16 rooms are spread across three buildings, with a beautiful wine cellar below. €€

Lyon and the Rhône Valley
Le Clos des Bruyères
Route Georges, 07150 Vallon Pont d'Arc
Tel: 04 75 37 18 85
www.closdesbruyeres.net
A modern hotel built in the Provençal style that's an ideal base for exploring the Gorges de l'Ardèche. The bright modern bedrooms, with balconies or terraces, surround a pool, and the restaurant serves local produce.
€–€€

Mercure Lyon Beaux Arts
73–75 rue du Président Edouard Herriot, 69002 Lyon
Tel: 04 78 38 09 50
www.mercure.com
Big-scale hotel in the centre of Lyon, with some Art Deco fittings in the public areas and all the reliable modern services associated with Mercure hotels. €€–€€€

The French Alps
Auberge du Bois Prin
69 chemin de l'Hermine, Les Moussoux, 74400 Chamonix-Mont Blanc
Tel: 04 50 53 33 51
www.boisprin.com
Beautiful, intimate chalet-auberge with a pretty garden and gorgeous views of Mont Blanc. Chef-owner Denis Carrier's restaurant is equally stunning, with tables on a terrace to enjoy the views in fine weather. Rooms are in great demand summer and winter. Closed 2 weeks Apr, and Nov. €€€–€€€€

Hôtel Christiania
73152 Val d'Isère
Tel: 04 79 06 08 25
www.hotel-christiania.com
Luxurious, modern ski-chalet hotel with opulent rooms with balconies offering magnificent views of the Val d'Isère, and an equally sumptuous restaurant. Spa has an indoor swimming pool. One of the hubs of this fashionable ski resort. €€€€–€€€€€

Hôtel Cristol
6 route d'Italie, 05100 Briançon
Tel: 04 92 20 20 11
www.hotel-cristol-briancon.fr
Traditional hotel, affiliated to Logis de France, with some rooms overlooking

Briançon's fortifications. The charming restaurant offers local dishes. **€**

Auvergne and the Limousin
Auberge le Pré Bossu
43150 Moudeyres
Tel: 04 71 05 10 70
www.auberge-pre-bossu.com
Remote and tranquil, this lovely old converted stone house is in a tiny village in the heart of the Auvergne, 25km (15 miles) southeast of Le Puy. The owners provide full information on walks, cycle routes and other activities in the area. Closed Nov–Easter. **€€€**

La Truffe Noire
22 boulevard Anatole-France, 19100 Brive-la-Gaillarde
Tel: 05 55 92 45 00
www.la-truffe-noire.com
This town hotel has been attractively renovated to combine modern comforts with its massive beams and other original features. The restaurant features local specialities such as Limousin beef and, of course, black truffles. **€€**

Le Val Vert
6 avenue Baptiste Marcet, 43000 Le Puy-en-Velay
Tel: 04 71 09 09 30
www.hotelvalvert.com
Good value Logis hotel on the outskirts of Le Puy, with brightly decorated bedrooms and a pleasant local restaurant. Rooms available for disabled guests. Pets allowed. **€**

RESTAURANTS
Wonderful wines aside, Burgundy and the Lyonnais are celebrated as two of France's greatest culinary regions. In the Alps, Savoyard mountain food is a highlight, while the Auvergne has its own rich, earthy cooking style.

Restaurant price categories
Prices are for a three-course meal for one (usually a set menu) with a drink.

€ = below €20
€€ = €20–45
€€€ = €45–90
€€€€ = over €90

Burgundy and Franche-Comté
Le Bistrot Bourguignon
8 rue Monge, 21200 Beaune
Tel: 03 80 22 23 24
www.restaurant-lebistrotbourguignon.com
Relaxed restaurant with Burgundy cuisine and a *bar à vins* for sampling local wines, with live jazz on some nights. Closed Sun and Mon. **€–€€**

La Bouzerotte-BBB
21200 Bouze-lès-Beaune
Tel: 03 80 26 01 37
www.labouzerotte.com
Dine on the sunny terrace or beside a cosy fire in winter at this stylish restaurant, where Olivier Robert takes a fresh approach to Burgundy's cuisine. Varied menus are great value. Closed Sun evening, Mon and (Nov–Easter) Tue. **€–€€**

L'Espérance
89450 Saint-Père-en-Vézelay
Tel: 03 86 33 39 10
www.marc-meneau-esperance.com
A sumptuous experience, Marc Meneau's celebrated hotel-restaurant has a palatial

Alfresco dining in Cluny

conservatory dining room, exceptional cuisine based on traditional Burgundy ingredients, and a wine cellar to match. Closed Mon midday, Tue, Wed midday, and Jan–Feb. €€€€

La Maison d'Olivier Leflaive
10 place du Monument, 21190 Puligny-Montrachet
Tel: 03 80 21 95 27
www.olivier-leflaive.com
In a village synonymous with fine wines, winegrower M. Leflaive has opened this delightful restaurant and small hotel in a typical stone Burgundy house. Meals are accompanied by wine tastings, and you can tour the vineyards. Closed Sun and Jan. €€

Le Pré aux Clercs
13 place de la Libération, 21000 Dijon
Tel: 03 80 38 05 05
www.jeanpierrebilloux.com
Rich traditional Burgundian cuisine cooked with panache by father-and-son team Jean-Pierre and Alexis Billoux, and served with prestigious wines. Nearby they have the more economical Bistrot des Halles (€–€€) and Brasserie Bg (€). Closed Sun evening and Mon. €€–€€€

Lyon and the Rhône Valley
Le Coq
Place du Marché, 69840 Juliénas
Tel: 04 74 04 41 20

Traditional *bouchon* in Lyon

www.coq-julienas.com
Sit on the terrace of this traditional Beaujolais bistro and enjoy the best regional cuisine, not least its *coq au vin*; there's also a pretty hotel, La Rose (€€). Closed Tue and Wed midday. €€

La Meunière
11 rue Neuve, 69001 Lyon
Tel: 04 78 28 62 91
www.la-meuniere.fr
One of the most classic *bouchons lyonnais* or traditional inns, where one goes prepared to eat one's fill of the city's famously generous cuisine – meaty salads, several aperitifs, fabulous cheeses, rich wines – in a very convivial atmosphere. Closed Sun, Mon. €€

Les Muses de l'Opéra
Place de la Comédie, 69001 Lyon
Tel: 04 72 00 45 58
www.lesmusesdelopera.com
Fashionable restaurant on the seventh floor of Lyon's opera house, with wonderful city views and stylish food at reasonable prices. Closed Sun. €€

Le Quai
17 rue Joseph Péala,
26600 Tain-l'Hermitage
Tel: 04 75 07 05 90
www.le-quai.com
An attractive brasserie beside the Rhône in the wine centre of Tain l'Hermitage, with creative cuisine and a fine range of Rhône wines. Owner Michel Chabran also has a gourmet restaurant under his own name (€€–€€€) in nearby Pont de l'Isère. €€

The French Alps
La Calèche
18 rue Dr Paccard, 74400 Chamonix-Mont Blanc
Tel: 04 50 55 94 68
www.restaurant-caleche.com
Traditional family-run restaurant serving Savoyard specialities, especially cheese and meat, with decor evoking Chamonix's history with old skis and a bobsleigh from the 1924

Winter Olympics. Enormously popular in the winter season. €€€

Le Chabichou
73121 Courchevel 1850
Tel: 04 79 08 00 55
www.chabichou-courchevel.com
One of the smartest restaurants in the glitzy ski resort of Courchevel, with suitably extravagant cuisine to accompany fabulous mountain views. Closed July–Nov. €€€€

L'Essentiel
183 place de la Gare, 7300 Chambéry
Tel: 04 79 96 97 27
Acclaimed as one of the best in Savoie, where mountain specialities are superbly prepared. Closed Sun, and Mon midday.
€€–€€€

Auvergne and the Limousin
Auberge Le Prieuré
Place de l'Eglise, 19500 Collonges-la-Rouge
Tel: 05 55 25 41 00
www.le-prieure.fr
A lovely traditional auberge in the centre of this old Corrèze town, with enjoyable regional dishes, and an idyllic terrace for fine weather. Closed Wed Sept–May. €–€€

Le Chabichou in glamorous Courchevel, located in the Trois Vallées

La Rotonde-La Table de Marlène
Boulevard de Lattre-de-Tassigny,
03200 Vichy
Tel: 04 70 97 85 42
www.restaurantlarotonde-vichy.com
Ultra-modern glass and chrome building beside the Lac d'Allier. La Table de Marlène on the first floor has wonderful panoramic views of the lake and contemporary cuisine, while Le Bistrot (€€) below has a terrace and more traditional menu. Closed Mon, Tue. €€€

NIGHTLIFE AND ENTERTAINMENT

Lyons' tourism website (www.lyon-france.com) has extensive information on local attractions, partly in English. All the big Alps ski resorts have loud and bright nightlife scenes during the winter season.

Café Face
Immeuble Christiania, 73150 Val d'Isère
Tel: 04 79 06 29 80
www.cafeface.com
The hippest après-ski spot in Val d'Isère, with good live music and DJ.

Opéra de Lyon
Place de la Comédie, 69001 Lyon
Tel: 08 26 30 53 25
www.opera-lyon.com
One of the largest of France's provincial opera houses, which also hosts ballet, concerts and other events.

La Terrasse
43 place Balmat, 74400 Chamonix-Mont Blanc
Tel: 04 50 53 09 95
www.laterrassechamonix.com
One of Chamonix's biggest venues, with a party bar downstairs and more chilled terrace above. Live music every night, and a menu consisting of burgers and nachos.

SPORTS AND ACTIVITIES

The French Alps of course form one of the world's greatest winter sports centres, and all kinds of activities are available. Most ski trips are booked as packages: Ski France (www.skifrance.co.uk) and Le Ski (www.leski.com) are two well-established specialists, and www.maddogski.com is a handy information source. For more on summer hiking, see *Exploring the landscape, p.34–5*. For rafting and canoeing in the Ardèche gorges, see *On the water, p.59*.

Kayaking in a gorge in the Ardèche

Alps Adventures
74400 Chamonix
Tel: 04 50 53 93 70
www.alpsadventures.com
Single-day hikes, a range of adventurous longer hikes lasting from 2 to 10 days, mountain trail runs and snowshoe treks around Chamonix and Mont Blanc, with an expert British guide. Accommodation is provided in a snug apartment.

Ardèche Adventures
Tel: (UK) 020 8123 0076
www.ardecheadventures.com
UK-based operator offering kayaking, climbing, mountain biking, caving and other adventure activities in and around the Ardèche Gorges, with camping trips and special programmes for families.

Evolution 2
Avenue de la Plage, 74400 Chamonix
Tel: 04 50 55 90 22
www.evolution2-chamonix.com
A very highly regarded, multinational ski school in winter, which offers rafting, canyoning, mountain hikes and every other kind of activity in summer.

France Raft-Savoie
73210 Centron
Tel: 04 79 55 63 55

www.franceraft.com
Based on the white-water River Isère between Albertville and Val d'Isère, and offering a whole mix of mountain adventures: rafting, kayaking, canyoning (a combination of climbing and swimming), high-mountain biking and more.

Mountain Guide Adventure
Chamonix-La Clusaz
Tel: 04 50 10 02 98
www.mountain-guide-adventure.com
Expert mountaineering guides who offer rock climbing, glacier hikes and other trips in summer, and adventurous skiing options in winter.

Progression Ski & Snowboard School
73150 Val d'Isère
Tel: (UK) 020 8123 3001, (France) 06 21 93 93 80
www.progressionski.com
British-run operator based in Val d'Isère and Tignes offering a full but flexible range of skiing and snowboarding lessons and services, including off-piste and kids' classes.

TOURS

A range of information on Burgundy wine tours is provided on www.burgundy-tourisme.com and www.burgundy-wines.fr, and on Rhône wine regions on www.rhone-wines-tourism.com. As throughout France, tourist offices have information on a variety of local tours. For more on wine tours in general, see *Foods and wines of France, p.25*. In Lyon, the tourist office provides guided walks in different languages (see www.lyon-france.com).

Bacchus Wine Tours/Safari Tours
21200 Beaune
Tel: 03 80 24 79 12
www.burgundy-tourism-safaritours.com
Easy-going, adaptable wine tours for non-experts.

Navig'Inter-Bateau Hermès
Quai Claude Bernard, 69001 Lyon
Tel: 04 78 42 96 81
www.naviginter.fr
Boat trips and lunch or dinner cruises on the Rhône and Saône from Lyon.

FESTIVALS AND EVENTS

In these regions many events inevitably centre on food and wine, with the biggest number of events naturally held around the time of the wine harvest in September and October.

November–May

Fête des Grands Vins de Bourgogne
Third weekend in Nov
Palais des Congès, Beaune
www.ot-beaune.fr
The place to see Burgundy's finest wines with wine auction, tastings and entertainment.

Festival de Musique Baroque de Lyon
Chapelle de la Trinité, Lyon
www.lachapelle-lyon.org
Late Nov–May
Throughout winter and spring Lyon's lovely Trinity chapel hosts Baroque music concerts.

Little World Festival
Méribel, near Moutiers
www.littleworldfestival.com
Mid-Mar
Five-day festival mixing skiing, snowboarding, live music and partying.

August–September

Fête du Lac
Annecy
www.lac-annecy.com

First Sat in Aug
Annecy's lake is lit up with one of Europe's largest fireworks displays.

Fête de la Vigne de Dijon
Dijon
www.ot-beaune.fr
End Aug–early Sept
A celebration not just of wines but of traditional music and dance.

Annecy's Fête du Lac takes place in August

The southwest

Green and rural, the southwest offers a slow pace of life far from the madding crowds. To the north is the gentle landscape of the Dordogne, to the south the Pyrenees. With only two large cities – Bordeaux and Toulouse – the farmed and forested hills are dotted with hamlets, villages and small market towns, each with their own weekly markets, each with their own preserved history.

Bordeaux and Toulouse

Population: 232,000 (Bordeaux), 445,000 (Toulouse)

Local dialling codes: Bordeaux 05 56; Toulouse 05 61

Local tourist offices:
Bordeaux: 12 cours XXX Juillet; tel: 05 56 00 66 00; www.bordeaux-tourisme.com.
Toulouse: Donjon du Capitole; tel: 08 92 18 01 80; www.uk.toulouse-tourisme.com

Main police stations:
Bordeaux: 23 rue François de Sourdis; tel: 05 57 85 77 77.

Toulouse: Capitole, rue La Fayette; tel: 05 61 22 34 14

Main post office: Bordeaux: 17 quai Louis XVIII. Toulouse: 25 rue Rémusat

Hospitals: Bordeaux: Centre Hospitalier Universitaire (CHU) de Bordeaux; tel: 05 56 79 56 79; Toulouse: CHU Purpan, place du Docteur Baylac; tel: 05 61 77 22 33.

Local media: Bordeaux: *Sud Ouest* (daily), *Spirit* (monthly English/French). Toulouse: *La Dépêche du Midi* (daily)

The southwest of France, comprising the regions of Aquitaine and Midi-Pyrénées, has preserved much of its heritage intact. And if it lacks the glamour of Provence and the Midi, it more than makes up for it with space, peace and a slower pace of life.

Framed by three natural frontiers – the Massif Central to the northeast, the Pyrenees to the south and the Atlantic coast to the west – the southwest offers an unbeatable combination of usually good weather and invariably green scenery, thanks to slow green rivers such as the Lot and the Dordogne, while the Canal du Midi runs across the flatter lands beneath the rising haunches of the Pyrenees. These are mountains par excellence, unbeatable for walking along routes that have been travelled for centuries by pilgrims and nature-lovers. Here the snow melts into crystal streams, and spas comfort the sick and provide opportunities for pampering and indulgence.

This region's history starts 20,000 years ago, as revealed by the extraordinary cave paintings found at Lascaux in the Dordogne. There is also a rich cuisine to discover, with specialities being truffles and *foie gras*. As for wines, the legendary *crus* of Bordeaux are a reliable place to start, but there are also many good but unsung local wines to try.

Aquitaine and the Dordogne

Bordeaux, the capital of the historic region of Aquitaine, grew wealthy from its wine industry, as its many fine buildings testify, and the country-side around is largely made up of vineyard estates, many dominated by magnificent châteaux.

To the northeast in the Dordogne, more châteaux, caves with prehistoric art and Roman remains abound in

Kayaking along a stretch of the Dordogne

this noble, rugged landscape, laced with broad and peaceful rivers.

The city of Bordeaux

Bordeaux ❶ proudly shows off its long-standing prosperity in the harmonious 18th-century style of its city-centre buildings, gleaming after a major facelift in recent years. The Romans were the first to exploit its strategic position on the Gironde, the tidal estuary of the Garonne, 80km (50 miles) from the sea. Later it grew rich on international trade, including slavery and commerce in sugar, coffee and spices.

Today, Bordeaux calls itself 'the wine capital of the world', and on the Esplanade des Quinconces stands the **Maison du Vin Ⓐ** (www.bordeaux.com; Mon–Thur 8.30am–12.30pm, 1.30–5.15pm, Fri until 12.30pm; free), incorporating a wine school and bar. Opposite, the tourist information office has all you need to know about the region's wines and organises trips to the surrounding vineyards. Going the other way down the street, you pass the **Grand Théâtre Ⓑ** and enter the city centre proper,

Many of Bordeaux's fine townhouses date from the 18th century

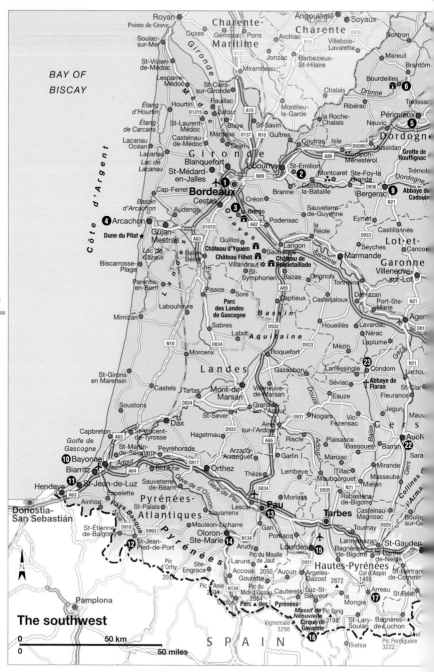

The southwest

0   50 km

0   50 miles

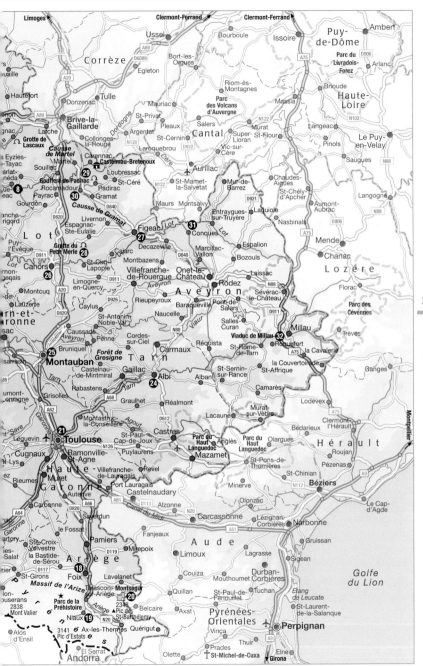

The Southwest

a maze of pedestrianised shops and small squares bordered on one side by the riverbank and on the other by the **Cathédrale St-André** and its adjacent Gothic belfry, the **Tour Pey-Berland**. Around the corner is the excellent **Musée d'Aquitaine** (www.musees-aquitaine.com; Tue–Sun 11am–6pm; free), tracing the history of the region.

The vineyards of Bordeaux

Many of the most prestigious wine estates are packed into the reclaimed marshland of the Médoc Peninsula north of Bordeaux. The D2 passes along the Gironde estuary near to the châteaux of Siran and Margaux, the latter a 19th-century neoclassical mansion, and Latour, to **Pauillac**, the largest of Médoc's towns, where a ferry crosses the estuary to Blaye. Beyond

are the châteaux Lafite-Rothschild, Mouton Rothschild and the oriental-style Cos d'Estournel.

On the east bank of the Gironde, the Dordogne river meets the Garonne after flowing past **St-Emilion** ❷, one of Bordeaux's most renowned wine villages. It also offers a wealth of religious architecture, including an 11th-century church tunnelled into the hillside. Not far away is the superb Roman villa of **Montcaret** (near Lamothe-Montravel on the road to Bergerac; June–Sept daily 9.45am–12.30pm and 2–6.30pm, Oct–May Sun–Fri 10am–12.30 and 2–5.30pm; charge). The extensive foundations of this house are visible, including ducts for a warm-air heating system, the baths and several complete mosaic floors.

Travelling south from Bordeaux, the Graves wine region along the

Sommelier in St-Emilion

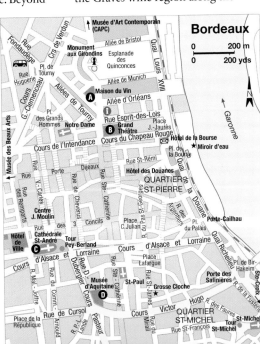

Descending the Dune du Pilat, the largest sand dune in Europe

left bank of the Garonne starts as soon as the suburbs give up. Here, the **Château de la Brède** ❸ (tel: 05 56 78 47 72; www.chateaulabrede. com; opening times vary; charge) is not a wine-producing château but home of the 18th-century philosopher Montesquieu. A few minutes away is the beautiful Renaissance **Château d'Yquem** (www. yquem.fr) in the tiny wine region of **Sauternes**, renowned for its sweet white dessert wine. Further on stands the fine 14th-century **Château de Roquetaillade**, embellished by the architect Viollet-le-Duc in the 19th century.

A long, straight strip of coastline extends south of the Gironde estuary, known as the **Côte d'Argent**. Almost halfway along lies **Arcachon** ❹, a popular resort of superb white sandy

Bordeaux transport

 Airport: Aéroport de Bordeaux Merignac; tel: 05 56 34 50 00; **www.bordeaux.aeroport.fr**; 13km (8 miles) east of city centre. Jet'Bus shuttle to city centre every 45 minutes, journey takes 45 minutes; €7 single. Local bus (TBC) Liane 1, every 10 minutes, takes 45 minutes; €1.40 single. Taxi, 30 minutes; around €30

 Trains: Gare SNCF St-Jean, rue Charles Domercq; tel: 36 35; www. sncf.fr, www.tgv.com, www.ter-sncf. com

 Buses and trams: TBC (Keolis Bordeaux): tel: 05 57 57 88 00; www.infotbc.com. There is an

extensive public transport network (called TBC) which includes buses, trams, a free city centre bus and a water shuttle. There is also a public bike-rental scheme (VCub). Single ticket for 1 hour, €1.40 for all TBC transport, 5 voyages, €5.40, 10 voyages €10.60; www.infotbc.com

 Taxis: bordeautaxi: tel: 05 56 32 43 00; **www.bordeauxtaxi.com**. Taxi Bordeaux: tel: 06 06 36 96 88; www. taxi-bordeaux-33.fr

 Car hire: Citadine Location, 8 rue Notre Dame; tel: 08 20 38 07 47; **www.citadinelocation.com**. Ada, 319 avenue Thiers; tel: 05 57 80 00 20; **www.ada.fr**

Brantôme is beautifully situated on the water

beaches, about 45km (28 miles) southwest of Bordeaux, with fantastically decorated villas, thermal baths and a casino resembling a fairytale castle. Around the point, you can stand on top of the extraordinary **Dune du Pilat** (also Pyla), the biggest sand dune in Europe. The giant bay or *Bassin* of Arcachon is full of seabirds, and loved by kayakers and windsurfers.

The Dordogne

The *département* of the Dordogne, to the northeast of Bordeaux, named after the river flowing through it, is often referred to by its old name, Périgord. Its capital, **Périgueux ❺**, built around the Cathédrale de St-Front, has cobbled streets lined with elegantly restored Renaissance facades. It began life as a Gallo-Roman city, reminders of which can be seen in the **Musée d'Art et d'Archéologie** (Apr–Sept Mon, Wed–Fri 10.30am–5.30pm, Sat–Sun 1–6pm, Oct–Mar Mon, Wed–Fri 10am–5pm, Sat–Sun 1–6pm; charge).

North of Périgueux, **Brantôme** is a romantic spot, encircled by the River Dronne, with five medieval bridges and striking riverfront architecture. Further along the river is the dramatic **Château de Bourdeilles ❻** (July–Aug daily 10am–7pm, Sept–June Wed–Mon 10am–12.30pm, 2–5.30pm, times may vary; charge), comprising two castles – one feudal, the other Renaissance – bordered by terraces overlooking the cliff.

In the eastern Dordogne, in the Vézère Valley between **Montignac** and **Les Eyzies-de-Tayac ❼**, is the world's most astonishing collection of prehistoric art *(see p.198–9)*, including some in the **Grotte de Rouffignac** (www.grottede rouffignac.fr; daily, July–Aug

9–11.30am, 2–6pm, Apr–June, Sept–Oct 10–11.30am, 2–5pm; charge). Les Eyzies styles itself as 'the prehistoric capital of France', and its **Musée National de Préhistoire** (www.musee-prehistoire-eyzies.fr; July–Aug daily 9.30am–6.30pm, Sept, June Wed–Mon 9.30am–6pm, Oct–May Wed–Mon 9.30am–12.30pm, 2–5.30pm; charge) is full of local archaeological discoveries.

The **Grotte de Lascaux** contains some of the most famous cave paintings in the world, which are about 17,000 years old; the extraordinary images of bulls, horses and other animals can only be seen in replica, at **Lascaux II** (www.lascaux.culture.fr;

tel: 05 53 05 65 65; tickets in advance only from the office in Montignac).

The Vézère river runs into the Dordogne south of Les Eyzies; between **Sarlat-la-Canéda**, a busy market town that could be the stage for a film set in the Renaissance, and Bergerac, there are some magnificent views combined with lovely villages and proud castles. From **Domme**, just south of Sarlat, the road plunges down to the river, and across the bridge, a few kilometres west, the beautiful village of **La Roque-Gageac**  8 looks as though it's glued to the cliff overhanging the river, and the 13th-century château perched above **Beynac-et-Cazenac** is a vision straight out of a medieval chronicle. Across the meandering river, south on the D25 from Le Buisson, is the unusual-looking **Abbaye de Cadouin**.

The western reaches of the Dordogne present a gentler landscape. The busy town of **Bergerac** 9 is the capital of the French tobacco industry, and the **Musée du Tabac** (place

The château at Beynac-et-Cazenac towers above the river

Black diamonds

Périgord is renowned for truffles, although even here they are now relatively rare and hard to find. Small underground mushrooms (*tuber melanosporum*) no bigger than a walnut, with a distinctive and penetrating scent, these precious delicacies are hunted like gold by the *Périgourdains*. They are found mostly under the roots of oak trees, and trained truffle hounds (or pigs) are often used to detect and grub them out. Virtually all Périgord truffles are found in the wild from September until Christmas.

du Feu; mid-Mar–mid-Nov Tue–Fri 10am–noon, 2–6pm, Sat until 5pm, Sun 2.30–6.30pm, mid-Nov–mid-Mar Tue–Fri only; charge), in the elegant 17th-century Maison Peyrarède, presents a fascinating look at the evolution of smoking.

The Basque Country and Béarn

The Basque Country, or Pays Basque, lies at the western end of the Pyrenees, cradled by forested hills and flanked by the pounding surf of the Atlantic (so great for surfers), where the long, golden beaches are strung with popular resorts. It shelters one of France's most distinct cultures, an ancient nation which has clung stoically to its own language and culture, especially in rural areas. But on the whole they are happy to be French, sharing the peaks and valleys, towns and villages of the Pyrénées-

Atlantiques *département* with Béarn, another society and culture of ancient origin.

The Basque coast

The capital of the Basque Country, **Bayonne** ❿ is situated at the confluence of the rivers Nive and Adour; its old town is a remarkably intact ensemble of tall, timbered mansions. The two main sights are the Gothic

> **Basque specialities**
>
> Bayonne is good for shopping, especially for Basque specialities such as the famous berets, espadrilles, linen and woollen blankets and of course jambon de Bayonne, the deliciously sweet air-dried ham of the region. Head for rue Port-Neuf, where under its shady arcades you will find all manner of cafés, and shops with seductive displays of Bayonne chocolate.

Bayonne is one of the most attractive towns in the southwest

With its fishing port and stylish streets, St-Jean-de-Luz is a typical Basque seaside town

Cathédrale de Ste-Marie and the **Musée Basque** (www.musee-basque. com; July–Aug daily 10am–6.30pm, Wed until 9.30pm, Sept–June Tue–Sun; charge), which gives an excellent introduction to the history and traditions of this singular corner of France.

Without leaving the built-up area, you find yourself in the very different town of **Biarritz**. 'Discovered' in the mid-19th century by Empress Eugénie and Napoleon III, it is still a charming and discreet resort of large houses and *salons de thé* (tearooms). The beaches of Biarritz extend past two cliff points to the northern beach of Chambre d'Amour ('Love Room'), famous for its spectacular waves and surfing competitions.

Continuing down the coast through Bidart and Guéthary, where the surf is considered to be the best in Europe, you reach **St-Jean-de-Luz** ⓫, a pleasing amalgamation of lively beach resort and colourful fishing port that once landed whale and cod but now supplies anchovies, sardines and tuna to the many restaurants in town. In 1660, Louis XIV came here to marry Marie-Thérèse, daughter of the king of Spain, and spent the night in the **Maison Louis XIV** (www. maison-louis-xiv.fr; guided visits only; July–Aug Wed–Mon 10.30am–12.30pm, 2.30–6.30pm, Apr–June, Sept–mid-Oct 11am–5pm; charge). St-Jean's fishing port is a beautiful chaos of fishing boats, masts and nets. Across it is the much smaller town of **Ciboure**, birthplace in 1875 of the composer Maurice Ravel.

From here an attractive coastal drive sets off south along the *Corniche basque* with spectacular views approaching **Hendaye** at the end of France. Another popular surfing town with a long sandy beach, it looks across an estuary at the Spanish

★ FRANCE'S PAINTED CAVES

From the dawn of human existence, yet often drawn with amazing ability and finesse, the ancient paintings that adorn many caves in southwest France are among the great wonders of the world. Mysterious but enormously vigorous, these images of stags, horses and giant bulls connect us with the earliest roots of human creativity. Direct access to the greatest is now restricted for their preservation, but any visit to these caves, even in replica, cannot fail to stir the imagination.

Some 35,000 years ago, early peoples found parts of southern France and northern Spain ideal places to settle. There was a temperate climate, cliffs and caves for shelter, abundant fresh water and thick forests with animals to hunt. The most important traces of their existence are hundreds of remarkable cave paintings.

These are so marvellously executed that when the first were discovered,

at Altamira in northern Spain in 1879, they were believed to be forgeries. The largest cluster is in the Dordogne, around Les Eyzies, but cave art extended over a wide area, and one of the finest caves open to visitors, Niaux, is in the Ariège south of Toulouse. In all, about 100 caves with prehistoric art have been found in these regions. Most were painted between 10,000 and 20,000 years ago. The most

Admiring the Great Hall of Bulls at Lascaux II

The Great Bull at Lascaux

famous Dordogne cave is Lascaux, a labyrinth of painted chambers discovered in 1940 by four boys. Unfortunately, the streams of visitors who poured in once they were open caused a deterioration in the paintings, and Lascaux has been closed to visitors since 1963. We must now make do with a replica, Lascaux II, but it is still a stunning experience.

Exactly why the paintings were produced remains a mystery, though a ritualistic role appears likely. The most important were executed in inaccessible, pitch-black caves. Most are of animals – deer, bears, horses and aurochs (wild ancestors of domestic cattle). Human figures are few, and crudely drawn by comparison with the animal paintings.

The artists must have worked by the light of a torch or animal-fat lamp. They learnt to exploit the contours of caves to accentuate the animals' shapes, and used a pencil of pigment or their fingers for line drawing, and colours made from minerals or charcoal. With such equipment, masterpieces like the Great Bull at Lascaux are an even greater testament to the genius of the first artists.

Lascaux has been considered the most spectacular cave, but in 1994 the oldest cave paintings in the world were found in the Chauvet Cave at Vallon-Pont d'Arc in the Ardèche. They have been dated to 32,000 years ago, and yet show astonishing sophistication. Access is strictly restricted, but they can now be seen in a film by German director Werner Herzog, *Cave of Forgotten Dreams*.

France's painted caves

Signs provide information about the prehistoric cave art at Grotte de Niaux

The lower reaches of the Pyrenees

Basque Country, where the assertion of Basque identity is more determined.

Basque Country heartland

Inland, the Basque Country is for the most part neat and picturesque. **Ainhoa**, 24km (15 miles) southeast of St-Jean-de-Luz, has some good examples of the stout old Basque farmhouses with white walls and timbers painted dark red or green. Further into the Pyrenees lies the historic town of **St-Jean-Pied-de-Port** ⑫, where pilgrims rest before crossing into Navarra on their long journey to Santiago de Compostela in Spain.

Where the Basque Country meets the Béarn is roughly marked in the lowlands by the two handsome towns of **Salies-de-Béarn**, where there are thermal baths, and **Sauveterre-de-Béarn**, and in the uplands by the quaint chapel of **Ste-Engrace**.

The departmental capital, **Pau** ⑬, was a favourite spot for wealthy Brits and Americans to spend the winter, and they left behind grand villas, promenades and English-style parks filled with flowers. This was also the birthplace of Henri IV (1589–1610) – his castle was transformed into the **Château de Pau** (www.musee-chateau-pau.fr; daily, mid-June–mid-Sept 9.30am–12.30pm, 1.30–5.45pm, mid-Sept–mid-June 9.30am–11.45pm, 2–5pm; charge), a charming Renaissance palace, rare for the region, full of Flanders and Gobelins tapestries.

From the Béarn eastwards the mountains start to impose, but two great valleys carve clear north–south routes, each ending with a border crossing and beginning in **Oloron-Ste-Marie** ⑭. The Ossau Valley climbs steadily towards the **Pic du Midi d'Ossau** (2,884m/9460ft), a distinctive, isolated peak plunging spectacularly into its surrounding lakes, including the Lac d'Artouste, which you can walk to or take a cog train.

Midi-Pyrénées

Whether you want to ski on crisp snow, ramble through pastures of wild flowers, trace the road to Santiago de Compostela, relax beside lakes or visit the sanctuary of Lourdes, the choice of what to do and see is wide in the Pyrenees. These stunning mountains dividing France from her Spanish neighbour may be lower than the Alps, but they are still popular among winter sports enthusiasts. As well as snow, another resource is hot mineral water, which is pumped to the surface in numerous thermal spas. The Pyrenees' greatest asset, however, is its exceptional but fragile wildlife.

The high Pyrenees

The best approach to the Pyrenees is through **Lourdes ⓯**, one of the most important Catholic shrines. The mountain surroundings and picturesque old town contribute to the climate of unrelenting hope and spiritual devotion. However, the thousands who crowd the streets each year in search of miracles can create a grim atmosphere of despair, along with a plethora of tacky souvenir shops.

In 1858, 14-year-old Bernadette Soubirous saw the Virgin Mary 18 times in a cave. The miracle drew crowds at once, and a sanctuary was set up; in 1871, a splendid basilica was built above it. The château in the old town houses the excellent **Musée Pyrénéen** (Apr–Sept 9am–noon, 1.30–6.30pm, Oct–Mar 9am–noon, 2–6pm, Fri until 5pm; charge), devoted to local traditions and pioneering climbers.

Heading south into the mountains, the valley forks into two gorges leading to extraordinary beauty spots. Up the Gorge de St-Savin is the large, elegant thermal resort of **Cauterets**, whose springs have been thought to benefit sterile women since Roman times. The road ends at the **Pont d'Espagne** (tel: 05 62 92 50 50; 15 May–26 Sept, call for opening times; charge) where you can take a chair lift to the **Lac de Gaube** for a superb

Pilgrims at Lourdes

view of Vignemale (3,298m/10,820ft), the highest peak in the French Pyrenees.

The other fork takes you to the natural wonder of the **Cirque de Gavarnie** ⑯, a mysteriously unreal 'monument' that has inspired countless writers and painters. Glacial erosion of the mountain has gouged out a magnificent natural amphitheatre, made up of three semicircular superimposed shelves, the top shelf being a succession of peaks, all above 3,000m (10,000ft), with waterfalls tumbling down them.

On the eastern side of the **Pic du Midi de Bigorre** (2,872m/9,423ft), which you can ascend by cable car, the picture-perfect balconied houses of the little town of **Arreau** ⑰ are enhanced by its setting at the confluence of two rivers. The simple, two-

The Tour de France

The highlight of this challenging race is its gruelling trek up and down the high passes (cols) of the Pyrenees. They all provide famous tests of endurance, and the advantage of seeing the cyclists climb up to these passes is that they travel relatively slowly – the first time it was included in the race was 1910, when bikes did not have multiple gears. Out of season, the cols provide a challenge for cyclists who can get a 'passport' stamped for their mettle in the saddle.

storey **Château des Nestes** (July–Aug daily 9.30am–1pm, 3–7pm, Sept–June Mon–Sat 9.30am–noon, 2–6pm; free) contains a tourist information office and the **Musée des Cagots**, telling the story of a fascinating but

Cirque de Gavarnie in the Pyrenees

preserved villages such as **St-Lizier**, which has a cathedral and bishop's palaces. **Foix** ⓲, the region's capital and only 75km (47 miles) south of Toulouse *(see p.204)*, is overlooked by the dramatically sited castle of the counts who bequeathed their name to the town when they ruled over large parts of southwest France in the Middle Ages. Probably the best time to visit Foix is on market day – Friday, and additionally on Tuesday and Wednesday in summer.

Up the valley from here at **Niaux** ⓳, near Tarascon-sur-Ariège, are some of France's best prehistoric painted caves (tel: 05 61 05 10 10; www.ariege. com/niaux; reservation required; opening times vary; charge) which have been kept open to visitors only by strictly controlling the number of people allowed to enter at any time *(see p.198)*.

A few kilometres to the east of Foix you can pick up the Sentier Cathar (Cathar Route) where the Cathars – a dualistic Christian sect – took refuge in the mountain fortresses from the king's army, sent to wipe out the 'heretics'. They withstood 10 months of siege by 10,000 soldiers at the fortress of **Montségur** ⓴ (tel: 05 61 01 06 94; www.montsegur.org; times vary; charge) in 1243–4, on the 1,216m (3,990ft) summit of a great dome of rock, before succumbing. Today, little remains but high defensive walls around an inner courtyard... and perhaps their lost treasure, explained in the local museum. **Mirepoix**, to the north, also sheltered Cathars in an

downtrodden minority group called the Cagots. From here, it is a relaxing 32km (20-mile) drive to **Bagnères-de-Luchon**, a handsome spa town in the foothills whose beneficial waters were first discovered by the Romans.

Rising from a hilltop, 30km (19 miles) to the north, the **Cathédrale Ste-Marie-de-Comminges** can be seen from afar. The fortified village of **St-Bertrand-de-Comminges**, founded by the Romans around 72BC, clusters around the Romanesque-Gothic church, with a beautifully sculpted portal.

To the east is the lush, forested and sparsely populated landscape of the Ariège, where rural traditions have been kept alive in scattered, well-

The southwest

Airport: Aéroport de Toulouse-Blagnac; tel: 01 70 46 74 74; **www.toulouse.aeroport.fr**; about 10km (6 miles) west of city centre. Shuttle bus (Tisseo Navette Aéroport) to city centre every 20 minutes, journey takes 20 minutes, 5am–12.15am; €5 single. Local bus (Tisseo), 3 different routes into the city; €5 single. Taxi (tel: 05 61 30 02 54), 15 minutes to centre; from €22

 Trains: Gare SNCF Matabiau, boulevard Pierre Sémard; tel: 08 36 35 35 35; **www.sncf.fr**, **www.tgv.com**, **www.ter-sncf.com**

 Métro, tram and buses: Tisséo: tel: 05 61 41 70 70; **www.tisseo.fr**; 2 métro lines A and B, last train Fri and Sat 1am, Sun–Thur midnight; 1 tram line between Aéro-constellation and Arènes; tickets can be used across the network, €1.50 single for 1 hour, Pass Journée €5.

Free electric buses operate Mon–Sat 9am–7pm around the centre, hail one to stop

 Taxis: Capitole Taxi: tel: 05 34 250 250; www.capitole-taxi.com. Taxis Radio Toulousains: tel: 05 61 42 38 38. La Toulousaine de Taxis: tel: 05 61 20 90 00. Taxis Touristiques offer tours for €50–65

 Taxi bicycles: CycloVille: tel: 05 61 48 06 35; www.cycloville.com; hail one in the street or go to pick-up points at place Esquirol, place Jeanne d'Arc, or allées Jean-Jaurès

 Car hire: Main car hire firms have offices at the airport and railway station

 Parking: www.vincipark.com; 13 car parks around the city with free parking if you have a ticket to travel at several métro stations

earlier siege in 1209. It has a charming main square of half-timbered houses with shady arcades beneath them.

The heart of Gascony

Emerging from the Ariège to the north, the landscape opens up into the ancient region of Gascony, where the **Canal du Midi** runs between Toulouse and the Mediterranean coast *(see p.58)*. Built in the 17th century, the canal is still a marvel of ingenuity and engineering, with 328 locks, bridges, aqueducts (including a modern one over Toulouse's motorway ring road) and other constructions. Boats are for hire in several places along its length,

or you can walk or cycle along the shady towpath. A permanent exhibition tells its story in a service area at **Port Lauragais** (near Avignonet-Lauragais), off the A61 autoroute.

France's fourth-largest city, **Toulouse** ㉑, stands plumb between

The Canal du Midi is an engineering marvel

Musée des Augustins, Toulouse

the Atlantic and the Mediterranean. Resolutely southern in both climate and way of life, it can claim to be the de facto capital of that indefinable southern territory, the Midi. The only material yielded by the plain of the Garonne river, on which the city stands, is clay for brick-making, which gives Toulouse the epithet of the *ville rose*, the 'pink city'.

Until the military campaigns against the Cathar heresy brought interference from northern France, the counts of Toulouse enjoyed great autonomy over their dominions in the southwest. In the 15th and 16th centuries profits from textile dyes financed several mansions in the city centre, which today add to the atmosphere of old-world charm and significant wealth.

Place du Capitole Ⓐ, the main square, has numerous cafés and restaurants and is a convenient spot from which to explore the city. To the north stands the 11th-century basilica of **St-Sernin Ⓑ**, the largest Romanesque church in France and an important halt on the pilgrimage route from Arles to Santiago de Compostela in Spain. South of place du Capitole, the pedestrianised **rue St-Rome** leads into a pleasant tangle of medieval streets, which runs down to the **Musée des Augustins Ⓒ** (Thur–Tue 10am–6pm, Wed 10am–9pm; charge), an art museum housed in an exquisite 14th-century convent, with a superb Gothic cloister.

Meanwhile, a walk west from place du Capitole will take you to the Garonne via the city's other glorious medieval cloister, part of the 13th-century church of **Les Jacobins Ⓓ**. On the west bank of the river is a museum of modern and contemporary art, **Les Abattoirs** (www.

lesabbatoirs.org; Wed–Fri 10am–6pm; Sat–Sun 11am–7pm; charge), housed in a former slaughterhouse. If you are with children, they might prefer the **Cité de l'Espace** 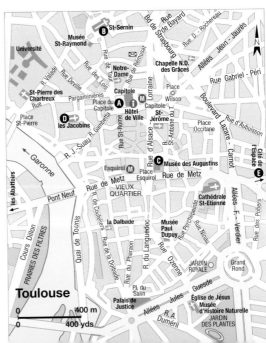 (in the eastern outskirts, on the Castres road; tel: 08 20 37 72 23; www.cite-espace.com; times vary; charge), a science museum dedicated to all things space-related, with plenty of hands-on exhibits and even a full-scale replica of the Mir space station.

Auch ㉒ (pronounced 'osh'), 70km (43 miles) west of Toulouse and the capital of the *département* of the Gers, is in what *Gersois* call the *pays des mousquetaires* – Musketeer Country. By the cathedral, which has a wonderful interior, is the **Escalier Monumental**, on which stands a bronze of d'Artagnan, the swashbuckling hero of Alexandre Dumas's *The Three Musketeers* (1844) who was based on a real Gascon, Charles de Batz.

A 52km (32-mile) detour to the southwest brings you to **Tillac**, a pretty *bastide* of one street, guarded at either end by fortified gates. In the northwest corner of the Gers, captivating and composed among the vineyards of armagnac country, is **Eauze**, where you can see a vast collection of Roman coins – the **Trésor d'Eauze** – discovered on the outskirts of the town in 1985.

Condom ㉓, 29km (18 miles) to the northeast of Eauze on the Baïse river, is a bright and prosperous cathedral town and a major armagnac centre. Its name, bizarre to English-speakers, is thought to have Vascon (later Gascon), or Roman origins. Getting down to the more serious business of armagnac, the **Musée de**

Cité de l'Espace in Toulouse

Auch and its cathedral from above

l'**Armagnac** (www.condom.org; Apr–
Oct Wed–Mon 10am–noon, 3–6pm,
Nov–Mar Wed–Sun 2–5pm; charge)
retraces the history of the renowned
eau-de-vie, and the tourist office provides a list of local producers to visit,
giving the opportunity to tour some
centuries-old Gascon residences.

High walls and stout ramparts
still guard **Larressingle**, just west
of Condom, a singular example of a
13th-century fortified village whose
tiny village houses now hold bijou
boutiques.

The Tarn and Aveyron
Albi ㉔, capital of the *département* of
the Tarn, is best known as the home
of the painter Toulouse-Lautrec.
Adjacent to the 13th-century red-
brick cathedral is the old episcopal
palace that houses the **Musée Henri
de Toulouse-Lautrec** (www.musee
toulouselautrec.net; times vary;
charge). It contains the most complete

collection of the artist's work and has
a delightful garden (daily 8am–6pm;
free) at the rear overlooking the river.

Northwest of Albi, wrapped around
a conical hill in a cloak of steep
cobbled streets, mellow stone and
mossy tiles, stands **Cordes-sur-Ciel**,
a perfectly restored medieval town

207

The southwest

Armagnac

France's oldest *eau-de-vie* is made by
some 5,000 *vignerons* (small producers)
by distilling white grapes grown in an
area covering about 130 sq km (50 sq
miles). From the still – quite often an old
copper alembic – it emerges colourless,
but time turns it golden. A quality
armagnac matures in an oak cask for
10 to 20 years. Once bottled, this ageing
process stops. Armagnac must be a year
old before it is sold. VO, VSOP or *Réserve*
on the label means it is at least four
years old. *Hors d'Age* indicates a blend of
spirits, none younger than 10 years.

and the first *bastide* to be built (1222), which grew prosperous from leather-working and weaving and now has a pedestrianised town centre.

The Aveyron cuts through the Tarn and just south of **St-Antonin-Noble-Val**, a town thought to have France's oldest surviving civic building, the river carves a small but picturesque gorge beneath the village of **Penne** and the spectacularly sited ruins of a 13th-century castle. The gorge comes to an end 6km (4 miles) further on, shortly after **Bruniquel**, another beautiful village with a castle.

The Tarn river passes through the *bastide* town of **Montauban** ㉕, 29km (18 miles) to the west, once a hotbed of Protestantism and now the *préfecture* of the somewhat amorphous *département* of Tarn-et-Garonne. Just before the Tarn merges with the Garonne to the northwest, it skirts **Moissac**, which has grown up around its abbey, one of the wonders of Romanesque architecture.

Apart from the Pyrenees, the most beautiful part of the Midi-Pyrénées region is the Lot. **Cahors** ㉖, its capital, 52km (32 miles) north of Montauban, has a magnificent fortified bridge, the Pont Valentré. A good round trip to make from here is up the valley of the Lot river – stopping for a walk around the exquisite village of **St-Cirq-Lapopie** – to the historic town of **Figeac** ㉗, birthplace of Jean-François Champollion (1790–1832), who cracked the code of Egyptian hieroglyphs. The return trip is down the delightful valley of the Lot's tributary, the Célé, stopping off at the pretty villages on the way.

In the wooded hills above Cabrerets, the **Grotte du Pech Merle** ㉘ (tel: 05 65 31 27 05; www.pechmerle. com; Apr–Oct daily 9.30am–noon and 1.30–5pm; booking recommended; charge) combines extraordinary rock formations with prehistoric paintings.

Across the austere *causses* (upland plateaux) to the north of the Lot Valley is another natural phenomenon, the **Gouffre de Padirac** ㉙ (www.gouffre-de-padirac.com; daily, Apr–June 9.30am–5pm, July until 6pm, Aug 8.30am–6.30pm, Sept–Nov 10am–5pm; charge), an enormous circular chasm or pothole, 99m (325ft) across and 103m (338ft) deep. Lifts and staircases take you down to a system of underground rivers and lakes.

Since the body of St Amadour was found uncorrupted in its grave

Looking out towards Rocamadour

The Viaduc de Millau, designed by Norman Foster

The southwest

in **Rocamadour** 30 15km (9 miles) to the south, in 1166, the site has been an important place of pilgrimage, with crypts, chapels and shrines clustered like the cells of a beehive against the cliff. The ancient ramparts, which overlook the valley, are all that remains of the 14th-century fortress that once defended the town.

Travelling up the Lot from Figeac, the landscape changes and the steeply rising wooded hills begin to give a feel of the Massif Central. A few kilometres southeast of the river is the charming village of **Conques** 31 and its magnificent Romanesque church, the 11th- and 12th-century Ste-Foy, one of the most important shrines on the medieval pilgrimage route to Santiago de Compostela in Spain.

Away in the far eastern corner of the Midi-Pyrénées region, en route to the Gorges du Tarn and the Cévennes (see p.224), are a group of diverse attractions beginning with the **Viaduc de Millau** 32, which carries the A75 over the Tarn Valley near Millau. This is not any old flyover but the world's tallest road bridge and has been attracting trippers since it was opened in 2004. It is 2.5km (1½ miles) in length and is also curved and slightly sloping. Read all about it at the aire des Cazalous (a small service station), on the D992 from Millau. Not far off the motorway, to the southeast of the viaduct, is **La Couvertoirade**, a remarkably compact, preserved medieval village founded by the Knights Templar that is still enclosed by its walls and towers.

Roquefort, a pretty village a few kilometres southwest of Millau, makes France's most famous blue cheese; steep streets lead to the caves where the cheese ripens.

ACCOMMODATION

Luxurious rooms in grand châteaux are among the accommodation options in the Bordeaux winelands, while elsewhere across the southwest there are delightful small hotels in the Dordogne and traditional Basque inns offering comfort and character.

Aquitaine and the Dordogne

Auberge de la Commanderie
3 rue Porte Brunet, 33330 St-Emilion
Tel: 05 57 24 70 19
www.aubergedelacommanderie.com
A pleasant, bright hotel with attractively modernised rooms in a venerable building in the heart of the old town of St-Emilion. A very good-value option in the winelands. **€€**

Bayonne Etche-Ona
4 rue Martignac, 33000 Bordeaux
Tel: 05 56 48 00 88
www.bordeaux-hotel.com
An impressive hotel in the Triangle d'Or district of Bordeaux with an 18th-century facade and modern interior. There's no restaurant, but rooms are excellently equipped. **€€€**

Hôtel Burdigala
115 rue Georges Bonnac, 33000 Bordeaux
Tel: 05 56 90 16 16
www.burdigala.com
One of Bordeaux's classic hotels, near the historic centre. Rooms are pamperingly

Château Cordeillan-Bages

comfortable, and the restaurant is renowned. **€€€€**

Château Cordeillan-Bages
Route des Châteaux, 33250 Pauillac
Tel: 05 56 59 24 24
www.cordeillanbages.com
A 17th-century château in the heart of the Médoc, elegantly restored incorporating chic modern styling. Jean-Luc Rocha's restaurant is exceptional, and the château also houses a school of wine. Closed late Dec–mid-Feb. **€€€€**

Le Chatenet
24310 Brantôme, Dordogne
Tel: 05 53 05 81 08
www.lechatenet.com
An *hôtel de charme* in a magnificent 17th-century Dordogne manor within its own grounds, with a pool. Its British owners ensure a welcoming, family atmosphere. Closed Jan–Easter. **€€–€€€**

Manoir d'Hautegente
24120 Coly, Dordogne
Tel: 05 53 51 68 03
www.manoir-hautegente.com
A lovely 13th-century Périgord manor in wooded grounds: spacious, comfortable bedrooms are furnished with antiques, there's a pool in the garden, and the vaulted dining room has excellent food. Closed Jan–Apr. **€€–€€€€**

Hôtel des Quatre Sœurs
6 cours du XXX Juillet, 33000 Bordeaux
Tel: 05 57 81 19 20
www.hotel-bordeaux-centre.com

An 18th-century building in the city centre, with simply decorated rooms and a cosy atmosphere. The same owners have the similarly good-value Hôtel de l'Opéra. €€

Relais de Margaux
5 route de l'Ile Vincent, 33460 Margaux
Tel: 05 57 88 38 30
www.relais-margaux.fr
This former wine cellar of the Château Margaux estate has been transformed into a luxury hotel, with a sumptuous spa and golf course. €€€€

Hôtel Rollan de By
3 route du Haut Condissas, 33340 Bégadan-Médoc
Tel: 05 56 41 27 75
www.hotelrollandeby.com
Intimate hotel with just six luxurious rooms in an 18th-century Charterhouse attached – of course – to a vineyard in the north of the Médoc. Charming and very tranquil. €€€€

Basque Country and Béarn

Hôtel Aquitaine
66 avenue Maréchal de Lattre de Tassigny, 40130 Capbreton
Tel: 05 58 72 38 11
www.hotelaquitaine-capbreton.com
A pleasant beach hotel near the surf beaches with a pool and breakfast bar; not brand new, but excellent value. €–€€

Hôtel Chantaco
Route d'Ascain, 64500 Saint-Jean-de-Luz
Tel: 05 59 26 14 76
www.hotel-chantaco.com
Luxurious facilities in a beautiful, giant 1930s villa with huge fireplaces and windows opening onto gardens with a pool and the hotel's own golf course. Closed Nov–Apr. €€€€–€€€€€

Hôtel-Restaurant Arcé
64430 Saint-Etienne-de-Baïgorry
Tel: 05 59 37 40 14
www.hotel-arce.com
Beautiful hotel in a typical Basque village house, with imaginatively modernised

Royal suite at the Hôtel du Palais

rooms, a garden and a riverside terrace for sampling Pascal Arcé's modern Basque cuisine. €€€

Hôtel du Palais
1 avenue de l'Impératrice, 64200 Biarritz
Tel: 05 59 41 64 00
www.hotel-du-palais.com
A splendid hotel overlooking the Grand Plage, harking back to Biarritz's Second Empire glory days. Facilities are eminently luxurious. €€€€€

Hôtel Les Pyrénées
19 place Charles-de-Gaulle, 64220 St-Jean-Pied-de-Port
Tel: 05 59 37 01 01
www.hotel-les-pyrenees.com
Very comfortable hotel where chef Firmin Arrambide prepares authentic Basque cooking. The garden, with pool, is especially pretty. Closed Jan. €€€

Midi-Pyrénées

Auberge du Sombral
46330 St-Cirq-Lapopie
Tel: 05 65 31 26 08
www.lesombral.com
A delightful old country inn in an exquisite village, with a convivial restaurant serving rich duck and other Cahors specialities. €

Hôtel des Beaux-Arts
1 place du Pont Neuf, 31000 Toulouse

Perched on the cliffs of Rocamadour is the Hôtel Sainte-Marie

Tel: 05 34 45 42 42
www.hoteldesbeauxarts.com
An individual hotel in the centre of Toulouse, near the Garonne, with 20 rooms in boutique style, great views, very comfortable lounges and an excellent traditional brasserie below. €€€

Hôtel-Restaurant Lons
6 place Georges Duthil, 09000 Foix
Tel: 05 34 09 28 00
www.hotel-lons-foix.com
A renovated old coaching inn in the middle of Foix, below the castle, with a bright terrace restaurant overlooking the river. Closed late Dec–mid-Jan. €–€€

La Réserve
81 route de Cordes, 81000 Albi
Tel: 05 63 60 80 80
www.lareservealbi.com
Standing in its own grounds on the banks of the River Tarn, this luxurious country-house hotel has a lovely pool, tennis courts and plenty of other facilities. The best rooms have delightful river views. €€€–€€€€

Hôtel Sainte-Foy
Rue Principale, Conques 12320
Tel: 05 65 69 84 03
www.hotelsaintefoy.com
A delightful stone village hotel furnished with antiques, in one of the Aveyron's most beautiful villages. The bar and garden are full of old-world charm. €€–€€€

Hôtel Sainte-Marie
Place des Senhals, 46500 Rocamadour
Tel: 05 65 33 63 07
www.hotel-sainte-marie.fr
The hotel is in the midst of the extraordinary cliff-village of Rocamadour, with fabulous views from the restaurant, terraces and best bedrooms. €

Hostellerie des 7 Molles
31510 Sauveterre-de-Comminges
Tel: 05 61 88 30 87
www.hotel7molles.com
Spacious hotel surrounded by meadows and trees, with a pool, amid lush countryside at the foot of the Pyrenees near Tarbes. Closed mid-Feb–mid-Mar. €€

Hôtel Terminus
5 avenue Charles-de-Freycinet, 46000 Cahors
Tel: 05 65 53 32 00
www.balandre.com
A slightly grand small-town hotel offering warm hospitality and light, spacious rooms. The restaurant, Le Balandre, is one of the area's best, with a pretty garden terrace. €–€€

RESTAURANTS

The southwest has several special food traditions, from the refined cuisines of Bordeaux or the Basque Country to the rich country cooking of the Dordogne and Gascony, land of *foie gras* and truffles.

Aquitaine and the Dordogne

Le Chapon Fin
5 rue Montesquieu, 33000 Bordeaux
Tel: 05 56 79 10 10
www.chapon-fin.com
Head for this Bordeaux restaurant, with original Art Nouveau decor, to sample great service and refined regional cooking, such as langoustines with caviar and sea bass with forest mushrooms. Closed Sun, Mon.
€€–€€€

Chez Yvette
59 boulevard du Général Leclerc, 33120 Arcachon
Tel: 05 56 83 05 11
Excellent fresh seafood combined with local vegetables in dishes like fricassee of octopus with hot Espelette peppers or *soupe de poisson d'Arcachon* (fish soup). A local favourite. **€–€€**

L'Esplanade
Rue Carral, 24250 Domme
Tel: 05 53 28 31 41
www.esplanade-perigord.com
There are wonderful views of the Dordogne Valley from this friendly, family-run hotel-restaurant, perched above the River Domme. The excellent local cuisine includes, each spring, a selection of truffle-based dishes. Closed mid-Nov–Jan.
€€–€€€

Le Moulin de L'Abbaye
1 route de Bourdeilles, 24310 Brantôme
Tel: 05 53 05 80 22
www.moulinabbaye.com
A beautiful old mill with a riverside terrace, where you can sample traditional Périgord dishes prepared with modern flair and

sophistication. Closed Mon–Fri midday in Nov–Apr. **€€–€€€**

Hostellerie de Plaisance
Place du Clocher, 33330 St-Emilion
Tel: 05 57 55 07 55
www.hostellerie-plaisance.com
Enjoy splendid views of medieval St-Emilion and its vineyards as you dine on the exciting cuisine of young chef Philippe Ethebest and – of course – the finest local wines at this seductively sumptuous luxury hotel. Reservations recommended. Dinner only except Sat, closed Sun, Mon and mid-Dec–mid-Feb. **€€€€**

Le Vieux Bordeaux
27 Rue Buhan, 33000 Bordeaux
Tel: 05 56 52 94 36
www.le-vieux-bordeaux.com
Classic Aquitaine dishes served in this charming restaurant include duck *au poivre et au foie gras*. The courtyard is a very restful spot within the city in summer. Closed Sun, Mon, two weeks Feb, three weeks Aug.
€€–€€€

Style and substance in a starter at the Hostellerie de Plaisance

Basque Country and Béarn

Auberge du Cheval Blanc
68 rue Bourgneuf, 64100 Bayonne
Tel: 05 59 59 01 33
This traditional restaurant in Petit Bayonne
has been serving classic Basque cuisine
for over 50 years, and current chef Jean-
Claude Tellechea has won a Michelin star.
Closed Sat midday, Sun evening and Mon.
€€€

Hôtel-Restaurant Chilo
64130 Barcus
Tel: 05 59 28 90 79
www.hotel-chilo.com
Family-run hotel in a village near Pau, serving exceptional Basque specialities made
with superb local produce. Guest rooms
are also charming, and there's a pool in the
garden. Closed Mon, Tue midday. €€

Hôtel-Restaurant Donibane
4 avenue Layatz, 64500 Saint-Jean-de-Luz
Tel: 05 59 26 21 21
www.hotel-donibane-saintjeandeluz.com
In summer, there are excellent views of La
Rhune mountain from this bright, airy restaurant. Chef Maxime Lacombe specialises
in modern variations on Basque cuisine. €€

Hôtel Euzkadi
285 Karrika Nagusia, 64250 Espelette
Tel: 05 59 93 91 88
www.hotel-restaurant-euzkadi.com
A citadel of traditional Basque cuisine, in a
classic, half-timbered village house hung
with clusters of Espelette's famous AOC
peppers every autumn. They feature in many
dishes, along with excellent seafood. Closed
Mon, Tue. €€

Le Galion
17 boulevard Général de Gaulle, 64200
Biarritz
Tel: 05 59 24 20 32
www.restaurant-legalion.net
In a wonderful location with a terrace overlooking the beach, Le Galion offers seafood
with a Basque flavour, and is excellent value.
Closed Mon, Tue midday. €€

Midi-Pyrénées

La Belle Epoque
Le Coustal Camboulit, 46100 Camboulit,
near Figeac
Tel: 05 65 40 04 42
www.domainelabelleepoque.com
Located 6km (4 miles) outside Figeac, this
restaurant in an old farmhouse forms part of
a low-key rural tourism centre that also has
B&B rooms and a campsite, shady terraces
and a pool. Cooking is enjoyably traditional.
€–€€

La Bohème
3 rue Lafayette, 31000 Toulouse
Tel: 05 61 23 24 18
www.la-boheme-toulouse.com
A romantic restaurant in a vaulted cellar
near the place du Capitole, specialising in
cassoulet, *magret aux cèpes* and other typical *toulousain* dishes. Closed Sat midday,
Sun. €€

L'Esprit du Vin
1 quai Choiseul, 81000 Albi
Tel: 05 63 54 60 44
A sophisticated restaurant in a historic
building in the centre of Albi, with a nicely
tranquil atmosphere. Dishes combine
tradition with originality. Closed Sun, Mon.
€€–€€€

Jambon de Bayonne

Michel Sarran
21 boulevard Armand Duportal,
31000 Toulouse
Tel: 05 61 12 32 32
www.michelsarran.com
Michel Sarran is one of France's celebrated chefs, and this townhouse, elegantly decorated in subtle colours, provides a suitable setting for his deliciously inventive cuisine. Closed Wed midday, Sat, Sun.
€€€–€€€€

Restaurant Le Victoria
24 place 8 Mai 1945, 81100 Castres
Tel: 05 63 59 14 68
www.restaurant81-levictoria.com
Set in the vaulted cellars of a 17th-century convent near the Musée Goya, Le Victoria presents inventive versions of regional dishes. **€€**

La Table d'Oste
7 rue Lamartine, 32000 Auch
Tel: 05 62 05 55 62
www.table-oste-restaurant.com

Dining room at Michel Sarran

This friendly restaurant has a terrace for summer dining, and specialises in Gascon duck, chicken and other rich meat dishes, with prime ingredients from local farms. Closed Sun, Mon midday Oct–Apr; Sat evening, Sun, Mon midday May–Sept. **€–€€**

NIGHTLIFE AND ENTERTAINMENT

Bordeaux and Toulouse are two of the liveliest cities in southern France, and their tourist office websites (www.bordeaux-tourisme.com, www.toulouse-tourisme.com) are good first stops for information. The pedestrianised streets in the city centre are a good place to start the evening. In the winter season, all the bigger Pyrenean ski resorts such as Tourmalet and Font Romeu have boisterous après-ski scenes.

Blue Cargo
Plage d'Ilbaritz, 64210 Bidart
Tel: 05 59 23 54 87
www.bluecargo.fr
Big, mellow restaurant-bar on the beach south of Biarritz, which becomes an open-air dance space at night. Popular with the wealthier surfing set.

Grand Théatre – Opéra National de Bordeaux
Place de la Comédie, 33025 Bordeaux
Tel: 05 56 00 85 95

www.opera-bordeaux.com
One of France's largest provincial opera houses and concert venues, which presents a full range of opera, dance and orchestral concerts.

Le Mandala
21 rue des Amidonniers,
31000 Toulouse
Tel: 05 61 21 10 05
www.lemandala.com
Hippest live venue in Toulouse, with rock, jazz, world music and more.

Théâtre du Capitole
Place du Capitole, 31000 Toulouse
Tel: 05 61 22 31 31
www.theatre-du-capitole.fr
The centre of Toulouse, this giant theatre
hosts a complete range of drama, music
and dance.

Théâtre National de Bordeaux
en Aquitaine
Place Renaudel, 33800 Bordeaux
Tel: 05 56 33 36 60
www.tnba.org
Bordeaux's prestigious theatre also has a
cabaret space and a very popular, hip bar-
restaurant, the Tn'Bar.

Nightlife on Place du Parlement, Bordeaux

SPORTS AND ACTIVITIES

The southwest has huge areas of beautiful countryside ideal for walking, and the
Pyrenees provide a location for all kinds of mountain activities, from winter skiing
and snowboarding to white-water rafting in summer. In addition, the Basque coast
near Biarritz has some of Europe's best surfing beaches. For more on hiking,
see *Exploring the landscape, p.31, 34–5*; for more on windsurfing at Arcachon,
surfing around Biarritz, water-skiing and inland kayaking on the Dordogne, see *On
the water, p.56–7, 59*. The French Pyrenees central website, www.lespyrenees.
net, has information on facilities at all ski resorts in the mountains.

Aquensis
Rue du Pont d'Arras, 653200 Bagnères-de-
Bigorre
Tel: 05 62 95 86 95
www.aquensis.fr
A feature of the Pyrenees is that the skiing
and hiking slopes are only a short distance from luxurious natural spas. This
stylish centre specialises in easy-access
treatments.

Climb Ariège
La Coupière, 09000 Serres-sur-Arget
Tel: 05 61 64 29 50
www.climbariege.co.uk
British climbers based near Foix in the eastern Pyrenees who offer climbing and a big
range of other mountain activities, such as
canyoning and rock climbing, with accommodation if required.

Mountain Bug
8 rue Mme de Maintenon, 65120 Barèges
Tel: 05 62 92 16 39
www.mountainbug.com
Skiing, snow-shoeing and other options in
winter; hikes, climbs and more in summer.

Pyractif
44 route Nationale, 65370 Bertren
Tel: 05 62 49 13 20
www.pyractif.com
Specialists in mountain-biking trips on
Pyrenean roads.

Traqueurs de Vagues
64260 Bilhères-en-Ossau
Tel: 05 59 82 64 32
www.rafting-pyrenees.com
Spectacular rafting, kayaking and other river
trips in the high Pyrenees. Open Mar–Oct.

TOURS

In Bordeaux good-quality wine tours are provided by the city tourist office, the Maison du Vin and local tourist offices in the wine towns; for more information, see *Foods and wines of France, p.27–8.*

33 Tours
12 allée Stendhal, 33000 Bordeaux
www.bordeaux-tours.com (contact by web + mail only)
Local guides providing easy-access tours of one or two days around the Bordeaux vineyards and châteaux, with a range of options available.

Aquitaine Bike Hire Dordogne
24220 Coux et Bigaroque

Tel: 05 53 30 35 17
www.aquitainebike.com
Cycling tours of the Dordogne and area.

Les Bateliers des Gorges du Tarn
48210 La Malène
Tel: 04 66 48 51 10
www.gorgesdutarn.com
Boat trips through one of the south's most spectacularly beautiful gorges. Open Apr–Oct.

FESTIVALS AND EVENTS

The festivals of the southwest reflect its cultural variety.

May–July
Week-end des Grand Crus
Around Bordeaux
www.ugcb.net
Early May
For one weekend the greatest names in Bordeaux wines invite devotees in for (often expensive) gourmet events.

Fêtes de Bayonne
Bayonne
www.fetes.bayonne.fr
End of July
Boisterous festival when the city streets fill with Basque music and dancing – and eating.

September–October
Festival Occitania
Various venues, Toulouse
www.festivaloccitania.com
Sept–Oct
Music, theatre and other arts from across southern France and the Mediterranean.

Fête du Safran du Quercy
Cajarc (Lot)

www.safranduquercy.com
One weekend late Oct
A cluster of Lot villages celebrate their traditional product – saffron.

November–December
Marché de Noël
Place du Capitole, Toulouse
www.toulouse-tourisme.com
Late Nov–Dec
Toulouse holds one of the south's biggest Christmas markets.

Basque parade

Mediterranean France

From Spain to Italy, the south of France is a melting pot of traditions and cultures. Roussillon guards its Catalan roots and Cathar hideouts litter Languedoc. Provence, with lavender fields and hilltop villages, is picture-postcard pretty, and the Côte d'Azur basks under dazzling blue skies. A ferry ride away lies the craggily beautiful island of Corsica.

Marseille, Toulon and Nice

 Population: 870,000 (Marseille), 170,000 (Toulon), 350,000 (Nice)

 Local dialling codes: Marseille: 04 91; Toulon: 04 94; Nice: 04 93

 Local tourist offices: Marseille: 4 la Canebière; tel: 08 26 50 05 00; www.marseille-tourisme.com. Toulon: 12 place Louis Blanc; tel: 04 94 18 53 00; www.toulon tourisme. com. Nice: 5 promenade des Anglais; tel: 08 92 707 407; www. nicetourisme.com

 Main police stations: Marseille: 66 la Canebière; tel: 04 88 77 58 00. Toulon: rue Henri Poincaré; tel: 04 98 03 24 00.

Nice: 1 avenue Maréchal Foch; tel: 04 92 03 60 89

 Main post offices: Marseille: 19 rue Henri Barbusse. Toulon: 16 rue Drouas. Nice: 23 avenue Thiers

 Hospitals: Marseille: Hôpital Timone, 264 rue Saint-Pierre; tel: 04 91 38 60 00; www.ap-hm.fr. Toulon: Centre Hospitalier Font-Pré, 1208 avenue Colonel Picot; tel: 04 94 20 48 51. Nice: Hôpital Saint-Roch, 5 rue Pierre Devoluy; tel: 04 92 03 33 75

 Local media: Marseille: *La Provence* (daily), *Métro Marseille* (daily); Nice: *Nice Matin* (daily), *Riviera Times* (English)

As one of the world's most glamorous holiday destinations, both winter and summer, the south of France, or Midi, has attracted visitors for almost two centuries, especially royalty and rock stars, with many making it their home. Along the southeast coast of the Mediterranean, the star-studded names of the Côte d'Azur, from Marseille to Menton, are strung like a glittering necklace. Their plentiful pleasures include not only sun and sea but magnificent art museums and medieval architecture, world-class yachts, casinos and festivals. It is a region best appreciated through the eyes of the many artists inspired by its luminous light. Inland, the cultural delights of Provence are set against a backdrop of windswept mountain plateaux, river gorges, lavender terraces and hamlets that cling to mountain crags. The more open, windswept coast of Languedoc-Roussillon curves round to the west, harbouring historic fishing ports and golden beach resorts; vineyards spread inland into medieval Cathar country, producing delicious wines, and towards the Pyrenees, French Catalonia has a distinct feel. Only four hours from Nice, the mountainous island of Corsica has an extraordinary variety of landscapes and a strong Italian flavour.

Lavender-cloaked fields of Provence

Languedoc-Roussillon

The ancient region of Languedoc extends westerly from the Rhône Valley to the Garonne in a great sweep of plains, mountains and vine-clad hills dotted with remote Cathar castles; nature reserves, interesting

Hilltop monastery of St-Martin-du-Canigou

towns and fishing ports line the shore. The name Languedoc comes from its own language, Occitan – *langue d'oc*. Though it is part of the Languedoc-Roussillon region, Roussillon is most distinguished by its Catalan character. Local architecture, landscapes and lifestyles all have an identity shared with the rest of Catalonia across the border, and the Catalan language is still fairly widely spoken.

French Catalonia

Coming from the Pyrenees and the Col de Puymorens, the scenic road winds down steeply, passing the ski resort of **Font-Romeu**, into a wide valley that separates France and Spain, before plunging into the narrow **Gorges de Carança** and not levelling off until it reaches **Prades ❶** at the foot of the Pic du Canigou. This was the favourite town of the cellist Pablo Casals (1876–1973), and a music festival is held in his honour in the magnificent 11th-century, restored Benedictine abbey of **St-Michel-de-Cuxa** every summer.

Above the abbey, the tiny road twists through **Vernet-les-Bains**, with

Mediterranean France

a spa cooled by a mountain torrent, to **Casteil** where a steep 30–50-minute hike leads to the spectacularly sited monastery of **St-Martin-du-Canigou** (tel: 04 68 05 50 03; www.stmartindu canigou.org; Feb–Dec, guided tours only; charge). One of the finest examples of Romanesque architecture in the region, it is still inhabited by a community of monks.

Perpignan, the heart of French Catalonia, is a lively city of moderate size, and a good way to approach it is by canal. The gem of the Catalan coast, however, and inspiration of 20th-century painters such as Matisse, Braque and Picasso, is **Collioure ❷**, 30km (19 miles) to the southeast. Encased in a small rocky bay, the seaside village, with the 13th-century **Château Royal** dividing the bay, has escaped the development that has devoured some of the coast of Roussillon. The scenic rocky coast road continues southwards – suffering traffic jams in summer – all the way to **Cerbère**, the last port before Spain.

Set in the Pyrenean foothills in

Airport: Aéroport de Marseille-Provence; tel: 04 42 14 14 14; www.mrsairport.com or www.marseille.aeroport.fr. Its location in Marignane is 26km (16 miles) northwest of the city centre. Trains depart regularly from Vitrolles Aéroport to Marseille, take 17–25 minutes and cost €4.90 for a single ticket. The shuttle bus to Marseille railway station runs every 20 minutes, takes 25 minutes and costs €8.50 for a single. *Navettes Blanches* (snow shuttles) to resorts in the southern Alps cost €35 for a return ticket, €90 for a family of four. For taxis, tel: 04 42 88 11 44; www.taxis-aeroport.com. The fare will be around €46 during the day, €57 between 7pm–7am

Trains: Gare SNCF Marseille Saint-Charles; tel: 04 95 04 10 00; www.gares-en-mouvement.com; TGV takes 3 hours from Paris; tel: 08448 484 064; www.tgv.co.uk

Buses, trams and métro: RTM, Espace Infos, 6 rue des Fabres; tel: 04 91 91 92 10 (bus), 04 91 36 58 11 (tram); www.rtm.fr, www.lepilote.com (for all travel info including trains). There are two métro lines (5am–10.30pm, until 12.30am Fri–Sun, Fluobus until 12.35am), almost 80 bus routes and two tram lines (5am–12.30am). Tickets cost €1.50 for a single, €5 for a visitor's day pass and €10.50 for a three-day ticket, valid on all public transport

Bicycle hire: city bike hire available 24 hours a day at 100 points with 1,000 bikes; tel: 0800 801 225; www.levelo-mpm.fr

By sea: Port Autonome, 23 place de la Joliette; tel: 04 91 39 40 00; www.marseille-port.fr. Harbour Office: quai Marcel Pagnol; tel: 04 91 73 93 63; www.marseille-provence.com. Ferries: CMN La Méridionale; tel: 08 10 20 13 20; www.lameridionale.fr. Up to 20 crossings a week between Marseille and Corsica. SNCM: tel: 3260 (say the acronym SNCM); www.sncm.fr, also make regular night crossings to Corsica

Taxis: Taxi Marseille: tel: 04 91 02 20 20; www.taximarseille.com. Accent Taxi: tel: 06 62 31 17 29; www.accenttaxis.com

Car hire: Europcar: 121 avenue du Prado; tel: 04 91 17 53 00; www.europcar.fr. Olympic Location: 28 rue des Orgues; tel: 04 91 34 05 25; www.olympiclocation.fr

the Tech Valley, about 25km (16 miles) south of Perpignan, **Céret** ❸ is a small medieval Catalan town steeped in traditions and famous for its excellent **Musée d'Art Moderne** (www.musee-ceret.com; May–Sept daily 10am–7pm, Oct–Apr Wed–Mon until 6pm; charge) containing works by Picasso and Braque, among others, who were all inspired by the remarkable surroundings.

The Languedoc

Strategically situated on what was once the border with Spain, and dominating the plain, **Carcassonne** ❹ is the only medieval monument of its kind in Europe, due to its two sets of intact fortifications, which surround a tiny town of 350 inhabitants overlooking the modern city. The first ramparts were built by the Romans in the 3rd and 4th centuries

Medieval Carcassonne

AD; the second lot were built in the 13th century by St Louis. In periods of siege during the Middle Ages, up to 10,000 people would take refuge here. In the 19th century Carcassonne was restored by the controversial Gothic Revivalist architect Viollet-le-Duc, so parts of it are deliberately more picturesque than the medieval originals.

Across the drawbridge, the bustling little town today is filled with cafés and restaurants, bakeries and antique shops. The medieval **Château Comtal** (daily, Apr–Sept 9.30am–6.30pm, Oct–Mar until 5pm; charge) is particularly impressive, the summer festival making use of its fabulous amphitheatre.

The journey between Carcassonne and Montpellier meanders past vineyards which produce the robust red Corbières and Minervois wines. To the south on the border with Roussillon, in the perfumed *garrigue* (scrubland), are the impressive former Cathar strongholds of Peyrepertuse and Quéribus. To the northeast about 34km (21 miles) from Carcassonne, surrounded by a sea of vines, is the Cathar town of **Minerve**, proud of its defiant past when it held out against Simon de Montfort in a siege that lasted seven weeks.

Carcassonne is connected to the coast by the **Canal du Midi** *(see p.58)*, which passes through **Béziers** ❺, 64km (40 miles) away. Prosperous under the Romans, Béziers was reduced to ruins by the crusade against the Cathars in 1209. Since the 19th century, however, thanks to the growing wine market, the typical Midi town has regained its vitality. On the coast, **Narbonne** ❻, 23km (14 miles) to the south, was once the capital of the Roman region of Narbonensis Prima, and has a well-restored medieval quarter.

During the 1960s, a major development programme on the Languedoc-Roussillon coast created a string of new resorts. Some, like Cap d'Agde and La Grande-Motte, came with dramatic (if controversial) modern architecture, but all were still interspersed with miles of windswept beaches and lagoons. **Sète 7** stands out as the most authentic town along this coast, its bridges and canals reminiscent of Venice, and its unsurpassed seafood restaurants particularly popular with the fishermen.

A few kilometres inland, **Montpellier 8**, 56km (35 miles) northeast of Béziers, is the capital of Languedoc-Roussillon and one of the liveliest and youngest cities in the Midi. It was revitalised during the 1990s by a dynamic mayor who initiated a programme of avant-garde public architectural developments.

The city has a large university and a medical school – the oldest in France, dating back to the early 13th century – whose student life focuses around the buzzing old town. Just to the east, on the salt flats and sun-bleached blue lagoons of the **Petite Camargue**, stands the perfectly preserved walled town of **Aigues-Mortes**, the 'place of dead waters' (referring to the surrounding saline marshes), built by St Louis as the embarkation point for the Seventh Crusade.

Nîmes and the Cévennes

Nîmes 9, 43km (27 miles) northeast of Montpellier, is a far-sighted city which successfully combines the old with the avant-garde. Once an important Roman city, Nîmes's 2,000-year-old amphitheatre still echoes with the sounds of bullfights that draw enormous crowds to the *Feria de Pentecôte* every May. Among other Roman relics and the lovely **Jardin de la Fontaine**, an 18th-century network of terraces, bridges and water pools, stands the **Carré d'Art** arts complex (Tue–Sun 10am–6pm; charge), a modern tribute in glass and steel by British architect Norman Foster.

Roman influences are everywhere, and 20km (12 miles) northeast of Nîmes is one of the finest remaining Roman aqueducts in the world. The massive stones of the **Pont du Gard** (daily; charge for visitor centre) have stood for more than 2,000 years, spanning 1km (½ mile) over the River Gardon. To the north in the rugged, scrub-covered hills, the town of

The lively old quarter of Montpellier

Uzès announces itself with a flourish of medieval towers; here, the central arcaded place aux Herbes hosts a colourful market laid out under the trees every Saturday morning.

The **Cévennes** rise abruptly about 60km (36 miles) north of the Mediterranean, offering some spectacular natural formations, along with the solitary peace of cooler mountain trails away from the torrid summer heat and the crowds of lower Languedoc. Among the large *massifs* are several *causses*, extremely dry plateaux, divided by deep gorges. En route to the Cévennes, partly protected as a national park, is the once remote Romanesque abbey of **St-Guilhem-le-Désert** , tucked into the head of a ravine overlooking the gorge of the Hérault river. There are several caves in the surrounding area, but none as spectacular as the **Grotte des Demoiselles** (www.demoiselles.com; guided tours daily, times vary; charge), 30km (19 miles) upriver in the foothills. Continuing along the Hérault, the pretty road ultimately leads to the

The home of denim

Nîmes is the spiritual home of blue jeans. Blue durable cloth called *serge* was introduced from Egypt by *Nîmois* tailors in the 17th century, and later exported to America. In 1853 Levi-Strauss, a German immigrant in California, saw the cloth and began to use it to make work clothes for farmers. The cloth had the mark 'de Nîmes' on it – and 'denim' was born.

highest peak of the Cévennes, **Mont Aigoual** (1,565m/5,140ft) for a view of the Alps to the east, the Mediterranean to the south and the Pyrenees to the southwest.

The **Maison du Parc National des Cévennes** (main information centre; daily, July–Aug 9am–7pm, Sept–June 9am–noon, 1.30–6pm) is in the 13th-century Château de Florac, in the pretty village of Florac at the eastern end of the magnificent **Gorges du Tarn** , extraordinary canyons carved through steep limestone cliffs by the Tarn river.

A marvel of Roman engineering, the Pont du Gard outside Nîmes

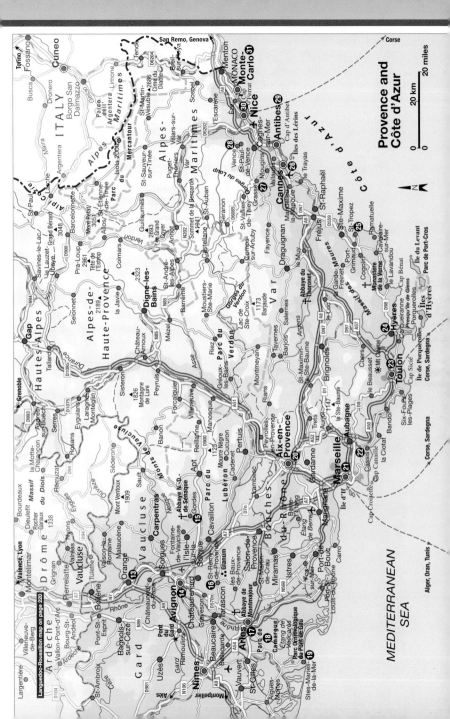

Provence and Côte d'Azur

0   20 km
0   20 miles

MEDITERRANEAN SEA

Central Provence

Stretching from the marshy Camargue to the Alpine foothills, Provence is a magical, light-infused world, where the scent of pine and lavender hangs under an azure-blue sky. Provence has a history as rich as its soil: the monuments of the Roman Empire still stand proudly in Orange, Arles and Nîmes. But the most important pleasure of Provence is not the sightseeing but the leisurely pace of life, the passionate Provençal people, the sun-soaked landscape, the wonderful cuisine and a bottomless pot of cultural activity.

The Rhône and its delta

Classified as the warmest city in France, **Orange ⑬**, at the northwestern tip of Provence, was founded by Julius Caesar's Second Legion and became a thriving Roman settlement. It possesses a majestic theatre and at

Travels with a donkey

The entire region of the Cévennes is full of long-distance GR footpaths *(see p.30)* that are well travelled in summer and have mountain lodges along the way. Scottish writer Robert Louis Stevenson walked through the Cévennes for 12 days in 1878 and published an account of his journey as *Travels with a Donkey in the Cévennes* the following year, drawing the world's attention to the region. The GR70 follows Stevenson's route.

the southern end of town the original **Arc de Triomphe**, built in AD26, is another great Roman monument.

Surrounding Orange, the department of the Vaucluse is richly fertile, producing melons, wild morel mushrooms, sweet tomatoes and peppers; in October the grape and olive harvests begin. The rich earth

The Avignon festival celebrates art, theatre and music throughout July

Abbaye Notre-Dame-de-Sénaque

com; Wed–Mon 10am–1pm, 2–6pm; charge) is worth visiting as much for the elegant architecture and gardens of the 18th-century *hôtel particulier* as for the collection of mainly French works and archaeological finds. However, the famous 'Pont d'Avignon', on which the nursery rhyme centres, is a disappointing four-arch ruin tumbling into the Rhône. Take a step back from the bustle to discover one of the prettiest streets within the ramparts, rue des Teinturiers. Tree-lined and cobbled, it borders the River Sorgue, and took its name (meaning dye-makers) from the 15th-century manufacturers of the brightly coloured fabrics called *indiennes*.

To the east of Avignon lies the **Lubéron**, the region described in Peter Mayle's 1991 bestselling book *A Year in Provence*. Still relatively untarnished, the Lubéron retains a mystical attraction, dotted with charming medieval villages such as **Cucuron**, often used as a film set, and **Gordes** ⓑ, perched on top of a hill. Though thronged with tourists in the summer, Gordes remains one of the most picturesque hilltop villages in Provence. The streets are steep and cobbled, the ancient stone houses are perfectly restored and the view out over the valley spectacular. Close by is the much-photographed 12th-century **Abbaye Notre-Dame-de-Sénaque**, which provides the backdrop to an immense lavender field.

At the foot of the rocky limestone hills of the Massif des Alpilles, among the vines and olive groves, is

nourishes some of the most prestigious vineyards, in particular those at **Châteauneuf-du-Pape**, renowned for their strong, full-bodied red and crisp white wines.

At the confluence of the Rhône and Durance rivers lies **Avignon** ⓮, a walled city packed with history and culture. The popes moved here from Rome in 1309 and for 70 years Avignon was the centre of European religion, art and prostitution. The clerics and brothels are long gone, but the **Palais des Papes** (www.palais-des-papes.com; daily 9am–7pm, times may vary; charge) remains one of the most breathtaking sights in Provence. **Place de l'Horloge** is the place to sip a *pastis* and watch the world go by. Among the many museums, **Musée Calvet** (www.musee-calvet-avignon.

Mediterranean France

The impressive setting of Les Baux-de-Provence

picturesque **St-Rémy-de-Provence**
⑯. Eighteen km (11 miles) south
of Avignon, it is a thriving market
town of fine 17th- and 18th-century
houses. The most famous residents
include Nostradamus, 16th-century
astrologer and scholar, and Van Gogh
(*see p.39*), who spent a year at the **St-
Paul-de-Mausole** (Maison de Santé;
guided tours daily, Apr–Oct 9.30am–
7pm, Nov–Mar 10.15am–4.45pm;
charge) which still serves as a monastery and mental hospital. You can

The Camargue's birdlife

Open all year, the **Parc Ornithologique
du Pont de Gau**, 4km (2½ miles), to the
north of Saintes-Maries-de-la-Mer, is an
ideal place to view birdlife from a series
of discovery trails that weave through
the marshlands of the Camargue.
In summer, thousands of flamingos
congregate on the lagoons, turning
the water pink, but the wetlands also
attract a further 500 species of visiting
birds. Along with a pair of binoculars,
be sure to arm yourself with plenty of
mosquito repellent.

follow a trail to the famous scenes he
painted, such as *Starry Night*. On the
town outskirts are two marvellously
sculpted Roman monuments, the
Arc de Triomphe and the **Mausolée**,
known as Les Antiques.

The Alpilles plateau is punctuated
only by the rock outcrop of **Les Baux-
de-Provence**, once famous for courtly
love and the songs of its troubadours
and now known as one of France's
most spectacular villages. Its medieval
citadel is perched above a tortuous
valley, and its windy summit provides
an unforgettable panorama over the
Crau Plain to Arles, the Camargue
and out towards the sea. The **Musée
d'Histoire des Baux**, which serves as
the entrance to the massive fortress,
illustrates the history of the castle and
its village through the centuries. Baux-
ite, named after the town, was discovered here in 1821. One of the disused
quarries provides a vast backdrop for
the Cathédrale d'Images. The 4,000
sq m (4,784 sq ft) stone walls provide
an immense screen for projected
images, creating an awesome visual
and musical display.

On the banks of the Rhône between Avignon and Arles, at the crossroads leading to the Alpilles and the Camargue, lies the medieval town of **Tarascon** with an almost perfectly intact 15th-century château. The legend of how the local dragon was tamed is celebrated at the end of June.

The soul of Provence lies in **Arles** ⑰, which has a Roman amphitheatre, **Les Arènes**, still used for bullfights. This is a place to wander and sit, following in the footsteps of Van Gogh *(see p.39)* and Gauguin, who was his house guest for two months before they quarrelled and Van Gogh cut his own ear. The lively Saturday market is often accompanied by gypsy guitars.

Arles is the gateway to the **Camargue** ⑱, a protected wild place of lagoons, rice fields and cowboys in the Rhône delta. Today the best way to experience the Camargue is still on horseback *(see p.32)*. A museum (Apr–Sept Wed–Mon 9am–12.30pm, 1–6pm, Oct–Mar until 5pm; closed Jan; charge) on the Camargue's history and ecosystems stands on the route between Arles and Saintes-Maries-de-la-Mer in an old sheep shed at **Mas du Pont de Rousty**. Outside there is a nature trail which leads to an observation tower. The beach at **Saintes-Maries-de-la-Mer** ⑲ is one of the longest in Provence: kilometres of white sand and shallow water. In late May, thousands of travellers flock to the village for the festival of the black Madonna, when a statue of the Virgin is carried into the sea surrounded by white horses.

Aix-en-Provence

Aristocratic **Aix-en-Provence** ⑳ is the intellectual heart of Provence. Its ancient, tree-lined streets, 17th-century residences and numerous squares are reminiscent of Paris

Mediterranean France

The famous, semi-wild white horses of the Camargue

Marseille – France's oldest city and a thriving port and cultural hub

– a Sunday afternoon in a café on the **Cours Mirabeau** is a lesson in crafted chic. Aix derives its name from the Latin for water, *aqua* – water is everywhere and fountains trickle in every corner. The Fontaine des Quatre Dauphins is one of the most beautiful in a small square of 17th-century townhouses. During the 19th century, novelist Emile Zola's father was the engineer responsible for building aqueducts to improve Aix's water circulation. Emile grew up in the city along with his friend, painter Paul Cézanne, and one of the best ways to see Aix is by taking the **Cézanne Trail** *(see p.38–9)*.

Marseille and Cassis

South of Aix, **Marseille ㉑** is France's oldest and second-biggest city. Founded by Greek traders in 600BC, Marseille has been a busy port for centuries. In recent years, it has done much to clean up its mafia-style image and has won the title of European Capital of Culture for 2013, resulting in more urban redevelopment.

Today the city is a vibrant, spicy concoction, worthy of its culinary gift to the world, the rich fish stew bouillabaisse, which can be savoured in the many restaurants around the colourful fish market in the **Vieux Port Ⓐ**. Running from the port is Marseille's most famous boulevard, **La Canebière**, a human tide of different nationalities by day but quieter by night. The streets around La Canebière are lively, with the **Opéra Ⓑ** a focal point for music-lovers. To the north of the Vieux Port is **Le Panier**, the city's oldest *quartier*, a charming labyrinth of narrow, steep streets and colourful tall houses. Now home to potters and artists, this shantytown was where dockers, sailors and fishermen lived until the 1960s. At the heart of Le Panier is **La Vieille Charité Ⓒ** (www.vieille-charite-marseille.org; June–Sept Tue–Sun 11am–6pm, Oct–May 10am–5pm; charge), a former hospice for the homeless built by Marseillais sculptor Pierre Puget in the 17th century.

Saved from demolition by Le Corbusier, it is now home to several fascinating museums. The city has a thriving art scene and several good art museums, including the **Musée Cantini** 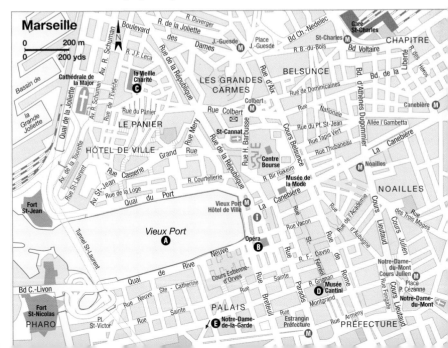 (June–Sept Tue–Sun 11am–6pm, Oct–May 10am–5pm; charge), with its fine Fauve and Surrealist collection. Rising above the city, the gleaming white 19th-century basilica **Notre-Dame-de-la-Garde** has wonderful views. On top of the campanile, looking seaward, is a statue of the Virgin Mary, entirely covered in gold leaf.

It's a 20-minute boat ride from the Vieux Port to **Ile d'If**, one of the cluster of islands that makes up the Frioul Archipelago. The imposing 16th-century fortress, built on the island by François I to guard the harbour, was never put to military use, and was converted into an escape-proof prison made famous by Alexandre Dumas's novel *The Count of Monte Cristo*.

The least developed part of a much-abused coastline lies between Marseille and Toulon. Here the shore is distinguished by Les Calanques, steep-sided fjords carved out of cliffs, popular with climbers and divers, and best viewed by boat from the little port of **Cassis**. A chic resort of restored houses, Cassis has a popular golden beach. It is known for its fragrant white wine which tantalises the palate with hints of the herbs which cover the hills. A little further down the coast is Bandol, home to another fine Provençal wine.

To the north, the high ridge of Le Gros-Cerveau (Big Brain) overlooks vineyards, orchards and fields of flowers – and on clear days, the distant harbour of Toulon.

✶ ST-TROPEZ WALK

The legendary Riviera resort of St-Tropez continues to be a bewitching mix of Provençal fishing village and jet-setters' hotspot, and a morning or afternoon's walk around it will reveal its hidden depths.

The pretty Vieux Port (Old Port), where visitors have disembarked since time immemorial, is the town's animated heart, lined with tall, colourful houses and busy quayside bars and brasseries. On the eastern side of the port on place Grammont, the **Musée de l'Annonciade** is one of the region's best 20th-century art museums.

Turn left onto rue Allard, busy with boutiques and celeb chef Christophe Leroy's Table du Marché, then right up

Backstreet near rue Sous de la Glaye, which can be reached from the beach of La Glaye

narrow rue Etienne Berny for another surprising museum, the **Maison des Papillons**, where over 4,000 species of butterfly are on display.

Return to the port and go right onto quai Suffren. Luxury yachts moor sternside to the quay, giving front-row views from the portside bars, such as Bar du Port and the neo-Baroque Café de Paris. Further along, Le Gorille dispenses drinks and standard brasserie fare day and night. Opposite, next to the **tourist office**, an archway leads to place aux Herbes, where there is a small fish market every morning. Continuing northwards on quai Jean Jaurès, Senequier is perfect for people-watching at aperitif hour, as are the elegant terraces of Le Quai Joseph and sister fish restaurant Joseph l'Escale a few doors up. Nearer the sea on quai Frédéric Mistral is a **memorial** to the Allied navies who liberated Provence on 15 August 1944.

Tips

- Distance: 2.25km (1½ miles)
- Time: 2–3 hours
- Start and end: Vieux Port
- To avoid summer traffic jams, use the ferry service from Ste-Maxime with Les Bâteaux Verts (tel: 04 94 49 29 39; www.bateauxverts.com)
- If driving, use the back roads from Ramatuelle rather than the coast road
- Avoid aperitif hour, Tuesday and Saturday morning market days and cloudy days
- Parking is at Nouveau Port beside the Vieux Port

Walk between the squat **Tour du Portalet** and La Tour restaurant, heading over the rocks to the pretty cove of **La Glaye**. From the beach, take the first archway into rue Sous de la Glaye, which exits on place de l'Hôtel de Ville – the **Château Suffren** is a remnant of the square tower built in 980, to protect against the North African Barbary pirates.

Take rue Sibille, turn left to the **Eglise Parossiale**, St-Tropez's parish church, and into rue du Clocher alongside the church through place de l'Ormeau to rue de la Citadelle, where the triangular **Tour Jarlier** is a remaining corner of the town ramparts. At the top of the road, steps lead to the **Citadelle**, built by Henri IV in the 17th century and housing a naval museum.

Retrace your steps, and at place Forbin turn left along rue du Petit Bal and descend rue de la Miséricorde, past the **Chapelle de la Miséricorde**, into rue Gambetta. Here, elegant

Vieux Port, the place to celebrity-spot and ogle the yachts from café terraces

18th-century doorways of merchants' houses punctuate upmarket shops, such as Vilebrequin, home-grown seller of men's swimwear.

Continue to the tree-lined **place des Lices**, where St-Tropez millionaires play at being Provençal villagers, renting boules from the Café des Lices, for games in the square. Return to the Vieux Port via rue Georges Clemenceau, source of St-Trop's classic sandals from Atelier Rondini and cream-filled cakes at La Tarte Tropézienne.

233

Walking tour of St-Tropez

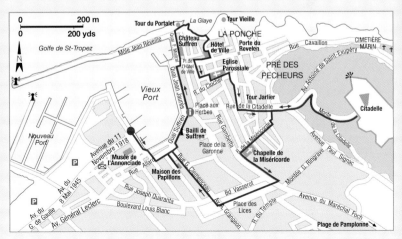

The medieval gate, Porte Massillon, leads to Hyères's compact old town

Toulon and Hyères

The prefecture of the *département* of the Var, **Toulon** ㉓, 66km (41 miles) east of Marseille, is France's principal naval base, with one of the region's most attractive deep, natural harbours. Toulon was badly damaged in World War II and much of the post-war building is ugly, especially along the quays, where boats depart for nearby islands. The port is also associated with the work of 17th-century sculptor Pierre Puget, who began his career carving ships' figureheads; two of his best works can be seen on the quay. Pieces by his followers stand in the **Musée de la Marine** (www.musee-marine.fr; July–Aug daily 10am–6pm, Sept–June Wed–Mon; closed Jan; charge), along with models of the many ships once made in the port.

Further east, the modern town of **Hyères** ㉔ combines charmingly with its backdrop of faded Belle Epoque grandeur. A Saturday morning food market takes place in the old town, entered via a 13th-century gate. This former port has long been a centre for sailing, scuba-diving, windsurfing and water-skiing *(see p.55–7)*. **Presqu'Ile de Giens**, which was once one of the **Iles d'Hyères** in the bay, is connected to the mainland by sandbars, enclosing the Salins des Pesquiers, the only salt marsh still worked along this coast.

The Côte d'Azur

In summer the coast from St-Tropez east to Menton, also known as the French Riviera, is extremely busy, but that's part of the fun. Most of the beaches are fabulous, and there is plenty of scope for people-watching, while lounging over a *pastis* on a terrace in the mostly wonderful weather. This azure-blue region has a rich artistic legacy, and the native umbrella pines sharing the landscape with acacia, eucalyptus and palm trees continue to be inspirational for modern-day artists.

St-Tropez and inland

Until the 18th century, the wild, wooded, hilly **Massif des Maures**, the backdrop to much of the Côte d'Azur, was almost deserted for fear of pirates. Today the inland roads remain quiet, passing through charming villages, waterfalls, and forests of cork-oak and chestnut – a stark contrast to **St-Tropez** ㉕ *(see p.232–3)* down at the water's edge, which receives up to 10,000 visitors in summer; even

A honeypot for artists

La Colombe d'Or, at the entrance to St-Paul-de-Vence, has developed from a café where pre-war artists gathered to paint the Mediterranean or the Alps over terraced hillsides to an exclusive hotel and restaurant patronised by well-known celebrities. As artists came and went they would often pay for their stay with a piece of their work. Today the hotel has a priceless art collection including Léger mosaics, a Calder mobile and an exquisite Braque dove.

the yachts number in the thousands. French painters and writers had discovered the fishing village by the late 19th century and recorded their findings on canvas, several of which are in the **Musée de l'Annonciade** (June–Sept Wed–Mon 10am–noon, 3–7pm, Oct–May 10am–noon, 2–6pm; charge). In the **Maison des Papillons** (May–Oct Wed–Mon 10am–noon, 3–7pm, Dec–Mar 10am–noon,

2–6pm; charge) you can see the painter Dany Lartigue's enormous collection of butterflies.

Fréjus and **St-Raphaël**, 33km (20 miles) to the east, have merged into one – although St-Raphaël is more fashionable – and divide the Massif des Maures from the Massif de l'Esterel. Fréjus has some important Roman ruins, including the 10,000-seat arena where Picasso liked to watch bullfights.

For fewer crowds, head inland to the vine-fringed villages of the Haut-Var with their legends of flying donkeys and fire-breathing dragons. The Abbaye du Thoronet is a beautiful 12th-century monastery hidden in the hills on the way to the spectacular Gorges du Verdon. The Verdon river cuts through limestone cliffs and plunges 600m (2,000ft).

Cannes and Antibes

In the 1830s, attracted by the temperate climate and lovely setting at the

Harbour at St-Raphaël, Napoleon's departure point when he was banished to Elba

The golden sand beach of Cannes is divided into public and private stretches

eastern end of the Esterel, British and Russian royals started wintering in **Cannes** ㉖ when it was an insignificant fishing village. The international film world's Festival de Cannes, launched in the late 1940s, consolidated its reputation for glamour, and boulevard de la Croisette became one of the most fashion-conscious seaside promenades on earth.

Two villages above Cannes are renowned for their famous artist resident, Pablo Picasso (1881–1973). At **Vallauris** he revived the ceramics and pottery industry almost single-handedly after World War II, leaving a bronze sculpture on the place Paul Isnard; his latter years were spent at **Mougins** working until the end *(for more on artists in the region, see p.40)*.

Beyond, 11km (7 miles) from Mougins, lies **Grasse** ㉗, a sheltered retreat of pink villas and palm trees, and home to perfume distilleries since the 16th century. At the **Musée International de la Parfumerie**, in

an elegant 18th-century mansion, you can smell the perfumed plants in a rooftop greenhouse (May–Sept daily 10am–7pm, garden until 8pm, Sat until 9pm, Oct–Mar Wed–Mon and Apr daily 11am–6pm; charge).

To the northeast of Grasse are the dramatic **Gorges du Loup**, which have a number of interesting villages and some spectacular walks. In **Vence** ㉘, 13km (8 miles) east of Pont-de-Loup, at the southern end of the gorges on the D2210, a wonderful legacy has been left by another important artist. Henri Matisse (1869–1954) considered the murals he completed in 1951 in his **Chapelle du Rosaire** (mid-Dec–mid-Nov Mon, Wed and Sat 2–5.30pm, Tue, Thur 10–11.30am, 2–5.30pm, Sun Mass 10am; charge) to be his masterpiece *(see p.41)*.

Artists who worked along the Mediterranean were attracted by the quality of the light, which has, by all accounts, always been especially fine at **St-Paul-de-Vence**, directly south of Vence. A walled town with 16th-century ramparts almost intact, St-Paul was 'discovered' by artists, such as Matisse and Chagall in the 1920s, but the perched village's popularity makes it very busy in summer. Just outside is the delightful **Fondation Maeght** (www.fondation-maeght.com; daily, July–Sept 10am–7pm, Apr–June until 6pm, Oct–Mar 10am–1pm, 2–6pm; charge), full of 20th-century paintings and outdoor sculptures (*see p.40–1*).

A few kilometres to the south, Impressionist painter Auguste Renoir (1841–1919) spent the last 12 years of his life in **Cagnes-sur-Mer**, where his home, **Maison Les Colettes** (Musée Renoir; May–Oct Wed–Mon 10am–noon, 2–6pm, Nov–Apr until 5pm; charge), remains almost as it was when he died. The old town is squeezed tightly into its walls and

is crowned by the 14th-century **Château-Musée Grimaldi** (May–Oct Wed–Mon 10am–noon, 2–6pm, Nov–Apr until 5pm; charge), containing a modern art museum.

Antibes 🈩, with Greek and Roman roots, faces Nice across the Baie des Anges (Bay of Angels) and shelters some of the world's most expensive yachts. Overlooking the sea is the 12th-century Grimaldi château containing the magnificent **Musée Picasso** (mid-June–mid-Sept Tue–Sun 10am–6pm, July–Aug Wed, Fri until 8pm, mid-Sept–mid-June 10am–noon, 2–6pm; charge), containing works that Picasso painted here in 1946.

Nice and Monaco

Prefecture of the Alpes-Maritimes and France's fifth-largest city, **Nice** 🈛 was a resort by the mid-18th century. The style of its architecture, from medieval to early 20th-century, is Genoese, but it was the British who created the Promenade des Anglais, now a 3km (2-mile) traffic-clogged boulevard. Its old town, with a colourful morning market and many terrace cafés, harbours the **Musée National Marc Chagall** (www.musee-chagall.fr; May–Oct Wed–Mon 10am–6pm, Nov–Apr until 5pm; charge), containing Chagall's masterpiece, *Le Message Biblique*. By the excavated Roman ruins in the chic **Cimiez** district is the **Musée Matisse** (www.musee-matisse-nice.org; Wed–Mon 10am–6pm; free), which contains the artist's bronzes.

Until 1860, when France annexed Nice, the Var river was the French border. The **Var Corniche** (avenue

Antibes's cobble-stoned old town

Mediterranean France

🚗 CORNICHES DRIVE

The three corniche coast roads abound with scenic views and dramatic settings. A day's drive from Nice will take you to Belle Epoque resorts, Roman ruins and picturesque medieval hill villages along the way.

From place Ile de Beauté on Nice's Vieux Port, take boulevard Carnot (D6098), start of the Basse (Lower) Corniche. After about 5km (3 miles), turn right off the corniche into **Villefranche-sur-Mer**, whose natural deep-water harbour was the main port of Nice for centuries and is now a stop for cruise ships. Fork left down avenue Sadi Carnot and park on place Wilson by the 16th-century **Citadelle**. Overlooking the harbour is the medieval **Chapelle St-Pierre**, known as the Cocteau Chapel because of its frescoes painted by writer and filmmaker Jean Cocteau (1889–1963). Up a few steps, place Amélie Pollonnais is home to a flea market on Sundays and the pleasant brasserie Le Cosmo. Beyond the chapel, quai Courbet is lined with fish restaurants, including La Mère Germaine.

Return to the D6098, then shortly after, take the D25 right towards **St-Jean-Cap-Ferrat**, a millionaires' enclave. A side road turns left to the Italianate **Villa Ephrussi de Rothschild** with beautiful gardens, and the tiny port has some upmarket restaurants, such as La Voile d'Or.

The D25 continues east into palmy Belle Epoque **Beaulieu-sur-Mer**, where you can visit the **Villa Grecque Kérylos**. Back on the Basse Corniche, another 7km (4½ miles) east of Eze-Bord-de-Mer, **Cap d'Ail** on the right has some Belle Epoque gems, such as the former Eden Palace hotel, where a footpath leads down to **Plage Mala**, a beautiful beach with the trendy Eden restaurant.

Continue through **Monaco**, taking the Tunnel du Serrouville to Port Hercule and follow signs for Menton. At the end of boulevard d'Italie return to France on the D6098; fork left onto the D6007 and left towards Roquebrune-Cap-Martin on the D2564, the Grande Corniche. Turn off right to **Roquebrune Village**, clinging to the hillside in a network of alleys, and park at the foot on place Birigliano, from where steps lead up to the square for lunch in La Grotte, or smarter Les Deux Frères. At the top sits a 10th-century château, enlarged

Tips

- Distance: 43km (27 miles)
- Time: one day
- Start: Vieux Port, Nice
- End: Eze Village
- The Basse and Moyenne corniches are now D roads, but you may still find road signs and maps indicating the N98 and N7
- Part of this tour is possible by public transport; frequent trains between Nice and Menton stop at Villefranche-sur-Mer, Beaulieu and Cap d'Ail
- Eze station is at Eze-Bord-de-Mer and not Eze Village; similarly, the nearest station for Roquebrune Village is Carnolès, followed by a steep footpath

A stunning view on the road to Eze

by the Grimaldis of Monaco, who ruled Roquebrune until 1860.

Heading west, the Grande Corniche zigzags for 8km (5 miles) to **La Turbie**, where the Café de la Fontaine is a superb place to eat. Park on the square and walk through one of the medieval gateways along narrow streets to **Le Trophée des Alpes**, built up high in honour of Emperor Augustus.

Continue westwards along the D2564, and turn left on the D45 which joins the D6007. This is the Moyenne Corniche, built in the 1920s. Park below **Eze Village**, a well-restored tourist village, perched on a rocky crag and accessible only on foot. Its Jardin Exotique is a feast of cacti and succulents.

It's another 10km (6 miles) along the D6007 to return to Nice.

Corniches drive

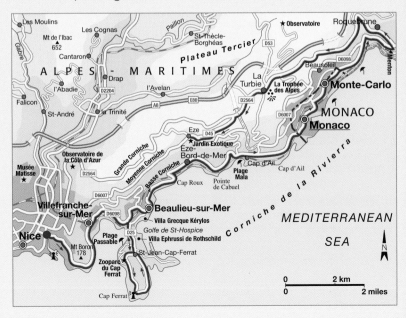

Auguste-Renoir from Cagnes) follows the west bank of the river, and three corniches, one above the other, traverse the 30km (20 miles) from Nice to Italy *(see p.238–9)*.

Merging with Nice to the east, **Villefranche-sur-Mer** is a surprisingly unspoilt little town, built around one of the deepest harbours in the world. Beyond is the refuge of the seriously rich, **Cap Ferrat**, where the **Villa Ephrussi de Rothschild** (www.villa-ephrussi.com; Feb–Oct daily 10am–6pm, July–Aug until 7pm, Nov–Jan Mon–Fri 2–6pm, weekends and school hols 10am–6pm; charge) gives a hint of the 1920s millionaire lifestyle. Just the other side of the Cap is **Beaulieu-sur-Mer**, with some of the best hotels on the Riviera, and which lays claim to the best climate on the coast, protected from the north wind by a great rock face. The **Villa Grecque Kérylos** (www.villa-kerylos.com; same opening hours as Villa Ephrussi; charge) is a complete reconstruction of an ancient Greek villa with cool courtyards open to the sea.

The tiny perched village of **Eze**, high above the sea with the finest views on the whole Riviera, is restored to the last stone: a bijou museum of medieval detail. High up on the Grande Corniche beyond Eze there is a dramatic view of Monaco from the Roman monument **Le Trophée des Alpes** (mid-May–mid-Sept Tue–Sun 9.30am–1pm, 2.30–6.30pm, mid-Sept–mid-May 10am–1.30pm, 2.30–5pm; charge) at **La Turbie**.

Between the 1870s and 1980s, **Monte-Carlo** ❸ was the roulette capital of Europe, and the wintering place of the very rich and of mothers with eligible daughters. Today, the administrative area of the prinicipality of Monaco has become the Miami of the Mediterranean. A stroll from the Palace through the old quarter leads to the cathedral and **Jardin Exotique**.

Browsing the cours Saleya market in Nice

Corsican *charcuterie*

Almost two-thirds of the island's interior is covered with the thick tangle of scented shrubs and wild flowers, known as *maquis,* which, along with the forests, provides the perfect habitat for wild pigs that feed mainly on acorns and chestnuts. During the hunting season they are turned into the delicious *charcuterie,* such as *prisutta* (smoked ham), *salamu* (smoked cured sausage) and *salsiccia* (spicy cured sausage) that Corsica is famous for. Make sure you buy from the small-scale traditional producers for the best quality.

Villa Ephrussi de Rothschild houses artworks and sits in exotic gardens

Further along the coast on the Italian border, **Menton**, pretty and well protected, remains more reserved than its neighbours, with a good beach, several exotic gardens and a lively lemon festival before Lent.

Corsica

The rugged, unspoilt island of Corsica offers beautifully dramatic coastlines and a wild interior of densely forested hills, and has a flavour as much Italian as French, apparent in the dialect. You can alternate days on the beach with some of the Mediterranean's best deep-sea diving, boat trips around coves, canoeing and fishing on inland rivers, and hikes in the mountains. Ajaccio has the main airport, and car ferries from Nice, Toulon and Marseille run to there and Bastia, Calvi, Porto Vecchio and Ile Rousse. However, the narrow, twisting roads need skill and a suitable car.

Ajaccio and the south

Ajaccio ❷, with palm-lined boulevards and a wonderful morning market, is Corsica's capital and the birthplace of Napoleon Bonaparte. His baptismal font is in the **Cathédrale Notre-Dame-de-la-Miséricorde** and his childhood home, **La Maison Bonaparte** (www.musees-nationaux-napoleoniens.org; Apr–Sept Tue–Sun 9am–noon, 2–6pm, Oct–Mar 10am–noon, 2–4.45pm; charge) is in rue St-Charles. His uncle's house, the recently renovated **Palais Fesch** (50–52 rue cardinal; May–Sept Mon, Wed, Sat 10.30am–6pm, Thur, Fri, Sun noon–6pm, Oct–Apr Mon, Wed, Sat 10am–5pm, Thur, Fri noon–5pm, third Sunday of the month noon–5pm; charge), has a notable collection of early paintings amassed during the Italian campaign.

Ajaccio heralds the island's southern *département*, Corse-du-Sud, whose coastline is studded with sandy bays

Mediterranean France

and long white beaches. Just off the N196 winding south, evidence of Corsica's earliest occupation by man can be seen in the mystical, majestic granite menhirs at **Filitosa** ❸❸ (www.filitosa.fr; Apr–Oct daily 8am–sunset; charge), carved into the shapes of warriors by megalithic man around 4,000 years ago. Further south, **Sartène** is an austere medieval town of grey granite blending into the surrounding rockscape, with a history of bandits and pirates.

At the southern tip, **Bonifacio** ❸❹ has superb seaward views as far as Sardinia, a fortified old town crowning the hilltop, and a bustling harbour, where you can dine at one of the many seafood restaurants lining the quay. The road north to the busy seaside resort of **Porto-Vecchio**, 28km (17 miles) away, passes the turn-off for the beautiful, long, sandy **Plage de Palombaggia**.

Northern Corsica

The coastline is at its wildest and loveliest between **Porto** and Calvi, especially around the **Golfe de Porto** ❸❺, 70km (43 miles) north of Ajaccio, where the red cliffs of the Calanche plunge a sheer 300m (1,000ft) into the sea. The Porto river, calm where it reaches the sea, can be followed inland to the point where several mountain torrents form the **Gorges de Spelunca**. The old mule track to the mountain village of **Evisa** passes through these gorges, and a walk in the lowest part gives an idea of what the island's former 'road system' was like.

Further along the northwest coast, one of Corsica's major seaside resorts, **Calvi** ❸❻, is where Admiral Nelson

The Corsican coastline is ideal for exploring by boat

Amble round Bonifacio to enjoy far-reaching sea views

lost an eye during an attack on the town in 1794. Although popular in summer – there's a good jazz festival in June – it maintains some charm, and in low season its cobbled streets are deserted.

Inland is the island's highest mountain, the 2,706m (8,877ft) **Monte Cinto**, where in winter you can ski. This is the **Niolo** region, the one part of Corsica where farming sheep and goats still provides the main income.

At the island's centre is **Corte ③⑦**, the 'spiritual capital' of the island and seat of Corsica's university. A steep climb up to the old town brings you to the ancient citadel, which houses the **Musée de la Corse** (www.musee-corse.com; July–Sept daily 10am–8pm, Apr–June and Oct Tue–Sun, Nov–Mar Tue–Sat until 5pm; charge), whose exhibits relate to the island and its people.

Between the 11th and 13th centuries, Corsica was ruled by the Italian city-state of Pisa, resulting in a crop of small, perfectly proportioned Tuscan Romanesque churches. One lies outside the sophisticated yachting centre of **St-Florent ③⑧** on the western neck of the Cap Corse Peninsula. On the other side lies **Bastia ③⑨**, the principal town of Haut-Corse, the island's northern *département*, and a major commercial port. It has a colourful Mediterranean flavour, with a lively square and **Vieux Port**. From there you can head north and explore remote **Cap Corse**, but allow time for the narrow, twisting road.

For 15 short but deeply felt years in the 18th century, Corsica tasted independence under the leadership of Pasquale Paoli. He was born in **Castagniccia**, a beautiful region of rocky crests and dramatic valleys, to the south of Bastia, covered in chestnut groves. This was once the island's most prosperous area, but is now all but deserted.

ACCOMMODATION

Places to stay around France's Mediterranean coast run from charming small hotels to some of the most famous luxury retreats in the world, so prices vary accordingly.

Languedoc-Roussillon

Best Western Hôtel l'Orangerie
755 rue Tour de l'Evêque, 30000 Nîmes
Tel: 04 66 84 50 57
www.orangerie.fr
Charming hotel with more character than most Best Western affiliates. Rooms are attractively decorated, and there's a garden, small pool and good restaurant. **€€**

Casa Pairal
Impasse des Palmiers, 66190 Collioure
Tel: 04 68 82 05 81
www.hotel-casa-pairal.com
Delightful villa in shady gardens close to the sea, in the Roussillon coast's prettiest village. The garden also contains a lovely pool. Exceptional value. Closed Nov–Mar. **€€**

Hôtel la Demeure des Brousses
538 rue du Mas de Brousse,
34000 Montpellier
Tel: 04 67 65 77 66
www.demeure-des-brousses.com
A lovely 18th-century manor house,

transformed into a special luxury retreat, in peaceful gardens on the edge of Montpellier. **€€–€€€**

Le Montmorency
2 rue Camille Saint-Saëns,
11000 Carcassonne
Tel: 04 68 11 96 70
www.lemontmorency.com
At the foot of the medieval ramparts, a stylish but very reasonably priced hotel with terrace, pool and log fires in winter. **€–€€**

Hôtel Saint-Louis
10 rue Amiral Courbet,
30220 Aiguës-Mortes
Tel: 04 66 53 72 68
www.lesaintlouis.fr
Charming balconied hotel in the walled town, with characterful rooms, a restaurant and a patio garden next to the ramparts. Closed Nov–mid-Mar. **€–€€**

Breakfast with a view at Château Eza

Central Provence
Hôtel d'Arlatan
26 rue Sauvage, 13631 Arles
Tel: 04 90 93 56 66
www.hotel-arlatan.fr
A venerable Provençal mansion with beamed ceilings and other original features, a rooftop terrace and courtyard-garden with pool. An ideal way to experience Arles. **€€**

Hôtel des Quatre Dauphins
54 rue Roux Alphéran,
13100 Aix-en-Provence
Tel: 04 42 38 16 39
www.lesquatresdauphins.fr
Overlooking the dolphin fountain, this small hotel has lots of fans, with good reason. It's inexpensive but has both charm and comfort, and the owners are very helpful. **€–€€**

La Sommellerie
Route de Roquemaure,
84230 Châteauneuf-du-Pape
Tel: 04 90 83 50 00
www.la-sommellerie.fr
In the heart of the vineyards, this 17th-century farm has lovely bright rooms, a garden pool and a Provençal-style dining room serving regional cuisine. **€€**

Résidence du Vieux-Port
18 quai du Port, 13002 Marseille
Tel: 04 91 91 91 22
www.hotelmarseille.com
This veteran hotel has been comprehensively renovated, and its rooms decorated in quirkily modern styles. Some have balconies with great views over the port, and there's an attractive restaurant. **€€€**

The Côte d'Azur
La Boulangerie
Route de Collobrières, 83310 Grimaud
Tel: 04 94 43 23 16
www.hotel-laboulangerie.com
Charming hotel situated in the Maures hills outside St-Tropez, with a Mediterranean garden, lovely pool and tennis courts, and a relaxed feel. Closed mid-Oct–Easter. **€€€**

La Réserve de Beaulieu

Hôtel Brise Marine
58 avenue Jean Mermoz,
06230 St-Jean-Cap-Ferrat
Tel: 04 93 76 04 36
www.hotel-brisemarine.com
A cosy small hotel in a superb location on Cap Ferrat, an institution on the Riviera; several rooms have sea views, and there's a terraced garden. Some rooms have either balconies or terraces. Closed Nov–Jan. **€€€**

Château Eza
Rue de la Pise, 06360 Eze
Tel: 04 93 41 12 24
www.chateaueza.com
Scarcely anyone who sees this castle-hotel, perched on the cliffs with one of the world's most stunning views, finds it anything other than fabulous. Rooms are naturally sumptuous and stylish, and the restaurant has a Michelin star. **€€€€€**

La Réserve de Beaulieu
5 boulevard du Général Leclerc,
06310 Beaulieu-sur-Mer
Tel: 04 93 01 00 01
www.reservebeaulieu.com
Utterly opulent Renaissance-style pink villa dominating the coastal corniche between Nice and Monaco, with private beach and other luxuries. Closed mid-Oct–mid-Dec. **€€€€€**

Listings

Villa Roseraie
Avenue Henri-Giraud, 06140 Vence
Tel: 04 93 58 02 20
www.villaroseraie.com
A small, friendly hotel in a 1930s villa which benefits from a lovely garden, a pool and a laid-back bar. Rooms are individually decorated. €€–€€€

Corsica
Hôtel-Residence du Centre Nautique
Quai Nord, 20169 Bonifacio
Tel: 04 95 73 02 11
www.centre-nautique.com
Warm-toned wooden walls and nautical accessories set the atmosphere for this original quayside hotel in Bonifacio's marina. Includes a seafood restaurant. €€–€€€

Kallisté Hôtel
51 cours Napoléon, 20000 Ajaccio
Tel: 04 95 51 34 45
www.hotel-kalliste-ajaccio.com

A stylish, boutique-like hotel in a typical Ajaccio apartment block, with a friendly atmosphere and good, new facilities. €€

U Santu Petru
20217 Casta
Tel: 04 95 37 04 60
www.usantupetru.net
The fabulous location is the big attraction of this small hotel, near empty beaches in the wild countryside of the Désert des Agriates west of Saint-Florent. There's a restaurant, and facilities are available to help guests explore the area. €

Le Vieux Moulin
20238 Centuri
Tel: 04 95 35 60 15
www.le-vieux-moulin.net
A very pleasant hotel overlooking a picturesque fishing harbour. It's worth staying here just for the lovely stone terrace. €€€–€€€€

RESTAURANTS
Delicious seafood and a lively use of Mediterranean ingredients are hallmarks of southern cooking, and on the Riviera there is, of course, a spectacular range of gourmet restaurants.

Restaurant price categories

Prices are for a three-course meal for one (usually a set menu) with a drink.

€ = below €20
€€ = €20–45
€€€ = €45–90
€€€€ = over €90

Languedoc-Roussillon
Casa Sansa
2 rue Fabriques d'en Nadal,
66000 Perpignan
Tel: 04 68 34 21 84
www.casa-sansa.fr
Lively Catalan restaurant in the old town, popular with locals, with enticing dishes such as grilled squid, *suquet* (fish stew) and chargrilled lamb. €€

La Côte Bleue
Avenue Louis Tudesq, 34140 Bouzigues
Tel: 04 67 78 31 42
www.la-cote-bleue.fr

Large, family-run hotel-restaurant ('The Blue Coast') overlooking the Bassin de Thau near Sète. In the family since 1961 and now run by a brother-and-sister team, it is one of the best in the area for langoustines, Bouzigues oysters and other fresh seafood. Closed Wed. €€

Le Languedoc
32 allée d'Iéna, 11000 Carcassonne
Tel: 04 68 25 22 17
After visiting Carcassonne's medieval *Cité*, head for this restaurant in the *basse ville* for an authentic *cassoulet* (meat and bean stew). Closed Sun evening and Mon. €€

Le Marché sur La Table
10 rue Littré, 30000 Nîmes
Tel: 04 66 67 22 50
This friendly modern bistro is just down the street from Nîmes's food market, so you can be sure the produce is fresh. Closed Mon, Tue. **€€**

Central Provence
Le Delta
1 place Mireille,
13460 Stes-Maries-de-la-Mer
Tel: 04 90 97 81 12
http://delta.camargue.monsite-orange.fr
This modest small hotel in the Camargue's main town has a likeable, local restaurant. Typical Camargue dishes served include the famous *viande de taureau*, the meat of the area's little black bulls. Closed Jan–Feb. **€–€€**

Les Deux Frères
4 avenue Reine Astrid,
13100 Aix-en-Provence
Tel: 04 42 27 90 32
www.les2freres.com
A smart, trendy modern bistro serving Provençal and globally influenced dishes on an attractive, well-shaded terrace. There are even vegetarian options. **€–€€**

Le Glacier de la Fontaine
19 boulevard Mirabeau,
13210 St-Rémy-de-Provence
Tel: 04 32 60 16 89
Original salads, tasty grilled meats and home-made pasta are specialities at this delightful restaurant. It's also an ice-cream parlour, with over 40 superb flavours – all made with local produce. **€**

Oustau de Baumanière
13520 Les Baux-de-Provence
Tel: 04 90 54 33 07
www.oustaudebaumaniere.com
A celebrated gourmet restaurant and hotel in a 16th-century manor in the spectacular fortress town of Les Baux, this is a place really to indulge the senses. Closed Wed, Thur Oct–Apr, and Jan–mid-Feb. **€€€€€**

La Table de Beaurecueil
66 allée des Muriers, 13100 Beaurecueil
Tel: 04 42 66 94 98
www.latabledebeaurecueil.com
The Jugy-Bergès family are renowned as being among Provence's finest cooks, and their restaurant at the foot of Cézanne's Montagne Ste-Victoire does not disappoint: ingredients are wonderfully fresh, including the treasured Vaucluse truffles, and menus generously priced. Closed Sun evening, Mon. **€€**

La Vieille Fontaine
Hôtel d'Europe, 12 place Crillon,
84000 Avignon
Tel: 04 90 14 76 76
www.heurope.com
This grand 16th-century townhouse hotel has a charming courtyard and terrace, a perfect setting for the creative cuisine of chef Bruno d'Angélis. Closed Sun, Mon. **€€–€€€**

Courtyard at La Vieille Fontaine in Avignon

The Côte d'Azur
L'Affable
5 rue Lafontaine, 06400 Cannes
Tel: 04 93 68 02 09
www.restaurant-laffable.fr
Contemporary bistro with an open kitchen
that turns out classic dishes and desserts
with an individual twist. Offers great-value
lunch menus. Closed Sat midday, Sun. **€€**

Auberge de la Madone
2 place Auguste Arnulf, 06440 Peillon
Tel: 04 93 79 91 17
www.auberge-madone-peillon.com
Mountain views are guaranteed from the
terrace of this delightful former inn above
Monaco, now a typical Riviera luxury hotel.
The excellent regional cuisine is strong on
fresh, light flavours. Closed Wed and Nov–
Jan except Christmas period. **€€€**

Café de la Fontaine
4 avenue du Général de Gaulle,
06320 La Turbie
Tel: 04 93 28 52 79
www.hostelleriejerome.com
Bruno Cirino of the Hostellerie Jérôme has
brilliantly revived the village café as a casual
but chic bistro, with a superb-value black-
board menu of homely specials, such as Nice-
style rabbit and home-made fruit tarts. Open
lunch and dinner. Closed Mon in winter. **€–€€**

La Colombe d'Or
Place du Général de Gaulle,
06570 St-Paul-de-Vence
Tel: 04 93 32 80 02
www.la-colombe-dor.com
One of the most famous spots in this celebrated artists' town, this exquisite small hotel
and restaurant is full of artworks donated by
Picasso, Braque, Miró and many more when
they came to what was then a village café in
the 1920s. Its lovely terrace is still a celebrity
draw. Closed Nov–mid-Dec. **€€–€€€**

Le Cosmo
11 place Amélie Pollonais,
06230 Villefranche-sur-Mer
Tel: 04 93 01 84 05

www.restaurant-lecosmo.fr
Friendly modern brasserie and cocktail bar
with an ample terrace overlooking the Cocteau chapel. Great for people-watching, and
the menu features inventive salads, steaks
and excellent fresh seafood. **€€–€€€**

Joseph l'Escale
9 quai Jean Jaurès, 83990 St-Tropez
Tel: 04 94 97 00 63
Ultra-fashionable quayside restaurant, the
essence of St-Tropez, with a menu focused
on intricate, globally influenced versions
of Mediterranean seafood. The bar is just
as popular as a late-night lounging spot.
€€€–€€€€

La Mérenda
4 rue Raoul Bosio, 06300 Nice
This little bistro in Nice's old town has a big
reputation; cognoscenti drop in to make a
reservation, since there is no phone (nor
does it accept credit cards). There are no
frills in the decor either, but it's celebrated
for the classic *niçoise* cuisine of deter-
minedly individual chef Dominique Le Stanc.
A gourmet experience. Closed Sat, Sun,
Easter, most of Aug, Nov–Christmas. **€€**

Corsica
L'Abri Côtier
Port de Plaisance, 20260 Calvi
Tel: 04 95 46 00 04
www.calvi-abricotier.com
Diners enjoy panoramic views of Calvi har-
bour from this quayside restaurant. There

Fresh fish in Cannes

Salade niçoise

are Corsican specialities such as *brucciu* cheese alongside more cosmopolitan choices. Closed Jan–Mar. €€–€€€

A Cantina di L'Orriu
5 cours Napoléon, 20137 Porto Vecchio
Tel: 04 95 70 26 21

Cosy old town restaurant with an open fireplace for winter, and pretty terrace for summer. Corsican favourites on the menu include stuffed aubergines, home-made ravioli and local wines. Closed Jan–Feb. €€

Aux Coquillages de Diana
Etang de Diane, 20270 Aléria
Tel: 04 95 57 04 55
www.auxcoquillagesdediana.fr
A floating restaurant on the lake of Aléria on Corsica's east coast, which is the source of the menu's oysters, mussels and fish. Great terrace with views over oyster beds. Closed evening Sun–Thur Oct–May, and all Jan. €€

U Rasaghiu
Port de Plaisance, 20130 Cargèse
Tel: 04 95 26 48 60
Unfussy quayside restaurant in the harbour of Cargèse, with a terrace for enjoying grilled seafood and pizzas, and live Corsican music on summer nights. Closed Nov–Mar. €–€€

NIGHTLIFE AND ENTERTAINMENT

Famed for its casinos and events like the Cannes Film Festival, the Côte d'Azur has both prestigious cultural venues and its own glitzy, expensive nightlife style.

Casino Barrière de Cannes – La Croisette
1 espace Lucien Barrière, 06406 Cannes
Tel: 04 92 98 78 00
www.lucienbarriere.com
Mix with the stars, or just see if you can spot them. Passport necessary for entry.

Casino de Monte Carlo
Place du Casino, MC 98000 Monaco
Tel: (00 377) 98 06 21 21
www.montecarlocasinos.com
Dress smartly to make the most of the world's most famous casino, one of five in the tiny principality.

Les Caves du Roy
Hôtel Byblos, avenue Paul Signac,
83990 St-Tropez

Tel: 04 94 97 16 02
www.lescavesduroy.com
This celebrity-heavy nightclub is the epitome of expensive cool on the Riviera.

Opéra de Monte Carlo
Place du Casino, MC 98007 Monaco
Tel: (00 377) 98 06 28 28
www.opera.mc
Renowned for its glittering productions.

Opéra de Nice
4–6 rue Saint-François-de-Paule,
06300 Nice
Tel: 04 92 17 40 00
www.opera-nice.org
The building has a colonnaded marble facade and is an elegant venue for opera, dance and symphony concerts.

SPORTS AND ACTIVITIES

The Mediterranean coast and Corsica are naturally meccas for all kinds of watersports, and the Southern Alps and the mountains of Provence contain wonderful locations for hiking, climbing and river-rafting. For more on riding and exploration in the Camargue, and hiking inland from the Riviera, see *Exploring the landscape, p.32, 34*; for more on sailing and windsurfing, diving and snorkelling, and rafting and kayaking in the Gorges du Verdon, see *On the water, p.59*.

Algajola Sport et Nature
20220 Algajola, Corsica
Tel: 04 95 44 08 32
www.algajola-sportetnature.com
Offers diving, water-skiing, windsurfing, kayaking and mountain biking, from a beach near Calvi.

Côté Plongée
Plage du Graillon, boulevard Maréchal Juin, 06600 Cap d'Antibes
Tel: 06 72 74 34 94
www.cote.plongee.com
Full-service dive centre in Antibes with English-speaking dive masters.

Tackling rock faces in the Gorges du Verdon

Les Lézards des Baous
23 rue du Château, 06640 Saint-Jeannet
Tel: 04 93 24 97 41
www.lezardsdesbaous.fr

Has expert rock climbing, mountain hiking and canyoning guides, based near St-Paul-de-Vence.

TOURS

Tourist offices provide a variety of local tours, particularly Avignon (www.avignon-tourisme.com) and Aix-en-Provence (www.aixenprovencetourism.com), which offers excellent information on Cézanne-related sites (see *On the artists' trail, p.38–9*). For more on vineyard visiting, see *Foods and Wines of France, p.29*.

Tours in Provence
Tel: 06 24 19 29 91
www.tours-in-provence.com
Made-to-measure tours to all the region's main attractions, led by a Provençal local fluent in English and Spanish.

Travel Provence
www.travel-provence.com
Australians Jim Llewellyn and Robbi Zeck provide a range of small-group trips

focusing on different themes – cuisine, the lavender fields, Van Gogh, the 'Heart of Provence' and more. Accommodation is provided in St-Rémy-de-Provence or Aix.

Le Vin à la Bouche
33 Grande Rue, 84550 Mornas
Tel: 04 90 46 90 80
www.levinalabouche.com
Individual wine tours and tastings in the southern Rhône and Provence.

FESTIVALS AND EVENTS

Annual events on the coast range from the very traditional to the athletic and the ultra-glamorous.

January–May
Carnaval de Nice
Nice
www.nicecarnaval.com
Late Jan or Feb–Mar
France's longest and most extravagant carnival celebrations.

Mondial du Vent
Port Leucate, north of Perpignan
www.mondialduvent.com
Late Apr
A celebration of windsurfing, kitesurfing and extreme sports spanning several days.

Festival de Cannes
Cannes
www.festival-cannes.com
Mid-May
Cannes's legendary film festival attracts the entire movie world, as well as celeb-spotters.

Pèlerinage des Gitans
Stes-Maries-de-la-Mer
www.camargue.fr
24–6 May
Twice a year (also 16–17 Oct) Romanies from across Europe converge on the Camargue for pilgrimages to the sea, in elaborate processions.

July–August
Chorégies d'Orange
Théâtre Antique, Orange
www.choregies.asso.fr
July–early Aug
France's oldest summer arts festival, held since 1860, is a lovely event which takes over Orange's Roman Amphitheatre for a programme of symphony concerts and opera, mainly Italian favourites by Verdi, Rossini and Puccini.

Festival d'Avignon
Avignon
www.festival-avignon.com
July
France's most important performing arts festival. The Palais des Papes is the main venue.

Festival Pablo Casals
Prades, Roussillon
www.prades-festival-casals.com
late July–early Aug
A beautiful chamber music festival, held in the Romanesque churches of Roussillon.

Listings

Kitesurfing at Mondial du Vent

Accommodation

There is a wide choice of places to stay in France, from luxury city hotels, rural châteaux and budget hotel chains on the outskirts of towns to campsites *au naturel*, farm stays and self-catering gîtes. In most of the country peak seasons are July, August, Easter and Christmas, when it's advisable to book in advance. However, some establishments may close in August in Paris, the big cities and many ski resorts.

HOTELS

Every comfort grade is offered by hotel groups such as Accor (www.accor.com) and Louvre (www.louvrehotels.com): upscale luxury and boutique hotels; reliable, good-value mid-range hotels, often good for children (Novotel); motel-like Campanile hotels; apartment hotels and the bargain-basement minimalist hotels. Very upmarket is the Relais et Châteaux (www.relais chateaux.com) group of luxury hotels, many with gourmet restaurants, and the Relais du Silence (www.relaisdu silence.com), offering high-end country-house hotels.

Independent, family-run, small hotels belong to the Logis group (www.logishotels.com). They guarantee a level of individuality the chains cannot. With their own grading system, they maintain high standards at very reasonable prices, and most have restaurants offering local cuisine.

All hotels in France carry national star ratings, from 1 to 5, set down by the government, but these can be

very deceptive, since they are based on a checklist of facilities rather than charm, individuality or overall quality of service.

Hotel prices are charged per room, not usually including breakfast. Many traditional hotels also have restaurants, and offer half-board (*demi-pension*) or full board (*pension complète*), as well as room-only bookings.

Hotel chains have their own central reservation facilities with special

The seafront Hôtel Normand in Yport

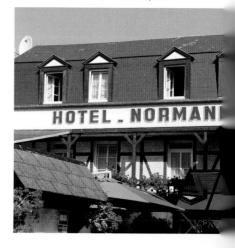

offers online. Lists of hotels for each area are provided in brochures and online by French tourist offices abroad and (more comprehensively) by regional, *département* and city tourist offices in France.

BUDGET ACCOMMODATION

The major hotel groups have budget brands such as Etap and Formule 1 (Accor) and Première Classe (Louvre Hotels), which are usually located on the outskirts of a town on the main road or industrial estate but include en suite bathrooms and Wifi. They are very practical for stop-offs en route to a holiday destination or for business trips. Prices start at around €25, and rooms can often sleep three or more. Many have special offers on their websites.

Holders of accredited Youth Hostel cards can stay in French hostels run by the Fédération Unie des Auberges de Jeunesse (FUAJ; tel: 01 44 89 87 27; www.fuaj.org), or the smaller Ligue Française pour les Auberges de Jeunesse (LFAJ; tel: 01 44 16 78 78; www.auberges-de-jeunesse.com). Expect to pay around €20 per night, or €25–35 in central Paris, sharing a room.

The British Youth Hostel Association (YHA; tel: 0800 0191 700; www.yha.org.uk) provides information on hostels around the world and Youth Hostel cards. In the US, apply to Hostelling International-USA (tel: 301 495 1240; www.hiusa.org).

Gîtes d'etapes offer hostel accommodation in country areas, particularly in national parks, and are popular with ramblers, climbers and horse riders.

De luxe room at Le Choiseul, the Loire

Prices are similar to youth hostels. For information and reservations, contact Gîtes de France *(see below).*

OTHER ACCOMMODATION

There is a broad range of bed-and-breakfasts, or *chambres d'hôtes,* across France, from simple rooms on farms to magnificent old manor houses, elegant townhouses and châteaux. Some, especially in the country, offer evening meals. Prices are usually lower than for comparable hotels in the same area.

Nearly all *chambres d'hôtes* are registered with one of three organisations: Gîtes de France (tel: 01 49 70 75 75; www.gites-de-france.com) takes bookings for rural accommodation; Clévacances (tel: 05 61 13 55 66; www.clevacances.com) covers rural, coastal and urban areas; Fleurs de Soleil (tel: 08 26 62 03 22; www.fleursdesoleil.fr.) is a small

Travelling by camper van

of accommodation and can usually arrange bookings. They should be made well ahead for the July–August season, when the best *gîtes* are highly prized. Bookings can be made through all the websites above.

CAMPING

There is a good choice of campsites in France, many near lakes or rivers and the coast. Regional and local tourist offices produce lists of all recognised sites welcoming camper vans and caravans as well as tents, with details of star ratings and facilities. As with other accommodation, book ahead for the high season. The *Michelin Green Guide – Camping/Caravanning France* is very informative and also lists sites with facilities for the disabled.

Packaged camping holidays are convenient for families, as all the camping paraphernalia is provided; mobile (trailer) homes are also available. Many sites offer facilities for sports such as windsurfing, kids' clubs and other activities for children. The campsites along the Mediterranean coast are tightly packed, so if you prefer peace and quiet, choose an *aire naturelle de camping* – grounds where facilities are absolutely minimal and have prices to match. The Fédération Française de Camping et Caravaning guide (FFCC; tel: 01 42 72 84 08; www.ffcc.fr) lists over 10,000 sites nationwide in French. Contact the Camping and Caravanning Club in the UK (tel: 0845 130 7632; www.campingandcaravanning club.co.uk) or the Caravan Club (tel: 01342 326 944; www.caravanclub.co.uk).

association that only handles *gîtes de charme*. In most areas, the more attractive *chambres d'hôtes* will probably cost around €60 or more in mid-season for a double room.

France has an excellent supply of self-catering holiday cottages *(gîtes)*, regulated and handled by the same organisations as B&Bs *(see above)*. The properties range from very simple farm cottages to grand manor houses and châteaux.

Farm stays (www.bienvenue-a-la-ferme.com) are becoming a popular form of accommodation with farmers looking to increase their income, either by offering rooms or a converted outbuilding from around €150 (low season) to €390 (high) a week. Holidaying on one of the many inland waterways is a wonderful way to see France *(see p.58)*; expect to pay from €850–1,650 a week for a 10m (30ft) cruiser sleeping four comfortably.

Regional, *département* and local tourist offices have lists of all types

Transport

GETTING TO FRANCE
By air

Paris has two airports: **Roissy-Charles de Gaulle (CDG)**, 23km (15 miles) northeast of the city, which handles all long-haul and most international flights; **Orly (ORY)**, 14km (9 miles) south of the centre, which handles French domestic and some short-haul international flights. For information on both airports tel: 3950 (or if calling from outside France +33 1 70 36 39 50; www.aeroportsdeparis.fr). Other principal international airports are at Lyon *(see p.165)*, Bordeaux *(see box p.193)*, Marseille *(see p.221)* and Nice (tel: 08 20 42 33 33; www.nice. aeroport.fr), but international flights go to many other French airports.

From the UK, the following have regular flights to France: **Air France** (www.airfrance.com); **bmi** (www.fly bmi.com); **Bmibaby** (www.bmibaby. com); **British Airways** (www.british airways.com); **easyJet** (www.easyjet. com); **Jet2** (www.jet2.com); **Ryanair** (www.ryanair.com).

Travellers from North America can obtain direct flights to Paris and major destinations in France, such as Nice and Lyon, via Air France and most national airlines. American Airlines, United Airlines and Delta also fly to France. Delta has a daily flight to Nice from New York.

By sea

Several ferry services operate between the UK, the Republic of Ireland, the Channel Islands and France with several crossings a day, or by night for the longer stretches. Most carry foot passengers as well as cars. Prices change by season, time of day and from weekdays to weekends. Dover–Calais and Dover–Boulogne, parallel to the Channel Tunnel, are the busiest routes (1½–1¾ hours); Ramsgate–Boulogne and Ostend are new services, and Dover–Dunkirk takes a little longer but is cheaper. The western Channel routes (to Dieppe, Le Havre, Caen, Cherbourg, St-Malo or Roscoff) are more expensive, but the crossings are longer and very comfortable.

Brittany Ferries (UK tel: 0871 244 0744; France tel: 08 25 82 88 28; www.brittany-ferries.com) operates routes between Portsmouth and Caen, Cherbourg and St-Malo, Poole to Cherbourg, and Plymouth and Cork

Choose from numerous ferry routes across the English Channel

to Roscoff. Sailing times generally take 5–9 hours, but fast catamarans operate on the Cherbourg routes from April to October, taking 2–3 hours.

Condor Ferries (tel: 0845 609 1024; www.condorferries.co.uk) ply routes from Portsmouth–Cherbourg, and Poole and Weymouth to St-Malo via Guernsey and Jersey.

Euroferries (tel: 0844 414 5355; www.euroferries.co.uk) run high-speed catamaran ferries between Ramsgate and Boulogne four times a day (75 minutes). **Transeuropa Ferries** (tel: 01843 595 522; www. transeuropaferries.com) started a Ramsgate–Ostend service in 2011.

Norfolkline (tel: 0871 574 7235; www.norfolkline.com) runs from Dover–Dunkirk and Rosyth, Scotland, to Zeebrugge in Belgium, conveniently close to the French motorway network. The Dunkirk route (runs every 2 hours) often has some of the lowest prices.

P&O Ferries (UK tel: 0871 664 5645; France tel: 08 25 12 01 56; www. poferries.com) sails Dover–Calais with up to 23 trips a day, as well as overnight sailings Hull–Zeebrugge.

SeaFrance (UK tel: 0871 423 7119; France tel: 03 21 17 70 33; www.sea france.com) has 13 round trips a day Dover–Calais.

Transmanche Ferries/LD Lines (UK tel: 0844 576 8836; France tel: 08 25 30 43 04; www.transmancheferries. com) sail Newhaven–Dieppe and Portsmouth–Le Havre.

By rail

Around 20 **Eurostar** (UK tel: 08432 186 186; France tel: 08 92 35 35 39; www.eurostar.com) high-speed trains

Eurostar runs between London and Paris and London and Lille

run through the Channel Tunnel each day between London St Pancras station and the Gare du Nord in Paris, in 2 hours 15 minutes, with several going via Disneyland Paris Resort. Eurostar fares vary considerably by season and time of day, so check alternative times when booking.

Eurostar trains also stop at Lille, which is a hub of the French TGV high-speed rail network, with direct services to many parts of the country (see p.101). Tickets combining Eurostar and internal French trains can be booked through **Rail Europe** (tel: 08448 484 064; www.raileurope.co.uk).

By road

The **Eurotunnel** (UK tel: 08443 35 35 35; France tel: 08 10 63 03 04; www.eurotunnel.com) shuttle takes cars through the Channel Tunnel from Folkestone to Calais, 24 hours a day, all year round, taking 35 minutes. Eurotunnel and the ferry companies compete on fares, and they vary widely between peak and off-peak times. The tunnel connects with the M20 motorway in the UK, and the A16 in France.

Eurolines (UK tel: 08717 818 181; France tel: 08 92 89 90 91; www.euro lines.com) provides coach services throughout Europe. There are seven daily services between London Victoria coach station and Paris, with less frequent services to other French cities. This is one of the cheapest ways of reaching France, with a return fare to Paris from £39.

GETTING AROUND

France has a very efficient rail network operated by the SNCF (*Société Nationale des Chemins de Fer*), so internal flights are only of use for the furthest distances. City transport authorities have been setting up cycle networks to link up with existing public transport networks. Autoroutes connect the main towns and cities; they are mostly toll roads (*péage*), so remember to budget for them.

Where to go next in the Loire valley

Domestic flights

Air France (*see p.257*) operates the majority of flights within France, but faces stiff competition from the budget airlines that now fly from the UK to many provincial airports.

Ferries

Corsica Ferries (tel: +33 04 95 32 95 95; www.corsica-ferries.fr) operate crossings from Toulon and Nice to Corsica. **SNCM** (tel: 3260 if within France; www.sncm.fr) sails from Toulon, Marseille and Nice to Corsica (*see p.221*).

Trains

SNCF (tel: 3635; www.sncf.fr, www. voyages-sncf.fr) operates the TGV (*train à grande vitesse*) ultra-comfortable high-speed trains.

Intercités and Téoz trains are more standard express trains, and Corail Lunéa are long-distance sleeper trains. TER trains are regional services that stop at every station.

Tickets can be bought at all SNCF stations, by phone and online or through Rail Europe. You must always remember to validate your ticket before boarding at machines marked *compostez votre billet*.

Intercity coaches

Intercity bus services are not as efficient as rail but they are usually cheaper. **Eurolines** (*see above*) operate between cities in France. In the Provence-Alpes-Côte d'Azur region, **Ligne Express Régionale** (LER; tel: 08 21 20 22 03; www.info-ler.fr) operates an extensive network of coaches.

Cycling along the Canal de Nantes at Brest, which crosses Brittany

Cycling

Bicycles (*vélos*) are readily available for hire – ask at the local tourist office. Public bicycle services, such as Vélo'V in Lyon, are becoming popular in big towns and cities. Bicycles can be hired and dropped off at stations, at very low cost.

DRIVING

Driving on French roads is a pleasant experience as long as you avoid going south on summer weekends. HGVs are banned from motorways at weekends, so for the rest of the year, the weekends are best. The numbers of roads have changed since 2008, with most of the N roads (*Route Nationale*) now the responsibility of the *départements* they pass through, meaning they are now called D roads.

Road conditions

Road safety has improved since the government had a crackdown on speeding and drink-driving. Be aware on the autoroute that your speed can be calculated between toll booths. Most French motorways are toll roads (*autoroutes à péage*). Rates vary, but to get from Calais to Paris costs around €19 in tolls. Information, including a toll calculator, is provided in English on www.autoroutes.fr.

Non-motorway main roads are often quite empty; look out for green holiday route signs (*Bis*) indicating alternative routes (tel: 08 00 10 02 00 in French; www.bison-fute. equipement.gouv.fr).

Petrol is readily available on autoroutes and in towns, with supermarkets offering the cheapest prices. *Sans plomb* is unleaded petrol (gas), *gazole* or *gas-oil* is diesel fuel.

Regulations

Fines can be levied on the spot, and in some circumstances your driving licence can be confiscated if you are caught breaking the rules. Have your driving licence, car insurance, European vehicle recovery insurance, car registration document V5, European accident statement form and passport to hand in case the police stop you and ask for '*Vos papiers?*'.
• Drive on the right.
• Full or dipped **headlights** must be used in poor visibility and at night and are compulsory all the time for motorcycles.
• The use of **seat belts** (front and rear) in cars, and crash helmets on motorcycles is compulsory. Children under 10 are not permitted to ride in the front seat.
• The French **drink-driving limit** is 0.5mg alcohol per litre of blood.

• **Speed limits**: toll motorways 130kph (80mph); urban motorways and dual carriageways 110kph (68mph); outside towns 90kph (56mph). Built-up areas unless signed otherwise are 50kph (31mph). The limits are reduced by 10–20kph when wet.

• Carry a high-visibility jacket (not in the boot/trunk), and a red triangle to place at least 30m (100ft) behind the car in case of breakdown.

Motoring associations

In an emergency, call the police (tel: 17) or use the free emergency telephones sited every 2km (1¼ miles) on motorways. It is wise to have internationally valid breakdown insurance. The AA (tel: 0800 085 2753, 24-hour European Breakdown Helpline 00 800 88 77 66 55; www.theaa.com) and RAC (tel: 0800 015 6000; www.rac.co.uk) insurance companies arrange breakdown cover.

Vehicle hire

You can get better deals hiring a vehicle when booking your plane or train tickets than on arrival in France. The minimum age to hire a car is 21. Some firms will not rent to people under 26 or over 60. All the major car hire companies have offices in most major towns, usually at the railway station or airport.

ACCESSIBILITY

Great improvements have been made for wheelchair access to public buildings and the international blue scheme applies for parking, so ensure you have all the

Approximate driving times	
Calais to Paris	3 hrs
Lille to Paris	2 hrs 13 mins
Bordeaux to Paris	5 hrs 30 mins
Lyon to Paris	4 hrs 15 mins
Marseille to Paris	7 hrs

documentation with you. Check out www.bluebadgeparking.com for designated parking spaces worldwide.

The French tourist office publishes a list of hotels with accessibility, but check directly for specific facilities. *Michelin Red Guide France* hotel guide and *Michelin Green Guide – Camping/Caravanning France* both include symbols for accessible accommodation. **Access Project** (39 Bradley Gardens, West Ealing, London W13 8HE; www.accessinparis.org) produces a free guide called *Access in Paris*, while **Tourism for All** (tel: 0845 124 9971; www.tourismforall.org.uk) provides comprehensive travel information.

Gridlock – if possible, avoid driving south on summer weekends

Health and safety

The urban *police municipale*

The standard of medical care in the French state health service (*Sécurité Sociale*) is among the best in the world. However, the main difference between the UK's National Health Service and the French state system is that you pay for any healthcare and drugs up front and then claim the costs back – sometimes all of it or at least 70 percent. To qualify for this, you must be an EU national in possession of a European Health Insurance Card (EHIC). You can apply free for an EHIC via the post office, by phone or online through the NHS (tel: 0845 606 2030; www.ehic.org.uk). The EHIC comes with a booklet outlining the procedures to be followed in each country.

To qualify for reimbursement of medical costs through the EHIC, when requiring medical treatment in France, you must only use the state health system, not private, and if possible present your card immediately. The EHIC will be fine for most situations and initial emergency care, but be aware that it does not cover you against all eventualities – notably the cost of repatriation in the event of a serious injury – or all of the costs, so it is important to take out private travel insurance as well.

To reclaim the cost of medical expenses, you must retain the *feuille de soins* or treatment form from the doctor or hospital, along with stickers from the packets of prescription drugs. Follow the instructions given with your EHIC to reclaim about 80 percent of the costs from the local health service office – Caisse Primaire d'Assurance Maladie (CPAM) – where you are staying, before you return home. Contact the Centre des Liaisons Européennes et Internationales de Sécurité Sociale (CLEISS; tel: 01 45 26 33 41; www.cleiss.fr) if you need further help. This can take time, so if it's not possible to be reimbursed before you leave, contact the Department for Work & Pensions (UK tel: 0191 218 1999) on your return.

If you see a doctor, expect to pay between €21–25 for a simple consultation, plus charges for any medicines.

If you have a medical emergency, there are hospitals with general casualty/emergency departments (*urgences*) in all cities and towns, or call the SAMU ambulance service *(see right)*. Consulates (and often hotels) can advise on English-speaking doctors in each area *(see fact boxes at the beginning of chapters for hospitals in your area)*.

Visitors from outside the EU should have full private travel and medical insurance, and if they have a medical emergency can use either private or public facilities, keep the same documentation as EU citizens *(see left)*, and then claim back on their insurance. IAMAT (USA, tel: 1-716-754 4883; Canada, tel: 1-416-652 0137; www.iamat.org) is a specialised travel health service that provides insurance and a directory of English-speaking doctors around the world.

Pharmacies are plentiful in French towns, and identified by a green cross sign that is lit up at night. French pharmacists have extensive training, and for minor ailments, bites and so on it will be easier to consult a pharmacist before looking for a doctor. Outside of normal shop hours and on Sundays, a card in the window of each

pharmacy will give the address of the nearest duty pharmacy *(pharmacie de garde)* staying open.

CRIME

Keep items of value in the hotel safe. Always lock your car and put valuables in the boot. You should have comprehensive travel insurance covering all your possessions against loss or theft. Watch your wallet in crowded public places. Any loss or theft should be reported immediately to the nearest police station *(commissariat de police)*, run by blue-uniformed *police municipale* in urban areas, or the *gendarmerie*, the force in charge of rural policing. If your passport has been lost or stolen, notify your embassy or consulate immediately.

EMBASSIES AND CONSULATES

Australia: 4 rue Jean Rey, 75724 Paris; tel: 01 40 59 33 00; www.france. embassy.gov.au
Canada: 35 avenue Montaigne, 75008 Paris; tel: 01 44 43 29 00; www.canada international.gc.ca/france
UK: 18bis rue d'Anjou, 75008 Paris; tel: 01 44 51 31 00; http://ukinfrance. fco.gov.uk
US: 2 avenue Gabriel, 75382 Paris; tel: 01 43 12 22 22; http://france.us embassy.gov

Pharmacy sign in Boulogne old town

Money and budgeting

Leaving an additional tip is suggested if you're happy with the service

CURRENCY

France's currency is the euro (€), which is available in 500, 200, 100, 50, 20, 10 and 5 euro notes, and 2 euro, 1 euro, 50 cent, 20 cent, 10 cent, 5 cent, 2 cent and 1 cent coins. There are 100 cents to one euro. At the time of going to press, exchange rates were: €1 = 88p or $1.44. If you enter or leave France with currency worth €10,000 or more, you must declare it.

CASH AND CARDS

Major credit and debit cards such as Visa, MasterCard and Maestro are widely accepted in France. Using your card in an ATM is the easiest way to exchange currency but can be expensive, so it is best to shop around before you go. At one time it was more economical to use a debit card to withdraw money from an ATM, but now it's best to find a credit card with a good deal. Banks and credit card companies keep changing their charging policies, so if you were getting a good deal on your previous holiday, check again. Some charge a percentage of the amount as well as a fee. Alternatively, you could get a prepaid credit card in which you download your holiday money onto it before you leave, but there may still be a charge at the ATM.

In French, cards are called *cartes bancaires*; a sign showing CB means that credit cards are accepted. There are automatic machines for paying at autoroute tolls and at many fuel stations but they don't always accept foreign cards, so make sure you have alternative means of paying. It is wise to notify your bank or other card issuer before you use a card abroad to prevent it being security blocked.

Cards in France use a chip-and-pin system exactly like that in the UK (the French for PIN is *code personnel*). When paying by card you may also be asked to show additional ID. If you have a US or Canadian card that is still not chip-and-pin coded you will have to ask that your card is swiped. Most waiters and shop staff, especially in Paris, are used to this.

When withdrawing currency from a Bureau de Change be aware that there is a cash withdrawal fee when paying with a credit card and some debit cards; you will need to produce your passport when changing money. Avoid buying currency at airports and ferry terminals, as they give the worst rates; you can get a better rate by pre-ordering up to four hours beforehand. Hotels always charge high commissions.

Banks have exchange (*change*) counters and in cities are usually open Monday to Friday 10am–5pm. Throughout the rest of France banks open Tuesday to Saturday 10am–1pm, 3–5pm, closing earlier the day before a public holiday.

Travellers' cheques are not so common now that ATMs are so widespread. A few hotels will accept them as payment, but not all banks will cash them. In remote rural areas you may have difficulty finding anywhere to cash travellers' cheques.

TIPPING

Most restaurant bills include a service charge (*service compris*). It is common to leave a small additional tip for the

A classic Parisian brasserie calls for waiters in traditional livery

waiter if the service has been particularly good. It is customary to tip taxi drivers 10 percent and to tip hotel chambermaids €1.50 per day.

TAX

There are two rates of tax, or TVA, on sales and services – the standard rate at 19.5 percent and reduced rate at 5.5 percent – which are always included at the appropriate rate in the price shown. A Tourism Tax is payable on accommodation with rates set by the local authority and can be between €0.20 and €1.50 a day per person, depending on the type of accommodation.

BUDGETING FOR YOUR TRIP

France is no cheaper than other Western countries, but a holiday on a low budget is possible with plenty of research. Often the earlier you book flights the better, although sometimes there may be last-minute deals available. A low-season economy return air fare from New York to Paris will cost around $950, and $1,200 in high season. If travelling first class, expect to pay around $16,000 at any time. Economy air fares from London to Nice in high season will be from £120 and in low season £80. A first-class fare will be £800.

For a budget, backpacker-style holiday you will need to set aside around €600 (£525/$850) per person per week. A standard family holiday for four will cost around €1,990 (£1,750/$2,845) per week. A luxury, no-expense-spared break can cost over €20,000 (£17,500/$28,500) per person per week.

Money and budgeting

Taking the tram is the most popular and easiest way to travel around Strasbourg

MONEY-SAVING TIPS

In cities, use public transport and buy a *carnet* (book) of tickets which can be shared around the family. In Paris, a *Paris Visite* card will cover public transport and some attractions. Museums around the country are sometimes free on the first Sunday of the month.

If breakfast is not included at your hotel, eat at a cheaper café instead. Eat your main meal at midday, as almost all restaurants serve a *menu du jour* at midday on weekdays, which is cheaper than ordering à la carte. Chinese and Vietnamese restaurants also offer particularly good lunchtime deals.

Budgeting costs

Top-class/boutique hotel: €850–1,480 for a double room per night
Standard-class hotel: €85–195 for a double room
Bed & breakfast: €50–70 for a double
Motel: €35–65 for a double
Youth hostel: €16–25 per person
Motor camp: €19–36 per caravan
Campsite: €22–42 per tent

Domestic flight: €68–282 Paris to Marseille
Intercity coach ticket: €30.80 Nice to Aix-en-Provence
Intercity train ticket: €45–66 Paris to Lyon
Car hire: €30 per day
Petrol: €1.60 a litre
10-minute taxi ride: €12–15 (in a city such as Bordeaux)
Airport shuttle bus: €5–10
Short bus ride: €1.70 (Paris)
One-day travel pass: €6.10 (Paris)

Breakfast: €6–12
Lunch in a café: €13–20
Coffee/tea in a café: €2.50–6
Menu (2 courses), budget restaurant: €13–20
Menu (3 courses) moderate restaurant: €20–35
Menu (3 courses) expensive restaurant: €35–80
Bottle of wine in a restaurant: €15–20
Beer in a pub: €3.50–8

Museum admission: €2–11
Day trip to Parc Astérix: €60 (adult), €46 (child) day pass and Parc Astérix Shuttle from the Louvre in Paris
Entry to Zoo de la Palmyre, Royan: €15 (adult), €11 (child)
Abbaye de Mont St-Michel: €9
Château de Chambord: €9.50
Theatre/concert ticket: Paris Lido dinner and show €150 per person
Shopping item: Camembert cheese €6

Responsible travel

GETTING THERE

It is greener to travel to Paris from the UK by train than plane. A family of four flying from London to Paris leaves a carbon footprint of 0.4 metric tonnes of CO_2, whereas going by train leaves a footprint of 0.01 metric tonnes. To offset the amount left by the flight would cost around £3. However, an even greener way to get to France would be as a foot passenger on the ferry.

A return flight for a family of four from New York would leave a carbon footprint of 4.25 metric tonnes of CO_2. To offset this would cost $41.65. Carbon Footprint (www.carbonfoot print.com), Clear (www.clear-offset. com and Terrapass (www.terrapass. com) have suggestions for ways to offset, including reforestation.

Travelling without the carbon emissions

ECOTOURISM

For those with a taste for adventure and who are happy to rough it, taking a bicycle and tent across the Channel to France is the way to leave the least impact on the environment. Campsites are dotted around the countryside, many at farms *(see p.256)*, but for the less hardy many travel companies offer cycling and walking holidays with baggage transfers to hotels along the route.

Many of the GR hiking paths *(see p.30)* through mountainous areas, such as the GR5 in the Alps, have basic eco-friendly refuges (communal lodgings) where you bunk down with other walkers and enjoy home-cooked food. For an eco-friendly self-catering holiday in a national park, the WWF has sanctioned *gîtes* as Gîtes Pandas (www.gites-pandas.fr) if they meet certain green criteria. Canal boat holidays *(see p.58)*, although fuel-driven, are a slow way of experiencing the country.

THINGS TO AVOID

Wherever you find beautiful landscapes that provide adventurous activities, or monuments and historic attractions, you will also find people. To reduce your environmental impact, use your common sense (see the Tourisme-Responsible section of the French tourist board's website www.uk.france guide.com). Keeping to marked footpaths, not leaving litter, and avoiding using air conditioning and plastic bags are just some of the general rules that help protect the environment.

Family holidays

A traditional way to keep the kids happy

PRACTICALITIES

All necessities are catered for, with baby food and nappies widely available in supermarkets and pharmacies. On the autoroutes and other public places most facilities with toilets have nappy-changing areas. If you are hiring a car, the rental company usually supplies car seats for an extra fee, or you can bring your own if the airline allows. It's best to bring your own buggy as you will need it at the airport, but if you are going to Disneyland Resort Paris via Eurostar you can hire them there.

ACCOMMODATION

Camping holidays are a great success with young children and parents alike, especially ones that have the tents and equipment already set up, with a swimming pool and Kids' Club, ensuring plenty of new friends.

The best ones do get booked up early though. Many self-catering *gîtes* have a swimming pool, and websites such as www.cheznous.com and www.owners direct.co.uk give details of how child-friendly the accommodation is.

Most hotels, especially the chains, have family rooms, and another bed or cot (*lit bébé*) can often be provided for a small charge, but check availability when booking.

FOOD AND DRINK

In France generally, children are treated as individuals not nuisances. It is pleasant to be able to take them out for a meal (even in the evening) without heads being turned in horror. French children, though, accustomed to eating out from an early age, are on the whole well behaved in restaurants.

Many restaurants provide high chairs and offer a children's menu; if not, they will often split a *prix-fixe* menu between two children. Crêperies – universal in Brittany, not hard to find elsewhere – are very popular with children. There are also plenty of fast-food outlets in towns and cities, often on the outskirts.

ATTRACTIONS AND ACTIVITIES

In Paris the Jardin d'Acclimatation in the Bois de Boulogne is an extensive amusement park featuring a menagerie, Explorodome museum, a mini-golf course, pony rides, a house of mirrors and a puppet theatre. Lyon has a similar but larger park – Parc Tête d'Or – with a zoo and go-karting circuit. Children can discover science through play at Parc de la Villette, and for those more artistically inclined the Centre Pompidou *(see p.68)* offers interactive expositions and workshops for children.

Disneyland Resort Paris, east of the capital, is the region's best-known attraction, drawing millions of visitors each year, and Parc Astérix (closed winter) to the north of Paris has stomach-churning rides and live shows. There are also the popular Walibi Parks, one situated in the Rhône-Alps region between Lyon and Chambéry, and the other near Agen in the Aquitaine region.

In the centre of France, near Poit-iers, the leisure park Futuroscope *(see p.155)* explores the moving image and high-tech visual effects in a futuristic architectural environment. Uncover the mechanics of volcanoes through games and hands-on activities at the state-of-the-art Vulcania centre *(see p.178)* in the Auvergne region.

In the summer, water parks are great fun for kids. Aqualand is a chain with parks at St-Cyprien, Port Leucate, Cap d'Agde, St Cyr-sur-Mer, Ste-Maxime and Fréjus. Outdoor adventure parks offer thrills for those who enjoy swinging from tree to tree attached to a cable; Via Ferrata has several in France.

Aquariums are fun whatever the weather, and the Aquarium de Paris has recently been restored and now houses 15,000 fish and four cinemas. Océanopolis at Brest and the Grand Aquarium in St-Malo take you on a voyage from warm seas to icy waters; Cité de la Mer in Cherbourg tells the story of man's relationship with the ocean and has the deepest aquarium in Europe, and at Boulogne-sur-Mer you can discover the many facets of marine life at the impressive Nausicaa sea life centre *(see p.101)*.

Zoos, themed animal parks, orni-thological parks and botanical gar-dens are appreciated by children and addresses can be obtained from local tourist offices.

Family holidays

Dizzyingly high rollercoaster ride at Parc Astérix near Paris

SETTING THE SCENE

History

BEGINNINGS

The earliest-known inhabitants of France can be traced back 1.8 million years thanks to the discovery of their stone tools in the Haute-Loire. In the Ardèche, man was making the earliest-known cave paintings near Vallon-Pont-d'Arc perhaps 32,000 years ago, while hunter-gatherers were becoming sedentary around 4000 BC, as evidenced by the megalithic sites in Brittany. Celtic tribes from Eastern Europe came looking for greener pastures in the areas that are now Franche-Comté, Alsace and Burgundy around 1000 BC.

At the same time, migrants from the Mediterranean countries were trickling into the south. The first recorded settlement was the trading post set up by Phocaean Greeks from Asia Minor at Massalia (Marseilles) *c.* 600 BC. But the Greeks developed few contacts with the interior, Gaul, beyond a little commerce, and when their position was threatened by Ligurian pirates and warlike tribes, the merchants of Marseille called on Rome for help.

FROM GAUL TO FRANCE

In 125 BC, the Romans conquered the 'Gallic barbarians' in the south and set up a fortress at Aquae Sextiae (Aix-en-Provence). From here they created Provincia (now Provence), from the Alps to the Pyrénées, to guarantee communications between Italy and Spain. When this province was endangered by fresh attacks, Julius Caesar took charge, conquering almost the whole of Gaul by 50 BC.

Christianity was introduced into Gaul in the 1st century AD and became the empire's official religion in the 4th century, cementing national solidarity. Clovis, leader of the Germanic Franks, defeated the last Gallo-Roman king in 486 and won the allegiance of most Gallo-Romans by converting to Christianity.

By around 800, the Frankish ruler Charlemagne had established an empire covering the whole of modern France, western Germany and northern Italy. However, the Franks' realm eventually broke up into fiefdoms, precursors of what are now the country's main provinces. Hugues Capet, count of Paris, was declared the first king of France in 987.

Charlemagne holding a model of Aachen Cathedral in Germany, where he is buried

THE MIDDLE AGES

France took the lead in the Crusades against the 'infidels' in Palestine. Louis IX (1214–70) was such a pious crusader he was made Saint Louis on his return. From 1309 to 1377, Avignon was the papal seat.

In 1066 William of Normandy successfully invaded England and became William the Conqueror. For the next 400 years, English and French monarchs fought over the sovereignty of various parts of France. During the Hundred Years War (1337–1453), a pious teenager named Jeanne d'Arc (Joan of Arc) was captured and burnt at the stake by the English in Rouen; her martyrdom stirred sufficient national pride eventually to oust the English from France.

THE ANCIEN REGIME

Absolute power was the dominant feature of what post-Revolutionary France called the *ancien régime*. François I (1515–47) strengthened central administration and abandoned an initially tolerant policy toward Protestants.

The 16th-century conflicts between Catholics and Protestants came to a head on 24 August 1572 with the St Bartholomew's Day Massacre in Paris, when 2,000 Protestants were killed. The conciliatory policies that emerged after the bloodshed brought the Protestant Henri IV (1589–1610) to the throne, but only after he promised to convert to Catholicism. The Edict of Nantes was signed in 1598 to protect Protestants.

In 1624, during the reign of Louis XIII (1601–43), Cardinal Richelieu took charge as prime minister. His main achievement was the centralisation of royal power, laying the foundations for the strong sense of national identity that has characterised France ever since.

THE SUN KING

When he began his rule at the age of 23, Louis XIV (1638–1715) adopted the emblem of the sun – he wasn't going to be outshone by anyone. His counsellors were wholly subservient and he never called upon the parliamentary assembly of the *états généraux*; he moved his court to Versailles. To enhance his glory, Louis turned to foreign conquest and developed the largest army in Europe. These ventures left France's once-thriving economy in ruins.

At home, his authoritarian rule required a brutal police force. Taxes soared to pay for his wars, and a growing number of peasants were pressganged into his armies. When Louis revoked the Edict of Nantes, the Protestant Huguenots – many of them highly skilled workers – fled abroad.

The Sun King died in 1715 and was succeeded by his five-year-old great-grandson, Louis XV (1710–74). However, government was in the hands of the late king's brother, Philippe d'Orléans.

THE REVOLUTION

Louis XVI (1754–93), grandson of Louis XV, was in trouble. The aristocracy and high clergy wanted to protect their privileges, the bourgeoisie longed for reforms that would give them greater opportunity, while peasants were no longer prepared to

Portrait of Napoleon

bear the burden of feudal extortion.

The *états généraux* convened for the first time in 175 years. Liberal reformers wanted a constitutional monarchy, not a republic. But on 14 July 1789, centuries of frustration and rage culminated in the storming of the Bastille – the prison-fortress of Paris, a symbol of royal power.

A National Assembly voted a charter for liberty and equality, the Declaration of the Rights of Man and of the Citizen. The aristocracy's feudal rights were abolished, and the Church's massive land-holdings were confiscated and sold off. A Republic was declared in 1792 and Louis XVI was guillotined in 1793.

The Jacobin-led revolutionary committee ordered sweeping measures of economic and social reform, which were accompanied by a wave of mass executions.

NAPOLEON BONAPARTE

A new wave of executions decimated the Jacobins and their supporters.

People called for order, and the more moderate leaders of the Revolution turned for help to a Corsican soldier triumphantly campaigning against the Revolution's foreign enemies – Napoleon Bonaparte (1769–1821). He returned to Paris in 1795 to crush the royalists and four years later, at the age of 30, seized power.

As First Consul, he established the Banque de France, created state-run *lycées* (high schools), and gave the country its first national set of laws – the Code Napoléon. The supreme self-made man, Bonaparte crowned himself Emperor Napoleon I in 1804. He managed simultaneously to pursue foreign conquests in Germany and Austria and domestic reforms that included a modernised university, a police force and proper supplies of drinking water for Parisians.

But Bonaparte led France into a succession of wars, which ended with a disastrous expedition to Russia in 1812. Exiled to Elba, he returned to France briefly but was finally defeated at Waterloo by a European coalition in 1815.

THE SECOND REPUBLIC

At the end of the Napoleonic era, the monarchy was restored. The new king, Louis XVIII (1755–1824), tried at first to reconcile the restored monarchy with the reforms of the Revolution and Napoleon's empire. But his nobles were intent on revenge and terrorised the Jacobins and Bonapartists.

Louis's reactionary successor, his brother, Charles X, was interested only in renewing the traditions of the *ancien régime*. However, the middle classes were no longer prepared to tolerate the restraints on their freedom, nor the worsening condition of the economy. This led to the insurrection of July 1830, paving the way for the 'bourgeois monarchy' of Louis-Philippe (1773–1850).

This last king of France encouraged the country's exploitation of the Industrial Revolution, but the new factories created an urban working class clamouring for improvement of its miserable working and living conditions. The regime's repression led to a third revolution in 1848, with the Bonapartists, led by Napoleon's nephew, emerging triumphant. The Second Republic ended four years later when he staged a coup to become Emperor Napoleon III.

THE THIRD REPUBLIC

Defeat at the hands of the Germans in 1870 shattered the Second Empire. While the new Third Republic's government negotiated the terms of surrender, giving Alsace-Lorraine to

One of the worst battles of World War I

Germany, the workers' commune in Paris refused to give in. In March 1871 they took over Paris for 10 weeks but were eventually crushed by government troops.

France resumed its industrial progress and expanded its overseas empire. In 1882, republican statesman Jules Ferry enacted legislation that education should be secular, which has formed the basis of France's state education system ever since.

On the right, nationalist forces were motivated by a desire to hit back at Germany, who were indeed defeated during the ensuing Great War. However, France lost 1,350,000 men. In the 1919 Treaty of Versailles, France recovered Alsace, but the national economy was shattered and political divisions were more extreme than ever.

WAR AND PEACE

The French were unprepared for the German invasion across the Ardennes in May 1940. Marshal Philippe Pétain capitulated on behalf of the French on 16 June. Two days later, on BBC radio's French service from London, General de Gaulle appealed for national resistance.

Based in Vichy, the collaborative French government often proved more zealous than its German masters in suppressing civil liberties and drawing up anti-Jewish legislation. Deliverance came when the Allies landed in Normandy on D-Day (6 June 1944). De Gaulle took a major step towards rebuilding national self-confidence by insisting that French armed forces fight with the Americans and British to liberate the country.

President Nicolas Sarkozy

But the general hated the political squabbles of the new Fourth Republic and withdrew from public life. He returned in 1958 ostensibly to keep Algeria French but gave it independence in 1962. A new constitution placed the president above parliament, where he could pursue his own policies outside of party politics.

MAY 1968

In May 1968, a general feeling of malaise erupted into aggressive demonstrations against the Vietnam War, government control of the media and the stagnant values of the older generation. The tension increased when the students removed paving stones in the Latin Quarter, built barricades and occupied the Sorbonne. Joined by the workers of the left, the student demonstrations escalated into a national crisis. Shaken badly by these events and by his failing foreign and economic policy, de Gaulle relinquished power to his former prime minister, Georges Pompidou, in 1969.

THE PRESIDENTS

In the ensuing presidential election, Gaullist Valéry Giscard d'Estaing beat socialist François Mitterrand. Despite his right-wing tendencies, Giscard d'Estaing's seven-year presidency incorporated reforms desired by the left: less restrictive divorce laws, legalised abortion, widely available contraception and a voting age of 18.

In 1981 Mitterrand defeated Giscard d'Estaing, bringing the left to power for the first time under the Fifth Republic. However, Mitterrand advocated only limited nationalisation of French industry. As the longest-serving president in French history, he played a significant role on the world stage.

INTO THE 21ST CENTURY

By the end of the 20th century the French economy was improving and a 35-hour week had been introduced. Nevertheless, labour disputes and protests continued to disrupt French life.

The victory of the left in 1997 brought about a period of cohabitation between the right-wing president, Chirac, and the left-wing government of Lionel Jospin. This ended in 2002, when in the first round of the presidential election, a large turn-out for the National Front resulted in Jospin's resignation. Chirac was re-elected with over 80 percent of the vote as the electorate united against the far right. The 2007 presidential election saw the country vote for the tough modernisation policies of centre-right Nicolas Sarkozy; in a 2010 French poll, he was voted the most unpopular French president ever.

Historical landmarks

1.8 MILLION BC
Earliest-known inhabitants in Haute-Loire.

32000BC
Cave paintings in the Ardèche.

1000BC
Celts invade France from east.

125–121BC
Romans establish colony of Provincia
(Provence).

59–50BC
Julius Caesar conquers Gaul.

AD486
'Barbarians' end Roman control.

987
Hugues Capet, first king of France.

1066
Duke William of Normandy conquers
England.

1337–1453
Hundred Years War.

1431
Joan of Arc executed.

1572
St Bartholomew's Day massacre.

1624–42
Cardinal Richelieu governs for Louis XIII.

1682
Louis XIV moves court to Versailles.

1789
French Revolution. Fall of the Bastille.

1804
Bonaparte becomes Emperor Napoleon I.

1815
Napoleon defeated at Waterloo, Louis XVIII
restored to throne.

1830–48
'Bourgeois monarchy' of Louis-Philippe.

1848
Liberal Revolution overthrows monarchy.

1852
Napoleon III proclaimed emperor.

1870–1
Franco-Prussian War.

1914–18
World War I.

1939–45
World War II. Germany occupies France.

1944
Allies invade Normandy (6 June).

1945–6
De Gaulle heads the Fourth Republic's
first government.

1958–69
De Gaulle is first president of the new Fifth
Republic.

1968
Student rebels shake government.

1981
Mitterrand elected Fifth Republic's first
socialist president.

1995
Jacques Chirac elected president.

2002
The euro becomes official currency. Chirac
re-elected.

2007
Centre-right Nicolas Sarkozy is elected
president.

2011
France leads a UN coalition military
campaign against Libya.

Culture

France is the world's most visited country, and it's not difficult to see why. Aside from the contrasting landscapes and enviable way of life, for centuries France was a cultural beacon to the world. Under the absolutist *ancien régime*, during the 18th-century Enlightenment and in the wake of its revolutions, France sent out ideas and influences to sympathisers and admirers everywhere.

If you were anyone, you spoke French to distinguish you from the riff-raff; if you could afford it, you built yourself a château in the French style; and if you were a penniless artist or writer, you headed straight to Paris or the Côte d'Azur. These days, while France is having to adapt to the challenges of a competitive world, the country still ensures its culture is supported and developed.

SOCIETY
Geographical divisions

The population of France is almost 63 million, with nearly 13 million people living in the Paris area. It's not unusual to hear foreigners refer to Paris and France as the same thing, but it's almost as if Paris and the rest of France are two different countries.

Move away from the capital or any other of the major cities and things look very different: the landscape is generally rural and less industrialised and the population is scattered. People living in provincial towns see life differently from those in tiny farming villages or *banlieues* (out-of-town ghettoes). It must also be remembered that France is a composite of quasi-nationalistic regions: for example, an Alsatian living near the German border will have a different view of France from a Breton living on the Atlantic coast.

Age and class

Age divides the French. The older generations remember the wars. The young, on the other hand, have grown up with hypermarkets and the internet. In between are the middle-aged, some of whom took to the barricades in May 1968.

Class divisions are more complicated. The French think of themselves as a classless society after seeing off the monarchy, and in

Faire les bises – how many times you kiss each cheek depends on the region you're in

theory anyone can succeed whatever his/her background. Only one class needs to be singled out – the elite that keeps the country functioning; it recruits new talent through the *grandes écoles* (universities for high flyers). However, it's important to point out that the elite identifies its interest with that of the country as a whole and not its own 'class'.

Republican values

Underpinning 'Frenchness' are the republican values established by the Revolution. The outward symbols of these – the cockerel, Marianne, the *Marseillaise* and the portrait of the incumbent president on the wall of the town hall – may look ridiculous to an outsider, but they represent the deep and enduring slogans of liberty, equality and fraternity.

The exception

The *exception culturelle française* is a concept which underpins the country's idea of itself. This is the assumption that France is different, unique and has something vital to contribute to the world and that its culture must be preserved and promoted.

Language is an important part of the *exception* and the Académie Française, set up by Cardinal Richelieu in 1635, is its watchdog. The state imposes a quota of French pop music that must be played on the nation's radio stations, and it collects a levy from cinema tickets to subsidise film production. The Ministry of Foreign Affairs is charged with disseminating French culture as far as it can.

People are proud of their regional heritage; this bookseller is a Breton from Carnac

Culture

The state

The agreed starting point of French politics is that there is only one legitimate power in the land – the state – and that it exists for the good of all; it is seen as an institution for preserving and applying the values of the Republic. The French state provides its citizens with a high standard of living through systems of health, education and transport that generally work well. As a result, life expectancy is in the world's top 10. The price for this is a centrally and highly controlled state which demands obedience and conformity – France must work together or it may not work at all. In light of this, politicians are expected to avoid divisive policies and to keep the status quo; when President Sarkozy recently announced plans to reform pensions, millions of people took to the streets.

Outside the synagogue in the Marais, Paris, a predominantly Jewish area of the city

Assimilation

Its obsession with keeping the country together and moving in a single direction explains France's attitude to its immigrant communities. France is not and does not aspire to be a multicultural society; it is a melting pot and new arrivals are expected to fit in.

However, this ideal scenario has not always gone to plan, and many immigrants, living in the edge-of-town *banlieues,* have often felt marginalised and discriminated against; this has led to civil unrest, most notably in 2005 when riots spread throughout France following the shooting of two Arab youths by the police in Paris.

In 2010, France became the first country in the world to ban women from wearing the burkha in public, which was met by protests and defiance.

Ethnicity and religion

Officially there are no ethnic or religious minorities in France, just French people and foreign residents who have their own beliefs and notions of self-identity. The state has not kept data about the faith or racial origins of its citizens since 1872. To identify a minority, even in order to give it assistance, could be a way of branding it non-French and leaving it open to persecution.

Theoretically, France is a predominantly Catholic country: while 25 percent tell pollsters that they don't practise any religion and only 13 percent say they do, about 65 percent of the population claim to be Catholic. The country's second religion is Islam at 6 percent and growing, while Protestantism counts for 2 percent. France has the highest population in Europe of Muslims, Buddhists and Jews. However, in France, religion is expected to be inconspicuous and separate from the state, including schools.

The invasion of liberalism

French politicians have often presented the neoliberalism of the UK and the US as more of a threat to France's culture than the changing religious and ethnic composition of its society. Politicians of both right and left have generally agreed on the need of the interventionist state to do what is necessary to uphold the job security and living standards of the populace. Currently, 29 percent of the working population are employed by the public sector, and many more work for companies that supply it. The workers see their jobs as safe and do not see any benefit in changing the arrangement. But in the new economic reality, France must get used to a life less subsidised, which means less job security, working longer before retiring, fewer teachers and a more restricted range of free healthcare.

ART

French painters have been prominent in most of the important artistic movements since the 17th century. This was the golden age of European art and produced France's first great artist, Nicolas Poussin (1594–1665), who painted landscapes and pastorals. In the 18th century, Rococo flourished and Jean-Antoine Watteau (1684–1721) reflected the decorative tastes of the aristocracy. Jacques-Louis David (1748–1825) was the official artist of the Revolutionary government and revelled in patriotic themes.

It was after the Revolution, though, that Paris and France really took over at the forefront of Western art, a position they held until World War II. The high priest of Romanticism was Eugène Delacroix (1798–1863), whose

Monet's waterlilies at the Musée de l'Orangerie, Paris

Liberty Leading the People is widely considered the last successful allegory ever painted. After the 1848 Revolution, artists began to paint people, and the father of this Realism was Gustave Courbet (1819–77). His work anticipated that of the Impressionists such as Edouard Manet (1832–83), trusting his eyes rather than traditional ways of seeing, or Claude Monet (1840–1926), the master of light and colour, whose work was initially scorned.

Paul Cézanne (1839–1906) is widely regarded as 'the father of modern art'. Two major movements arrived in the early 20th century: Fauvism, led by Henri Matisse (1869–1954), which believed colour to be an emotional force, and Cubism, led by Georges Braque (1882–1963) and Picasso, which sought to flatten space. After the war, Yves Klein (1928–62) and Pierre Restany (1930–2003) created New Realism, often compared with Pop Art. Contemporary art has a high profile in France, with specialist museums in Paris, Lille, Metz, St-Etienne and Nice.

CINEMA

As the birthplace of cinema and the host of the world's most famous film festival (Cannes), France has long given movies a special place in its cultural life. The first 'film' was made by the Lumière brothers in Lyon in 1895. The 1930s were dominated by Jean Renoir, son of the Impressionist painter Pierre-Auguste, whose 1939 film *La Règle du Jeu* (*Rules of the Game*) is regarded by many critics as one of the best films ever made. After the war, more diverting entertainment came in the form of the silent comedy of Monsieur Hulot and then Brigitte Bardot, whose sex-kitten characters symbolised all that was desirable about France. In the 1960s, directors including Godard and Truffaut, making films with small crews using hand-held cameras, created the *Nouvelle Vague* (New Wave) genre.

Jean-Jacques Beineix and Luc Besson introduced the concept of *cinéma du look* in the 1980s, where style was as important as plot. Contemporary France has a strong cinema culture, with more films produced per head of the population than any other country thanks to government subsidies. In recent years, the fashion has been for films inspired by cartoon art (*Delicatessen, Amélie*), documentaries (*Etre et Avoir, Home*), gritty realism (*La Haine, Un Prophète*) and biopics (*La Môme, Gainsbourg*).

LITERATURE

France has a long tradition of literary excellence, starting in the 11th century with epic poems which told tales of heroic knights. Across the ages, French literature has had a number of roles and forms: in the 16th century, Rabelais's *Gargantua* (1535) expressed the author's feelings about the Renaissance, and Michel de Montaigne invented the personal essay style to explore humanism.

The golden age of French literature came in the 17th century, when some of France's greatest dramatists appeared: Racine, Corneille and Molière; Madame de Sévigné raised letter-writing to an art form, while Réné Descartes's *Discours de la Méthode*

(*Discourse on Method*, 1637) established the author as the first modern philosopher. In the 18th century, poetry was used to express the changes brought about by the recent social and political upheavals. The star of the 19th century was Honoré de Balzac, whose epic *Comédie Humaine* (*Human Comedy*, 1842–8) was the forerunner of Realism. In the 20th century, France gave the world Surrealism, existentialism and the 'Theatre of the Absurd'. Today, literature remains as important as ever – *Un Livre Un Jour* (*One Book One Day*) is one of the country's most popular daily television programmes. No wonder France has received more Nobel prizes for literature than any other country.

MUSIC

French music has come a long way since its 10th-century plainchants. Late 19th-century France gave the

The annual Fête de la Musique in June celebrates music of all kinds

world some of its greatest composers: Berlioz, Bizet, Debussy and Ravel. The popular music era started with the *chanson française* in 19th-century music halls and was sung by the likes of Edith Piaf and Charles Trenet in the 1930s, then Georges Brassens and Charles Aznavour in the 1950s.

Rock and roll arrived from the USA and made a star of Johnny Hallyday – 'the French Elvis'. The clever lyricist Serge Gainsbourg spanned a range of styles from the 1960s to 1980s, then, in the nineties, French House took the dance music world by storm. Hip-hop, coming out of the immigrant *banlieues*, and Raï, developed in Algeria and sung in Arabic, are popular today. France's regions, each with its own strong identity, have their folk music traditions: for example, Corsica is known for its polyphonic singing.

SPORT

Sport is a major part of French life, be it as a participant or a spectator. Football is the country's most popular sport – the top clubs are Olympique Lyonnais and Olympique de Marseille – followed by tennis; Paris hosts the French Open, a Grand Slam tournament, at the Stade Roland Garros in May/June. Rugby Union is very popular in the south, as is the French version of boules called *pétanque*, while the 3,400km (2,100-mile) coastline is dotted with marinas filled with the boats of keen sailors. Many of the regions have their own traditional sports: in Brittany, *gouren* is a kind of wrestling. The Formula One races at Magny-Cours and Monaco attract visitors from all over the world in June,

You'll see *pétanque* played in village squares throughout the country

Culture

as does the Tour de France cycle race in July. In winter, the Alps and the Pyrénées are the places to head for snow sports.

ETIQUETTE

Be sure to say '*Bonjour Monsieur*' or '*Bonjour Madame*' to anyone you meet, including when going into a small shop or restaurant. It's also polite to say '*au revoir*' when leaving and '*bon appétit*' just before eating.

When introduced to someone in a business or social setting, it's usual to shake hands and, in informal situations, to kiss on each cheek (except between men unless they are related or close friends); the number of kisses depends upon the region.

Jeans and casual clothing are worn almost everywhere except in business situations. Skimpy clothing remains out of place except in seaside resorts.

Food and drink

Food plays a major role in life in France, and the French take eating very seriously. This is primarily because France, a land of great climatic and agricultural diversity, offers an enormous variety of top-quality produce. In 2010, French cuisine was added to the Unesco 'intangible' World Heritage List for being a 'social custom aimed at celebrating the most important moments in the lives of individuals and groups'.

WHERE TO EAT AND DRINK

In larger towns and cities you'll have a wide choice: upmarket gourmet restaurants, large all-day brasseries, traditional local bistros, cafés, *salons de thé* (tearooms) and street stalls selling kebabs, crêpes or spicy merguez sausages; you'll probably find cuisine from all four corners of the globe.

Most villages, towns and cities will have restaurants specialising in the region's cuisine: for example, Brittany has its crêperies and Lyon its *bouchons* serving offal-based dishes; there are many Italian restaurants in and around Nice. In the countryside, *fermes-auberges* (farm-inns) are farms that serve home-cooked food using their own produce; the pub-like *estaminets* are specific to Flanders, and Alsace has its timber-framed *winstübs*.

It may challenge every stereotype, but France is the second-most profitable territory in the world for McDonald's hamburgers (*McDo*, in French slang) after the USA; there are other fast-food outlets too, like the Quick chain, Flunch and Délifrance. Non-meat-eaters are increasingly being catered for, with vegetarian restaurants popping up in most cities, but you'll struggle to find something suitable in a traditional French restaurant.

Set-price menus are posted outside all restaurants, making it easy to choose where you want to eat; it's a good idea to book in advance if you're going somewhere small or fashionable. Many eateries will close for at least a day between Sunday and Tuesday and, traditionally, will also shut for at least two weeks in July or August.

Alcohol is sold in all restaurants, bars and cafés (unless otherwise specified); by law, these last have to display a list of prices somewhere prominent. Wine bars have been fashionable

Lunch alfresco with the house red

for the past 20 years, as have English and Irish pubs, and there's even an absinthe bar in Antibes.

MAKE A MEAL OF IT

Breakfast (*le petit déjeuner*) is usually a croissant, brioche or bread with butter and jam with coffee, tea or hot chocolate; bowls are traditionally used for drinking in place of cups. However, larger hotels offer buffet-style breakfasts with cereal, bacon, eggs, cheese and cooked meats. It's usually cheaper and more authentic to have breakfast in a local café than in your hotel; and it's cheaper to stand at a café counter than sit at a table.

Lunch (*le déjeuner*) is a good time to eat your main meal of the day, as you can usually find a three-course fixed-price menu (*menu*) for less than €20. A *formule* is either starter and main course or main course and dessert. Cafés usually serve salads, omelettes, sandwiches and *croque-monsieurs* (ham and cheese toasted sandwich). Most establishments offer a *plat du jour* (dish of the day).

Dinner (*le dîner*) tends to be more expensive than lunch, as dishes are generally à la carte, but this means there's usually more choice. A jacket is expected in smart establishments, but only a few insist on a tie. Tap water is free – ask for *un carafe d'eau* – and house wine (*cuvée du patron*) offers the best value. A small coffee (*un café*) can add €2 or more to your bill.

Starters (*entrées* or *hors d'œuvres*) usually include *crudités* (raw vegetables), *charcuterie* (cooked meats) and soup; main courses will be meat, fish and regional specialities often

The ubiquitous baguette

accompanied by green salad and fries, while the dessert menu will generally feature chocolate mousse, ice cream, sorbets, fruit tarts – especially *tarte*

Meal times

Breakfast: 6.30am–9.30am
Lunch: noon–2pm
Dinner: 7.30pm–9.30pm
Times vary from restaurant to restaurant
French people tend to eat at regular times, especially in small towns and the countryside, and restaurants operate accordingly. Country restaurants expect to take orders for lunch from around 12.30–1.30pm, and for dinner from 8.30–9pm, and if you arrive even at 1.45pm for lunch you might find that a place can no longer serve you. Once you have sat down and given your order, though, you can stay as long as you like. In cities, restaurants and especially brasseries are more flexible.

Food and drink

Fresh seafood by the sea can't be missed

tatin (caramelised apple tart) – and cheese. Note that steaks are cooked rarer than in many other countries: extra-rare is *bleu*, rare is *saignant*, medium is *à point* and well done *bien cuit*; don't be surprised to see raw minced beef being delivered to a neighbouring diner – this is the popular dish *steak tartare*.

WHAT TO DRINK
Aperitifs

Typical choices for pre-dinner drinks (*apéritifs* or *apéros*) would be *pastis* (anise-flavoured drink), kir (white wine with a dash of blackcurrant liqueur) or vermouth. Most regions have their own offerings: for example, in Provence there's Figoun (made from figs) and in the Basque Country, Txapa (wine infused with fruits and spices). Champagne is usually quaffed on special occasions.

Wine

When confronted with a list of wine names, producers and vintages, the choice can be daunting. The best restaurants will have extensive wine lists covering all the regions of France, but smaller restaurants will usually only offer a small selection of local wines, often sold in a carafe or *pichet* (jug). It's a good idea to ask the *patron* (boss) or waiter for a recommendation.

Local wines are at their best with local food. This is to do with the wine's overall characteristics such as body, acidity, tannin, fruitiness, grape variety and barrel ageing, which create their overall flavour. Full-bodied reds, like a Rhône, will overpower a delicate sauce yet complement a rich *bœuf bourgignon*. The acidity in wine is important since it lifts a rich, buttery dish or oily fish; for example, Muscadet is the ideal wine to accompany Loire fish dishes. Champagne is the best match for oysters, and Alsatian whites accompany perfectly the region's sausages.

Tannins in red wines also have a similar cutting effect. Wines with strong tannins, such as Bordeaux, are enhanced by local dishes such as *confit de canard* (preserved duck). But not all red wines are tannic. Loire red and Beaujolais, for example, are fruity and accompany fish well and can even be drunk chilled. Young wines tend to have more upfront fruit and are a good choice for duck à l'orange. Sweet wines combine well with both sweet and savoury foods – a glass of chilled Sauternes or the less expensive Barsac is delightful with *foie gras*, Roquefort cheese or fruit. In the south, a chilled rosé is drunk with pretty much everything.

Beer, cider and non-alcoholic drinks

Thanks to its Germanic heritage, Alsace is France's largest producer of beer and the home of major brands such as Fischer, Karlsbrau and Kronenbourg. Beer-lovers might find it more interesting to seek out the more characterful beers of smaller artisan breweries in the Pas-de-Calais and Flanders, such as Ch'ti in Benifontaine near Lens. Beer goes particularly well with Toulouse sausages and Alsatian *choucroute*. There are also good small breweries dotted throughout Normandy and Brittany, like Mor Braz in Morbihan, which uses sea water in its brewing.

Normandy cider comes in two basic varieties, *doux* (sweet) and *brut* (dry), and the best is *cidre bouché* (corked), which doesn't have a screw top. The Pays d'Auge around Cambremer is the most renowned cider district, the only one with an AOC, but excellent, slightly drier ciders are found in Perche and the Cotentin Peninsula.

Brittany also produces many good ciders along the Rance river; it's traditionally drunk with crêpes.

France has many springs and sources, and there are lots of different brands of bottled water. Still water *(eau plate)* brands include Evian and Volvic, while Perrier and Badoit are well-known examples of sparkling water *(eau gazeuse)*. Fizzy soft drinks include Orangina; Brittany produces Breizh Cola.

Digestifs

For an after-dinner drink, as well as cognac and the mellower armagnac, there's a wide range of fruit brandies *(eaux-de-vie)* made from pear, plum, cherry or raspberry, as well as the famous apple-based calvados.

Some of the best beer is from Alsace

Seasonal foods

The first pressings of the new season's AOC olive oil appear in January in Nyons, then in February lemons take centre stage on the Côte d'Azur. Lobsters start rearing their claws in March, and when asparagus from the Loire Valley appears in the shops you know that spring is in the air. The charming Roussillon town of Céret produces the first cherries of the season in mid-April. In June in Provence, Cavaillon's famous melons start brightening up the market stalls. Lavender covers many southern fields in July and August, while autumn sees AOC chestnuts harvested in the Ardèche. Much-coveted truffles start getting sniffed out in November, and on the third Thursday of the same month, the first wine of the season, Beaujolais Nouveau, is eagerly tasted.

Food and drink

PHRASE BOOK

t'as de beaux

you talkin' to me?

yeux tu sais

y connaît pas le raoul

j'suis sur l'point de conclure

tmosphère

okay!

izarre,

je t'aime

et mes seins...

qu'est-ce que je peux faire? je sais pas quoi faire!

dégueulasse

les oiseaux

si vous n'aimez pas la mer, si vous n

SAUF
ERVICE

la mort ne m'aura
pas vivant...
tomorrow is
another day
rosebud
jusqu'ici tout va
phone
les jambes des femmes sont des
la belle
la bête
nobody is
que la
si vous
allez vous

Phrase book

There are approximately 129 million native French-speakers worldwide. French *(français)* is an official language in 30 countries and is one of the five official languages of the United Nations. Like Italian and Spanish, it is a Romance language, derived from Vulgar Latin, and is spoken by 4 million people in Belgium, 7 million in Canada (principally Quebec), 60.5 million in France and 1.3 million in Switzerland. It is also an official language of 22 African nations.

PRONUNCIATION

This section is designed to make you familiar with the sounds of French using our simplified phonetic transcription. You'll find the pronunciation of the French letters and sounds explained below, together with their 'imitated' equivalents. This system is used throughout the phrase book; simply read the pronunciation as if it were English, noting any special rules below.

In French, all syllables are pronounced the same, with no extra stress on any particular syllable. The French language contains nasal vowels, which are indicated in the pronunciation by a vowel symbol followed by an N. This N should not be pronounced strongly, but it is there to show the nasal quality of the previous vowel. A nasal vowel is pronounced simultaneously through the mouth and the nose.

In French, the final consonants of words are not always pronounced. When a word ending in a consonant is followed with a word beginning with a vowel, the two words are often run together. The consonant is therefore pronounced as if it begins the following word.

Example	*Pronunciation*
comment	*koh • mawN*
Comment allez-vous?	*koh • mawN tay • lay • voo*

Consonants

Letter	*Approximate Pronunciation*	*Symbol*	*Example*	*Pronunciation*
cc	1. before e, i, like cc in accident	ks	**accessible**	*ahk • seh • see • bluh*
	2. elsewhere, like cc in accommodate	k	**d'accord**	*dah • kohr*
ch	like sh in shut	sh	**chercher**	*shehr • shay*
ç	like s in sit	s	**ça**	*sah*
g	1. before e, i, y, like s in pleasure	zh	**manger**	*mawN • zhay*
	2. before a, o, u, like g in go	g	**garçon**	*gahr • sohN*
h	always silent		**homme**	*ohm*
j	like s in pleasure	zh	**jamais**	*zhah • may*
qu	like k in kill	k	**qui**	*kee*

| r | rolled in the back of the mouth | r | **rouge** | *roozh* |
| w | usually like v in voice | v | **wagon** | *vah • gohN* |

The letters b, c, d, f, k, l, m, n, p, s, t, v, x and z are pronounced as in English.

Vowels

Letter	*Approximate Pronunciation*	*Symbol*	*Example*	*Pronunciation*
a, à, â	between the a in hat and the a in father	ah	**mari**	*mah • ree*
e	sometimes like a in about	uh	**je**	*zhuh*
è, ê, e	like e in get	eh	**même**	*mehm*
é, ez	like a in late	ay	**été**	*ay • tay*
i	like ee in meet	ee	**il**	*eel*
o, ô	generally like o in roll	oh	**donner**	*doh • nay*
u	like ew in dew	ew	**une**	*ewn*

Sounds spelled with two or more letters

Letter	*Approximate Pronunciation*	*Symbol*	*Example*	*Pronunciation*
ai, ay, aient, ais, ait, aî, ei	like a in late	ay	**j'ai** **vais**	*zhay* *vay*
ai, ay, aient, ais, ait, aî, ei	like e in get	eh	**chaîne** **peine**	*shehn* *pehn*
(e)au	similar to o	oh	**chaud**	*shoh*
eu, eû, œu	like u in fur but short like a puff of air	uh	**euro**	*uh • roh*
euil, euille	like uh + y	uhy	**feuille**	*fuhy*
ail, aille	like ie in tie	ie	**taille**	*tie*
ille	1. like yu in yucca	eeyuh	**famille**	*fah-meeyuh*
	2. like eel	eel	**ville**	*veel*
oi, oy	like w followed by the a in hat	wah	**moi**	*mwah*
ou, oû	like o in move or oo in hoot	oo	**nouveau**	*noo • voh*
ui	approximately like wee	wee	**traduire**	*trah • dweer*

English	French	Pronunciation
Hello	**Bonjour**	*bohN • zhoor*

French words and phrases appear in bold. A simplified pronunciation guide follows each French phrase; read it as if it were English. Among English phrases, you will find some words included in square brackets; these are the American English equivalents of British/English expressions.

General

0	**zéro** *zay • roh*	100	**cent** *sawN*
1	**un** *uhN*	500	**cinq-cent** *sehNk • sawN*
2	**deux** *duh*	1,000	**mille** *meel*
3	**trois** *trwah*	1,000,000	**un million** *uhN meel • yohN*
4	**quatre** *kah • truh*	Monday	**lundi** *luhN • dee*
5	**cinq** *sehNk*	Tuesday	**mardi** *mahr • dee*
6	**six** *sees*	Wednesday	**mercredi** *meehr • kruh • dee*
7	**sept** *seht*	Thursday	**jeudi** *zhuh • dee*
8	**huit** *weet*	Friday	**vendredi** *vawN • druh • dee*
9	**neuf** *nuhf*	Saturday	**samedi** *sahm • dee*
10	**diz** *dees*	Sunday	**dimanche** *dee • mawNshh*

Hello/Hi.	**Bonjour/Salut**. *bohN • zhoor/sah • lew*
Goodbye.	**Au revôir**. *oh ruh • vwahr*
See you later.	**A bientôt**. *ah beeyehN • toh*
Yes.	**Oui**. *wee*
No.	**Non**. *nohN*
OK.	**D'accord**. *dah • khor*
Excuse me! (to get attention)	**Excusez-moi!** *ehk • skew • zay • mwah*
Excuse me. (to get past)	**Pardon**. *pahr • dohN*
I'm sorry.	**Je suis désolé/désolée**. *zhuh swee day • zoh • lay*
How are you?	**Comment allez-vous?** *koh • mawN tah • lay • voo*
Fine, thanks.	**Bien, merci**. *beeyehN mehr • see*
I'd like…	**Je voudrais...** *zhuh voo • dray…*
How much?	**Combien?** *kohN • beeyehN*
Where is…?	**Où est...?** *oo ay…*
Please.	**S'il vous plaît**. *seel voo play*
Thank you.	**Merci**. *mehr • see*
You're welcome.	**De rien**. *duh reeyehN*
Please speak slowly.	**S'il vous plaît, parlez lentement**. *seel voo play pahr • lay lawN • tuh • mawN*
Can you repeat that?	**Pouvez vous répéter cela?** *poo • vay • voo ray • pay • tay suh • la*
I don't understand.	**Je ne comprends pas**. *zhuh nuh kohN • prawN pah*
Do you speak English?	**Parlez-vous anglais?** *pahr • lay • voo zawN • glay*
My name is…	**Je m'appelle...** *zhuh mah • pehl…*

Arrival and departure

I'm on holiday [vacation]/business.	**Je suis en vacances/voyage d'affaires.** *zhuh swee zawN vah • kawNs/vwah • yahzh dah • fehr*
I'm going to…	**Je vais à …** *zhuh vay ah…*
I'm staying at the Hotel…	**Je reste à l'hôtel…** *zhuh rehst ah loh • tehl…*

Money and banking

Where's…?	**Où est…?** *oo ay…*
– the ATM	**– le distributeur automatique de billets** *luh dee • stree • bew • tuhr oh • toh • mah • teek duh bee • yay*
– the bank	**– la banque** *lah bawNk*
– the currency exchange office	**– le bureau de change** *luh bew • roh duh shawNzh*
When does the bank open/close?	**Quand est-ce que la banque ouvre/ferme?** *kawN tehs kuh lah bawNk oo • vruh/fehrm*
I'd like to change pounds/dollars into euros	**Je voudrais échanger des livres sterling/dollars en euros** *zhuh voo • dray ay • shawN • zhay day doh • lahr/lee • vruh stayr • leeng awN nuh • roh*

Transport

How do I get to town?	**Comment vais-je en ville?** *koh • mawN vay • zhuh awN veel*
Where's…?	**Où est…?** *oo ay…*
– the airport	**– l'aéroport** *lah • ay • roh • pohr*
– the train [railway] station	**– la gare** *lah gahr*
– the bus station	**– la gare routière** *lah gahr roo • tee • yehr*
– the underground [subway] station	**– le métro** *luh may • troh*
Is it far from here?	**C'est loin d'ici?** *say lwehN dee • see*
Where do I buy a ticket?	**Où puis-je acheter un billet?** *oo pwee • zhuh ah • shtay uhN bee • yay*
A single [one way]/return [round trip] ticket to…	**Un billet aller simple/aller-retour…** *uhN bee • yay ah • lay sehN • pluh/ah • lay • ruh • toor…*
How much?	**Combien ça coûte?** *kohN • beeyehN sah koot*
Which gate/line?	**Quelle porte/ligne?** *kehl pohrt/lee • nyuh*
Which platform?	**Quel quai?** *kehl kay*
Where can I get a taxi?	**Où puis-je prendre un taxi?** *oo pwee • zhuh prawN • druh uhN tahk • see*
Take me to this address.	**Conduisez-moi à cette adresse.** *kohN • dwee • zay • mwah ah seh tah • drehs*
Can I have a map?	**Puis-je avoir une carte?** *pwee • zhuh ah • vwahr ewn kahrt*

Accommodation

Can you recommend a hotel?	**Pouvez-vous me conseiller un hôtel?** *poo • vay • voo muh kohN • say • yay uhN noh • tehl*
I made a reservation.	**J'ai fait une réservation.** *zhay fay ewn ray • zehr • vah • seeyohN*
My name is…	**Mon nom est…** *mohN nohN may…*
Do you have a room…?	**Avez-vous une chambre…?** *ah • vay • voo ewn shawN • bruh…*

– for one/two	**– pour un/deux** *poor uhN/duh*
– with a bathroom	**– avec salle de bains** *ah • vehk sahl duh behN*
– with air conditioning	**– avec climatisation** *ah • vehk klee • mah • tee • zah • seeyohN*
For …	**Pour…** *poor…*
– tonight	**– ce soir** *suh swahr*
– two nights	**– deux nuits** *duh nwee*
– one week	**– une semaine** *ewn suh • mehn*
How much?	**Combien ça coûte?** *kohN • beeyehN sah koot*
Is there anything cheaper?	**N'y a-t-il rien de moins cher?** *Nee • yah • teel reeyehN duh mwehN shehr*
When's check-out?	**Quand dois-je quitter la chambre?** *kawN dwah • zhuh kee • tay lah shawN • bruh*
I'll pay in cash/by credit card.	**Je paierai en espèces/par carte de credit.** *zhuh pay • ray awN nehs • pehs/pahr kahrt duh kray • dee*
Can I have my bill/a receipt?	**Puis-je avoir ma facture/un reçu?** *pwee • zhuh ah • vwahr mah fahk • tewr/uhN ruh • sew*

Internet and communication

Where's an internet café?	**Où y a-t-il un cyber café?** *oo yah • teel uhN see • behr kah • fay*
Can I access the internet/check email?	**Puis-je me connecter à Internet/consulter mes mails?** *pwee • zhuh muh koh • nehk • tay ah ehN • tehr • neht/kohN • sewl • tay may mehyl*
How do I connect/log on?	**Comment est-ce que je me connecte/j'ouvre une session?** *koh • mawN ehs kuh zhuh muh koh • nehkt/zhoo • vruh ewn seh • seeyohN*
A phone card please.	**Une carte de téléphone, s'il vous plaît.** *ewn kahrt duh tay • lay • fohn seel voo play*
Hello. This is…	**Bonjour. C'est…** *bohN • zhoor say…*
Can I speak to…?	**Puis-je parler à…?** *pwee • zhuh pahr • lay ah…*
Can you repeat that?	**Pouvez-vous répéter cela?** *poo • vay • voo ray • pay • tay suh • lah*
I'll call back later.	**Je rappellerai plus tard.** *zhuh rah • peh • luh • ray plew tahr*
Where's the post office?	**Où est la poste?** *oo ay lah pohst*
I'd like to send this to…	**Je voudrais envoyer ceci à…** *zhuh voo • dray zawN • vwah • yay suh • see ah…*

Sightseeing

Where's the tourist information office?	**Où est l'office de tourisme?** *oo ay loh • fees duh too • ree • smuh*
What are the main attractions?	**Quelles sont les choses importantes à voir?** *kehl sohN lay shoh zehN • pohr • tawN tah vwahr*
Do you have tours in English?	**Proposez-vous des visites en anglais?** *Proh • poh • zay • voo day vee • zeet awN nawN • glay*
Can I have a map/guide?	**Puis-je avoir une carte/un guide?** *pwee • zhuh ah • vwahr ewn kahrt/uhN geed*

Shopping

Where's the market/shopping centre [mall]?	**Où est le marché/centre commercial?** *oo ay luh mahr • shay/sawN • truh koh • mehr • seeyahl*
I'm just looking.	**Je regarde seulement.** *zhuh ruh • gahrd suhl • mawN*
Can you help me?	**Pouvez-vous m'aider?** *poo • vay • voo meh • day*
I'm being helped.	**On s'occupe de moi.** *ohN soh • kewp duh mwah*
How much?	**Combien ça coûte?** *kohN • beeyehN sah koot*
That one please.	**Celui-ci/Celle-ci, s'il vous plaît.** *suh • lwee • see/sehl see seel voo playr*
Where can I pay?	**Où puis-je payer?** *oo pwee • zhuh pay • yay*
I'll pay in cash/by credit card.	**Je paierai en espèces/par carte de crédit.** *zhuh pay • ray awN neh • spehs/pahr kahrt duh kray • dee*
A receipt, please.	**Un reçu, s'il vous plaît.** *uhN ruh • sew seel voo play*

Culture and nightlife

What's there to do at night?	**Que peut-on faire le soir?** *kuh puh • tohN fehr luh swahr*
What's playing tonight?	**Qui joue ce soir?** *kee zhoo suh swahr*
Do you have a programme of events?	**Avez-vous un programme des festivités?** *ah • vay • voo uhN proh • grahm day fehs • tee • vee • tay*
Where's…?	**Où est…?** *oo ay…*
– the city centre [downtown area]	**– le centre ville** *luh sawN • truh veel*
– the bar	**– le bar** *luh bahr*
– the dance club	**– la discothèque** *lah dees • koh • tehk*

295

Business travel

I'm here on business.	**Je suis ici pour affaires.** *zhuh swee zee • see poo rah • fehr*
Here's my business card.	**Voici ma carte.** *vwah • see mah kahrt*
Can I have your card?	**Puis-je avoir votre carte?** *pwee • zhuh ah • vwahr voh • truh kahrt*
I have a meeting with…	**J'ai une réunion avec…** *zhay ewn ray • ew • neeyohN nah • vehk…*
Where's…?	**Où est…?** *oo ay…*
– the business centre	**– le centre d'affaires** *luh sawN • truh dah • fehr*
– the convention hall	**– le palais des congrès** *luh pah • lay day kohN • greh*
– the meeting room	**– la salle de réunion** *lah sahl duh ray • ew • neeyohN*

Travel with children

Is there a discount for children?	**Y a-t-il une remise pour les enfants?** *yah • teel ewn ruh • meez poor lay zawN • fawN*
Can you recommend a babysitter?	**Pouvez-vous me recommander une baby-sitter?** *poo • vay • voo muh ruh • koh • mawN • day ewn bah • bee-see • tuhr*
Do you have a child seat/high chair?	**Avez-vous un siège enfant/une chaise haute?** *ah • vay • voo zuhN seeyehzh awN • fawN/zewn shehz oht*
Where can I change the baby?	**Où puis-je changer le bébé?** *oo pwee • zhuh shawN • zhay luh bay • bay*

Phrase book

Disabled travellers

Is there…?	**Y a-t-il…?** *yah • teel…*
– access for the disabled	**– un accès pour handicappés** *uhN nahk • say poor awN • dee • kah • pay*
– a wheelchair ramp	**– un accès pour chaises roulantes** *uhN nahk • say poor shehz roo • lawNt*
– a disabled-accessible toilet [restroom]	**– des toilettes accessibles aux handicappés** *day twah • leht ahk • seh • see • bluh oh zawN • dee • kah • pay*
I need…	**J'ai besoin…** *zhay buh • zwehN…*
– assistance	**– d'aide** *dehd*
– a lift [an elevator]	**– d'un ascenseur** *duhN nah • sawN • suhr*
– a ground-floor room	**– d'une chambre au rez-de-chaussée** *dewn shawN • bruh oh ray • duh • shoh • say*

Emergencies

Help!	**Au secours!** *oh suh • koor*
Get a doctor!	**Allez chercher un docteur!** *ah • lay shehr • shay uhN dohk • tuhr*
Call the police!	**Appelez la police!** *ah • puh • lay lah poh • lees*
Where's the police station?	**Où est le commissariat de police?** *oo ay luh koh • mee • sah • reeyah duh poh • lees*
There was an accident/attack.	**Il y a eu un accident/une attaque.** *eel • yah ew uhN nahk • see • dawN/ewn ah • tahk*

Health

I'm ill [sick].	**Je suis malade.** *zhuh swee mah • lahd*
I need an English-speaking doctor.	**J'ai besoin d'un docteur qui parle anglais.** *zhay buh • zwehN duhN dohk • tuhr kee pahrl awN • glay*
It hurts here.	**Ça fait mal ici.** *sah fay mahl ee • see*
I'm in pain.	**J'ai mal.** *zhay mahl*
Where's the chemist [pharmacy]?	**Où est la pharmacie?** *oo ay lah fahr • mah • see*
What time does it open/close?	**À quelle heure ouvre-t-elle/ferme-t-elle?** *ah kehl uhr oo • vruh • tehl/fehrm • tehl*
I'm allergic to…	**Je suis allergique à…** *zhuh swee zah • lehr • zheek ah…*

Eating out

Can you recommend a good restaurant/bar?	**Pouvez-vous me conseiller un bon restaurant/bar?** *poo • vay-voo muh kohN • say • yay uhN bohN reh • stoh • rawN/bahrr*
Is there a traditional French/an inexpensive restaurant nearby?	**Y a-t-il un restaurant traditionnel français/bon marché près d'ici?** *yah • teel uhN reh • stoh • rawN trah • dee • seeyohN • nehl frawN • say/bohN mahr • shay pray dee • see*
A table for…, please.	**Une table pour…, s'il vous plaît.** *ewn tah • bluh poor…seel voo play*
A menu, please.	**La carte, s'il vous plaît.** *lah kahrt seel voo play*
I'd like…	**Je voudrais…** *zhuh voo • dray…*
The bill [check], please.	**L'addition, s'il vous plaît.** *lalah • dee • seeyohN seel voo play*

l'agneau *lah • nyoh*	lamb	**le jambon** *luh zhawN • bohN*	ham
l'ail *lie*	garlic	**le jus** *luh zhew*	juice
l'ananas *lah • nah • nah*	pineapple	**le lait** *luh lay*	milk
l'artichaut *lahr • tee • shoh*	artichoke	**la laitue** *lah lay • tew*	lettuce
le beignet *luh beh • nyay*	fritter	**les légumes** *lay lay • gewm*	vegetables
le beurre *luh buhr*	butter	**le maïs** *luh mah • ees*	sweet corn
la bière *lah beeyehr*	beer	**le miel** *luh meeyehl*	honey
le bifteck *luh beef • tehk*	steak	**les moules** *lay mool*	mussels
le bœuf *luh buhf*	beef	**les noix** *lay nwah*	nuts
le bouillon *luh boo • yohN*	broth	**l'œuf** *luh*	egg
le café *luh kah • fay*	coffee	**l'oignon** *loh • neeyohN*	onion
le canard *luh kah • nahr*	duck	**le pain** *luh pehN*	bread
le champignon *luh shawN • pee • nyohN*	mushroom	**les pâtes** *lay paht*	pasta
le citron *luh see • trohN*	lemon	**les pâtisseries** *lay pah • tee • suh • ree*	pastries
la confiture *lah kohN • fee • tewr*	jam	**le petit pain** *luh puh • tee pehN*	bread roll
les coquilles *lay koh • keeyuh*	scallops	**les petits pois** *lay puh • tee pwah*	peas
la côtelette *lah koh • teh • leht*	chop	**la pintade** *lah pehN • tahd*	guinea fowl
la crevette *lah kruh • veht*	shrimp/prawn	**le poisson** *luh pwah • sohN*	fish
la dorade *lah doh • rahd*	sea bass	**le poivre** *luh pwah • vruh*	pepper
l'eau *loh*	water	**le piment** *luh pee • mawN*	chilli pepper
les épinards *lay zay • pee • nahr*	spinach	**le poivron** *luh pwah • vrohN*	pepper (vegetable)
l'escalope (de poulet) *lehs • kah • lohp (duh poo • lay)*	breast (of chicken)	**la pomme** *lah pohm*	apple
l'escargot *lehs • kahr • goh*	snail	**la pomme de terre** *lah pohm duh tehr*	potato
le filet *luh fee • lay*	loin	**le porc** *luh pohr*	pork
le foie *luh fwah*	liver	**le potage** *luh poh • tahzh*	stew
la fraise *lah frehz*	strawberry	**le poulet** *luh poo • lay*	chicken
la framboise *lah frawN • bwahz*	raspberry	**le raisin** *luh reh • zehN*	grape
les frites *lay freet*	chips [French fries]	**le riz** *luh ree*	rice
le fromage *luh froh • mahzh*	cheese	**le rôti** *luh roh • tee*	roast
les fruits de mer *lay frwee duh mehr*	seafood	**la saucisse** *lah soh • sees*	sausage
le gigot *luh zhee • goh*	leg	**le saucisson** *luh soh • see • sohN*	salami
la glace *lah glahs*	ice cream	**le sel** *luh sehl*	salt
les haricots verts *lay ah • ree • koh vehr*	green beans	**la tarte** *lah tahrt*	pie
le homard *luh oh • mahr*	lobster	**le thon** *luh tohN*	tuna
l'huile d'olive *lweel doh • leev*	olive oil	**le veau** *luh voh*	veal
l'huître *lwee • truh*	oyster	**la volaille** *lah voh • lie*	poultry

297

Phrase book

Index

298

Index

Accommodation Index

Credits for Berlitz Handbook France

Written by: Nick Rider
and Caroline Radula Scott
Series editor: Tom Stainer
Commissioning editor: Siân Lezard
Copy editor: Catherine Dreghorn
Map production: Stephen Ramsay and Apa
Cartography Department
Production: Linton Donaldson, Rebeka Ellam
Picture manager: Steven Lawrence
Picture and design editor: Tom Smyth
Photography: All photography APA/Sylvaine Poitau
except: Alamy 199; Art Archive 272; An Tour Tan
143; AWL Images 8TL, 205; Courtesy best Weston
115; Brittany Tourism 56, 57, 133, 134, 141, 142;
Burgundy Tourism 189; Bordeaux Tourism 216;
Courtesy Hotle Castel Blue 139; Courtesy Café de
la Paix 93; Comite Régional du Tourisme Poitou-
Charentes 68R; Corbis 4TR, 175B; CDT Somme/Alba
Bayes 104; Courtesy Charmont su Loire; Courtesy
Hotel de Crillon 90; Courtesy Chateau Cordillion
Bages 210; APA Kevin Cummins 6TL, 7B, 51, 65T,
69T, 71, 72, 73/T, 74, 75B, 78, 80, 81, 83/T, 84,
85, 86, 96, 261, 262, 265, 268, 280, 281, 285,
288/289; courtesy Hotel des Iles 138; Courtesy
Disney Land Paris 87; Fotolia 58R/TL, 34, 58, 89,
119, 121B, 127B, 145B, 147, 163B, 166, 172,
173, 175T,179, 187, 207, 219B; Fotolia 9L&
37; Getty Images 14, 15, 126T, 159, 276; Pascal
Greboval/Tourism Ile de France 40; Robert Harding
5ML; Courtesy Hostellerie des Pigeons Blancs 158;
Courtesy Hotelerie de Palisance 213; Courtesy Hotel
du Palais 211; APA Ilpo Musto 60/61, 65B, 69B, 70,
75AT, 76, 107, 283; istockphoto 58L, 7TR, 88L/BR,
9TR, 55, 82, 135, 176, 201, 239, 256; Wadey James
230; 32, 43, 219T, 228, 229, 232, 234, 235,
236, 237; Courtesy Le Chabrichou 185; Courtesy
le Chalet des iles 94; Courtesy Hotel le Cep 181;
Courtesy Lam Choisel 157; Courtesy Les Crayer Parc
117; Courtesy Hostellerie Le Marechal 116; Courtesy
Hotel Lutetia 92; Marc Ginot/Montpellier Tourism 52,
223; Marseille Tourist Board 30; Pairs Tourist Board
97; Courtesy Parc Asterix 269; Courtesy Pavillion
de Raine 91; Photolibrary/hemis 126, 198; Picture
Colour Library 4B, 4TL; Photolibrary 68L; Courtesy
Michel Sarran 215; Specialist Stock 174; Superstock
79, 124; Toulouse Tourism 206; Union des Grands
Crus de Bordeaux 27

Cover: front: photolibrary.com; back left: Fotolia.
co.uk; back middle and right: iStockphoto.

Printed by: CTPS-China

© 2012 APA Publications (UK) Limited

First Edition 2012

Berlitz Trademark Reg. US Patent Office and
other countries. Marca Registrada. Used under
licence from the Berlitz Investment Corporation
No part of this book may be reproduced.
stored in a retrieval system or transmitted
in any form or by any means (electronic,
mechanical, photocopying, recording or
otherwise), without prior written permission
of APA Publications. Brief text quotations with
use of photographs are exempted for book
review purposes only. Information has been
obtained from sources believed to be reliable,
but its accuracy and completeness, and the
opinions based thereon, are not guaranteed.

Contacting Us

At Berlitz we strive to keep our guides as
accurate and up to date as possible, but if
you find anything that has changed, or if you
have any suggestions on ways to improve
this guide, then we would be delighted to
hear from you. Write to Berlitz Publishing, PO
Box 7910, London SE1 1WE, UK or email:
berlitz@apaguide.co.uk

Worldwide: APA Publications GmbH & Co.
Verlag KG (Singapore branch), 7030 Ang
Mo Kio Ave 5, 08-65 Northstar @ AMK,
Singapore 569880; tel: (65) 570 1051;
email: apasin@singnet.com.sg

UK and Ireland: Dorling Kindersley Ltd,
a Penguin Group company
80 Strand, London, WC2R ORL, UK;
email: customerservice@dk.com

United States: Ingram Publisher Services,
1 Ingram Boulevard, PO Box 3006, La Vergne,
TN 37086-1986; email: customer.service@
ingrampublisherservices.com

Australia: Universal Publishers, 1 Waterloo
Road, Macquarie Park, NSW 2113;
tel: (61) 2-9857 3700; email: sales@
universalpublishers.com.au

www.berlitzpublishing.com

S La Sommellerie
(Châteauneuf-du-Pape) 245
T La Truffe Noire (Brive-la-
Gaillarde) 183

U U Santu Petru (Casta) 246
V Le Val Vert (Le Puy-en-Velay)
183
Le Vieux Carré (Rouen) 138

Le Vieux Moulin (Centuri) 246
Villa Reine Hortense (Dinard)
139
Villa Roseraie (Vence) 246